HOW TO STUDY PICTURES

HOW TO STUDY PICTURES

BY MEANS OF A SERIES OF COMPARISONS OF THE PAINTERS' MOTIVES AND METHODS

BY

CHARLES H. CAFFIN

WITH ADDITIONS BY
ROBERTA M. FANSLER
Instructor at the Metropolitan Museum of Art

EDITED BY
ALFRED BUSSELLE, JR.
Instructor at the Metropolitan Museum of Art

REVISED EDITION

Essay Index Reprint Series

BOOKS FOR LIBRARIES PRESS
FREEPORT, NEW YORK

LIBRARY OF CONGRESS CATALOG CARD NUMBER:

68-58776

MANUFACTURED
BY
HALLMARK LITHOGRAPHERS, INC.
IN THE U.S.A.

TO
DOROTHY
AND
FREDA

CONTENTS

[vii]

CONTENTS

ILLUSTRATIONS

ILLUSTRATIONS

[x]

ILLUSTRATIONS

ILLUSTRATIONS

EDITORS' NOTE

IN writing his book on how to study pictures, Mr. Caffin used what he called in his Author's Note the "parallel method: 'Look on this picture and on this.' Not, as a rule, to suggest that one is more admirable than another; but to stimulate interest and the faculty of observation, and to show how various are the motives which have prompted artists and the methods which they have adopted."

"The object of the study," he says, "should be to put oneself in touch with each artist in turn, to enter into his point of view, to see as far as possible with his eyes, and to estimate his work, not for what it does *not* contain, but for what it *does*. In this way only can our appreciation of painting become catholic and intelligent. Then, we are no longer content to say 'I know what I like,' but 'I know *why* I like'; and our likings are multiplied."

In preparing the present text we have made a minimum of changes in the earlier edition in order to meet the shifting interests of modern taste. Chapters written by Mr. Caffin on El Greco, Vermeer, Ingres, and Cézanne have been introduced into this edition for the first time, while the two chapters on Manet and on Matisse have been re-written to include such important masters as Degas and Picasso. Finally a chapter has been added to bring the material down to the present day.

In his original plan Mr. Caffin disclaimed any intention "to pick out a list of the most famous names in painting; my real aim being to unfold the gradual progress of the art, to show how various motives have from time to time influenced artists, and how the scene of vital progress has shifted

EDITORS' NOTE

from country to country. I have tried to present a survey of the whole field of painting, not to write a history of artists or schools." In treating the material of the twenty-five years between Mr. Caffin's final chapter and our own, we have tried to follow in general his plan, to suggest clues to an understanding, not to define and classify the contemporary trends.

ROBERTA M. FANSLER
ALFRED BUSSELLE, JR.

New York City

HOW TO STUDY PICTURES

CHAPTER I

INTRODUCTION

" Having eyes, see ye not ? "

THE world is full of beauty which many people hurry past or live in front of and do not see. There is also a world of beauty in pictures, but it escapes the notice of many, because, while they wish to see it, they do not know how.

The first necessity for the proper seeing of a picture is to try and see it through the eyes of the artist who painted it. This is not a usual method. Generally people look only through their own eyes, and like or dislike a picture according as it does or does not suit their particular fancy. These people will tell you: " Oh! I don't know anything about painting, but I know what I like "; which is their way of saying: " If I don't like it right off, I don't care to be bothered to like it at all."

Such an attitude of mind cuts one off from growth and development, for it is as much as to say: " I am very well satisfied with myself, and quite indifferent to the experiences and feelings of other men." Yet it is just this experience and feeling of another man which a picture gives us. If you consider a moment you will understand why. The world itself is a vast panorama, and

[3]

from it the painter selects his subject: not to copy it exactly, since it would be impossible for him to do this, even if he tried. How could he represent, for example, each blade of grass, each leaf upon a tree? So what he does is to represent the subject as he sees it, as it appeals to his sympathy or interest; and if twelve artists painted the same landscape, the result would be twelve different pictures, differing according to the way in which each man had been impressed by the scene; in fact, according to his separate point of view or separate way of seeing it, influenced by his individual experience and feeling.

It is most important to realize the part which is played by these two qualities of experience and feeling. Experience, the fullness or the deficiency of it, must affect the work of every one of us, no matter what our occupation may be. And if the work is of a kind which appeals to the feelings of others, as in the case of the preacher, the writer, the actor, the painter, sculptor, architect or art-craftsman, the musician or the dancer, it must be affected equally by the individual's capacity of feeling and by his power of expressing what he feels.

Therefore, since none of us can include in ourselves the whole range of possible experience and feeling, it is through the experience and the feeling of others that we deepen and refine our own. It is this that we should look to pictures to accomplish, which, as you will acknowledge, is a very different thing from offhand like or dislike. For example, we may not be attracted at first, but we reason with ourselves: " No doubt this picture meant a good deal to the man who painted it; it embodies his experience of the world and his feeling toward the subject. It represents, in fact, a revelation of the man himself; and, if it is true that ' the noblest study of mankind is man,' then possibly in the study of this man, as revealed in his work, there may be interest for me."

I am far from wishing you to suppose that all pictures will repay you for such intimate study. We may get inside the man to find that his experience of life is meager, his feeling commonplace and paltry. There are not a few men of this sort in the occupation of art, just as in every other walk of life, and their pictures, so far as we ourselves are concerned, will be disappointing. But among the pictures which have stood the test of time we shall always find that the fruits of the artist's experience and feeling are of a kind which makes lasting appeal to the needs of the human heart and mind, and that this fact is one of the causes of their being held in so high esteem. There is also another cause.

If only experience and feeling were necessary to make an artist, many of us would be better artists than a considerable number of those who follow the profession of art. But there is another necessity—the power of expressing the experience and feeling. This, by its derivation from the Greek, is the primary meaning of the word " art ": the capacity to " fit " a form to an idea. The artist is the " fitter " who gives shape and construction to the tenuous fabric of his imagination; and this method of " fitting " is his technic.

So the making of a picture involves two processes: a taking in of the impression and a giving of it out by visible expression; a seeing of the subject with the visual and mental eye, and a communicating of what has been so seen to the visual and mental eyes of others; and both these processes are influenced by the experience and feeling of the artist and make their appeal to our own. And, I think, it should be clear from what we have been saying that the beauty of a picture depends much less upon its subject than upon the artist's conception and treatment of it. A grand subject will not of itself make a grand picture, while a very homely one, by the way in which it has been treated, may impress us profoundly.

The degree of beauty in a picture depends, in fact, upon the feeling for beauty in the artist and upon his power to express it. I have spoken of these two qualifications as if they influenced the picture separately; but, as a matter of fact, conception and technic are blended together in a picture, and as we pursue our study, we shall find ourselves embracing them simultaneously.

But at the outset we must proceed step by step, alternately studying the conception and the technic; and, in order that we may discover how variously, at successive times and in diverse countries, different men have conceived of life and have expressed their feeling and experience in pictures, I propose that we shall study them through a series of comparisons.

Our plan, therefore, will be:

"Look here, upon this picture, and on this";

not to decide offhand which we like the better, for in some cases perhaps we may not like either, since they were painted in times so remote from ours as to be outside our habit of understanding; but in order that we may get at the artist's way of seeing in each case, and reach some appreciation of his methods. In this way I hope that we may be able to piece together the story of modern painting; beginning with its rebirth in the thirteenth century, when it emerged from the darkness of the middle ages, and following it through its successive stages in different countries down to our own day.

It will very much increase the usefulness of this method if the student can obtain reproductions of other work by each artist, so as to test, by a particular study of them, the general principles that are being discussed.

CHAPTER II

GIOVANNI CIMABUE
1240(?)–1301
Italian School of Florence

GIOTTO DI BONDONE
1266–1336
Italian School of Florence

FOR the first comparison I invite you to study the two examples of *The Madonna Enthroned*—one by Cimabue, the other by his pupil Giotto. Both are painted on wooden panels in distemper—that is to say, with colors that have been mixed with some gelatinous medium, such as the white and the yolk of an egg beaten up together; for it was not until the fifteenth century that the use of oil as a medium was adopted. The colors used in Giotto's panel are tints of blue and rose and white; in Cimabue's the blues and reds are deep and dusky; the background in each case being golden.

We notice at once a general similarity between these two pictures, not only in choice of subject, but in the manner of presentation: Madonna, the queen of heaven, upon a throne; her mantle drawn over her head; her right hand resting on the knee of the infant Saviour, who has two fingers of his right hand raised in the act of blessing; kneeling angels at the foot, and figures in tiers above them; all the heads being surrounded by the nimbus, or circular cloud of light, symbolic of their sacred character.

[8]

The reason for this general similarity is that the choice of subject and the manner of its presentation were fixed by tradition; and long before this thirteenth century the tradition of Greek art had been lost, and in place of it was the Byzantine tradition, interpreted and enforced by the Christian church.

Briefly, the cause of the change was this. Greek art and Greek religion were indissolubly connected. The gods and goddesses were represented as human beings of a higher order; physical perfection was the ideal alike of religion and art. Therefore Christianity, in waging war upon heathenism, could not help attacking its art. Moreover, as the morals of the Empire became baser and baser, Christianity was driven more and more toward asceticism; meeting the ideal of physical perfection with the spiritual ideal of mortifying the flesh. So that pagan art, which itself had grown grosser as morals declined, became an object of exceeding hatred to the church. But some form of pictorial representation was needed to bring the truths of religion before the eyes of the faithful, and the church found what it required in the art of Byzantium.

This city was the gateway between the eastern and the western world, and the original Greek character of its art was speedily influenced by artists from the Orient. Now the ideals of the East and West are very different. Briefly, the longing of the East is for the Ultimate and Universal, while the West loves to dwell on the Particular, and to dwell upon the means rather than the end. While the Greek artist carved or painted some particular form, striving to give it perfection of shape in every part, so that through a series of means he might express his ideal of physical and spiritual perfection, the artist of the East reached his ideal through the abstract perfection of beautiful lines, of beautiful patterns of form and color. Thus, the one art is represented most characteristically by the sculpture on the Parthenon, the other by a decorated porcelain vase.

The arrival therefore, at Byzantium, of this art, so far removed from the Greek and Roman study of the human form, so beautifully decorative, was hailed by the church, both for the decorating of its sacred buildings and for the illuminating of the sacred manuscripts; and it was as decorators and illuminators that the Byzantine artists did their finest work. But, as the study of the nude figure had been abandoned, the ignorance of the artists regarding the real character of the human form increased; their types of figure became less and less like nature, and more and more according to a convention established by the church. Asceticism was preached, so the figure must be thin and gaunt, the gestures angular, the expression of the emaciated faces one of painful ecstasy. Moreover, there were certain dogmas to be enforced, and the church gradually dictated the manner of their representation; so that in time all that was required of or permitted to a painter was to go on producing certain conventional subjects in a purely conventional way. The divorce of art from nature was complete, and the independence of the artist lost in the domination of the church.

The story of the Italian Renaissance, which commenced at the end of the thirteenth century, relates how the artist gradually emancipated himself and his art, giving new life to the latter by inoculating it with nature and with something of the classic spirit.

Now, therefore, we can understand why these two pictures of *The Madonna Enthroned* by Cimabue and Giotto are so similar in arrangement. They followed the tradition prescribed by the church. Yet the Florentines of Cimabue's day found his picture so superior to anything they had seen before, so much more splendid in color, if not much nearer to the true representation of life, that when it was completed they carried it in a joyous procession from the artist's home through the streets of Florence, and deposited it with ceremony in the Cappella de' Rucellai in the Church of Santa Maria Novella. The English artist Lord Leighton, in his picture commemorating the event, has represented Cimabue walking in front of the Madonna, with his pupil Giotto at his side; and in the procession appears Dante, who left this mention of the two:

> Cimabue thought
> To laud it over painting's field; and now
> The cry is Giotto's, and his name eclipsed.
> > PURGATORIO, XI, 94. (*Cary.*)

The story is that Cimabue had chanced upon the boy as, like David of old, he watched his flock upon the mountain; and he found him drawing the form of one of the goats upon a rock with a sharp piece of slate. The master must have found some hint of genius in the work, for he straightway asked the boy if he would like to be his pupil; and, having received a glad assent and the father's permission, carried him off to Florence to his *bottega*. This, the artist's studio of that period and for long after, was rather what we should call a workshop, in which the pupils ground and prepared the colors under the master's direction; and it was not until they had thoroughly mastered this branch of the work—a procedure which in Giotto's time was supposed to occupy about six years—that they were permitted to use the brushes. How often, as he worked in the gloom of the *bottega,* must the shepherd boy have peeped wistfully at the master standing in the shady garden, before a great glory of crimson drapery and golden background, and wondered if he should ever himself acquire such marvelous skill.

He was destined to accomplish greater things, for his young mind had not been tutored to traditions, nor his young eyes constrained to admire the conventional. In the free air of the mountains the boy's spirit had wandered where it listed, and the eager eyes had learned to love and study nature. It was the love of form that had set him to try and picture a goat upon the surface of the rock; it was the actual appearance of objects that he sought to render when, in due time, he learned to use the brush.

If you turn again to a comparison of his Madonna with that of Cimabue, you will see what strides he had already made toward natural truth. Observe how the figure of the Virgin is made real to us, notwithstanding that it is covered, as in Cimabue's, with drapery; and while the Christ-child in each picture is represented in a similar garment, the form in Cimabue's does not

MADONNA ENTHRONED   CIMABUE

RUCELLAI CHAPEL, SANTA MARIA NOVELLA, FLORENCE

MADONNA ENTHRONED   GIOTTO

ACADEMY. FLORENCE

appear to be as strong and firm and life-like as in Giotto's. And if you examine the other figures in his picture you will find the same suggestion of substantial form that could be touched and grasped in the arms. Notice, further, how Giotto's feeling for truth has affected his arrangement of the forms. The throne actually occupies space of three dimensions—length, breadth, and thickness; so do all the figures, and they rest firmly upon the ground; the artist has called in the aid of perspective to enforce the reality of his group.

Now, how has he accomplished this appearance of reality? By the use of light and shade, and by making his lines functional—expressive, that is to say, of the structure and character of the object. Compare, for example, the figure of the infant Saviour in the two pictures. In Cimabue's the drapery is scored with lines which vaguely hint at folds and obscure the shape of the limbs beneath; but in Giotto's certain parts of the figure are made to project by the use of high lights, and others are correspondingly depressed by shade, while the lines of the drapery serve to indicate the shape of the form beneath.

This use of light and shade by Giotto, while it marks a distinct advance from the flat pattern-like painting of the Byzantine school, is still rudimentary; and, as if conscious of the fact, the artist has selected the most simple arrangements of drapery. Indeed, breadth and simplicity are characteristic of the whole picture. It was painted probably during the years of his apprenticeship to Cimabue, or, at any rate, under his influence, and shows much less freedom and assurance than the works of his maturity. These are to be found in frescoes upon the walls of the Upper and Lower Churches at Assisi; the Arena Chapel, Padua; the Bardi and Peruzzi Chapels, S. Croce; and the Chapel of the Bargello, Florence. Giotto was the first to introduce the faces of contemporaries into his pictures, and the *Paradise* on the walls of the Bargello contains the famous portrait of Dante in his early manhood. It had remained covered with whitewash for two hundred years, until once more brought to light in 1840. All these paintings were executed in fresco—that is to say, on the plaster before it was dry, with water-colors mixed in a glutinous medium, so that as the surface hardened the colors became incorporated in it. While the technical knowledge displayed in them is rudimentary, they are so simple and unaffected, so earnest and large in feeling, and tell the story with such dramatic effect, that they command the interest and enthusiasm of the modern student.

In his own day Giotto's fame as a painter was supreme; he had numerous followers, and these Giotteschi, as they were styled, perpetuated his methods for nearly a hundred years. But, like all the great men of the Florentine school, he was a master of more than one craft. "Forget that they were painters," writes Mr. Berenson, "they remain great sculptors; forget that they were sculptors, and still they remain architects, poets, and even men of science." The beautiful Campanile, which stands beside the Cathedral in Florence, and represents a perfect union of strength and elegance, was designed by Giotto and partly erected in his lifetime. Moreover, the sculptured reliefs which decorate its lower part were all from his designs, though he lived to execute only two of them. Thus, architect, sculptor, painter, friend of Dante and of other great men of his day, Giotto was the worthy forerunner of that galaxy of brilliant men who thronged the later days of the Italian Renaissance.

CHAPTER III

TOMMASO MASACCIO
1401–1428
Italian School of Florence

ANDREA MANTEGNA
1431–1506
Italian School of Padua

SINCE the death of Giotto nearly a hundred years have elapsed, during which his followers in Florence and certain painters in Siena, notably the brothers Lorenzetti, have been continuing the effort to emancipate painting from the flat formalism of Byzantine art. But, although they have learned something more about expressing the roundness of form, have studied more closely the action of light upon objects and the expression and character of faces, and have begun to acquire some insight into the principles of foreshortening and perspective, they are inferior to Giotto in originality of feeling and grandeur of design. He had been a solitary genius.

However, at the beginning of the fifteenth century, there arose in Florence a new genius, who became to this century what Giotto had been to the fourteenth. At a bound he leaped above all competitors, set painting free from its shackles, and continued to be a stimulus to hosts of other painters, including Michelangelo and Raphael. This new genius was Masaccio; and he, after his short life of twenty-seven years, was followed by the Paduan

Mantegna; this man, too, a genius, whose influence was wide-spread. By these two men painting was completely emancipated and set upon that sure and certain path along which it marched with gathering splendor toward the climax of the High Renaissance of the sixteenth century.

The great achievement of both these men, the original force from which all other improvements followed, was to realize for themselves and to impress upon others the independent dignity of painting as an art. Hitherto it had been regarded as the handmaid of religion, its highest function to set before the eyes of men the doctrines of the church. We have seen to what a condition it had thus been brought under Byzantine influences. Nor was Giotto able to do more than accept this secondary use of painting and then try to infuse more life into it. A century had to drag its length before Masaccio and Mantegna could say, in effect: " Before everything else we are painters; practisers of an art that, like sculpture, but much more than it, can make the external appearances of things visible to the eye. The invisible things of the spirit we will embody in our pictures if we can, but it is not with them that painting is first concerned. Its first duty is to develop that which belongs exclusively to itself. The teaching of doctrine, the telling of sacred stories and legends, we share with the men who use spoken or written words, and their power in this respect is fuller than ours; the suggestion of beautiful thoughts is quite as much, and more, within the power of the musician; but the representation of the external appearance of things, and especially of humanity, the crown of things, is the one point in which painting excels all other modes of expression. This is its special province; and our aim as painters must be, first and foremost, to represent the external appearances of things. This is at once our peculiar province and delight."

The joy of the painter in external things, we shall find, was shared at this time by thousands who were not painters. It was a symptom of the age. But, before discussing it, let us turn to the two pictures: Masaccio's *St. Peter Baptizing the Heathen* and Mantegna's *Gonzaga, Marquis of Mantua, Welcoming Home from Rome his Son, the Cardinal Francesco.* The former is religious in subject; but is it not clear that what chiefly occupied Masaccio's mind was to represent the incident as it may actually have occurred, with real men conducting themselves as they naturally might do under the circumstances? Observe especially the young man on the right with his arms crossed. In the first place, it is an enormous advance on Byzantinism that the artist, in this figure and the kneeling one, has represented the nude. Giotto had made a tentative step in this direction when, in his picture of the *Entombment,* he painted the figure of Christ nude as far as the waist. But here the baptism justified a nude representation of the whole of the figure, and Masaccio made full use of the opportunity. Note also in each case with what a regard for character as well as correctness of form; with an intent to make the nude a vehicle of expression. Compare the reverential composure of the young man who kneels with the trembling attitude of the other who stands on the bank shivering and nervously waiting his turn. Moreover, in each case, note the truth to nature represented in the pose: the shoulders, being drawn forward, are balanced by the bending of the knees and the drawing back of the body. For the present it will be sufficient to contrast with these nude figures the grand figure of St. Peter. The drapery is broadly and simply treated, as in Giotto's paintings, but with still greater ease and fluency of lines and masses that more thoroughly suggest the attitude and bulk of form of the figure. Lastly, observe the dignity of the saint's head, and the character and individuality portrayed in all the faces. It is humanity for its own sake, as separately represented in the individual, not the use of form for symbolical purposes, that interested Masaccio. With him painting became emancipated finally from Byzantinism.

When we turn to the Mantegna, it is probably again the character and individuality of the heads which first arrest our attention. They are portraits of the marquis, his sons, and courtiers: not beautiful, except perhaps in the case of the youth in the foreground. He is already a prothonotary of the holy see at Rome, one of the twelve ecclesiastical clerks who keep a record of the pontifical proceedings, and is destined to be a bishop. The gravity of life has weighed his young face with seriousness; in remarkable contrast to his elder brother, the Cardinal Francesco. The latter is soft and fleshly, as if fond of easy living; we are not surprised to learn that he is a lover of music, a connoisseur and collector of works of art, a man of refined and comfortable tastes. The faces of these two sons are curiously reflected in the stern, strong, but not untender head of the old father on the left, while the two little children have a strange infantile resemblance to the other members of the family. The remainder of the group consists of courtiers, men of pronounced character, shrewd and masterful. Throughout the whole there is a tendency toward stiff attitudes and liny draperies, at first sight not agreeable; but there is no mistaking the reality of these people; and we shall better appreciate the picture when we have discovered the influence that helped to form Mantegna's style.

It was through the lessons learned from sculpture that painting recovered its independent force. Both Masaccio and Mantegna displayed their genius by making these lessons so completely their own that they themselves became the models for succeeding painters. Being a Florentine, Masaccio must have been familiar from childhood with the bronze doors of the Baptistery by Andrea Pisano, the finest sculptural work of the fourteenth century in Italy; and, before he began the painting of *St. Peter,* Ghiberti had finished the first pair of his doors for the same Baptistery, and Donatello had executed, among other works, his statue of *St. George.* The last-named is remarkable for its naturalistic and at the same time elevated treatment of the human figure in the complete round, while Ghiberti's pictorial panels, which Michelangelo thought worthy of decorating the Gates of Paradise, no less naturalistic than the *St. George,* are richly elaborate compositions containing numerous figures—in some cases as many as a hundred —associated with architecture and landscape. The *St. George* is an example of the grandeur of form in the round; Ghiberti's work, of the illusion which can be

ST. PETER BAPTIZING   MASACCIO

BRANCACCI CHAPEL, CHURCH OF THE CARMINE, FLORENCE

GONZAGA WELCOMING HIS SON   MANTEGNA

CAMERA DEGLI SPOSI, CASTELLO DI CORTE, MANTUA

produced by varying the elevation of the surfaces, so that, although nothing is in the round, everything has the appearance of being; and also by regulating the direction of lines and the gradations of planes, so that the scene depicted seems to extend back in a distant perspective.

This latter quality is conspicuous in Masaccio's as compared with earlier work. There is no longer a stretching of the figures across the picture in a flat band, almost on the same plane, with other figures placed above them, whose position in a further plane is only indicated by a diminution of their size; instead, a natural and concentrated grouping, in which the figures and landscape occupy in a natural way their several planes in the receding space. For this picture is no longer flat, but hollow and filled with air. Whatever Masaccio may have learned from the sculptors, this he gained from a direct study of nature. He proved himself a true painter by the skill with which he surrounded his figures with air and represented the varying effects of light upon the different objects. And these qualities, added to his knowledge of the human form and his strong, sincere treatment of it in composition and drawing, are the secrets of his greatness.

His chief works are the frescoes in the Brancacci Chapel of the Church of the Carmine in Florence, of which this *St. Peter* is one: a series finished later by Filippino. In 1428 he .was summoned to Rome, and all further knowledge of "Careless Thomas" (for that is the meaning of his name) ceases. It was nearly fifty years before a worthy successor to him appeared in Florence, and meanwhile the story shifts to Padua and to Mantegna.

In 1305 Giotto had gone to that city and commenced the series of thirty-eight frescoes in the Chapel of the Arena, which are among his most famous works. But they bore no immediate fruit in Padua. More than a hundred years afterward, however, one Squarcione, a tailor and embroiderer, began to take an interest in art. Having considerable means, he proceeded to make a collection of pictures; and, traveling through Italy and, some say, Greece, made drawings and took casts of ancient marbles. Returned to Padua, he placed these on exhibition and opened a school of art. The most famous of his pupils was Andrea Mantegna, the son of a small farmer. The master had thought so highly of the boy that he adopted him as a son, thereby securing additional control over his labors. His shrewdness was justified, for at the age of twenty-one the young man was already executing important work on behalf of his master. The latter, in time, received a commission to decorate the chapel of the Ovetari family in the Church of the Eremitani; and here, quite close to the garden inclosing Giotto's chapel, Squarcione's pupils painted a series of frescoes, which became to the painters of North Italy what those by Masaccio in the Brancacci Chapel were to Florence.

At the commencement of this series, which was designed to represent incidents in the lives of St. Christopher and St. James, the master's best pupil was Niccolo Pizzolo, whose most promising career was cut short in a street brawl; but before the work's completion it was clear that the greatest of all was Mantegna. While the latter was still engaged upon this work, he made the acquaintance of the Venetian painter Jacopo Bellini, who, with his two sons, later to be so famous in the annals of Venetian painting, Gentile and Giovanni, was then sojourning in Padua. The acquaintance ripened into a close attachment, which was cemented by Mantegna's marriage to Jacopo's daughter.

His growing reputation caused him to be summoned to Verona, and while he was working in that city there came an invitation, frequently repeated, from Lodovico Gonzaga, Marquis of Mantua. For, by this time, the municipal authority of the free cities, which had flourished during the fourteenth century, had been usurped by powerful families.

The Communes, the Republics of Italy, after their period of self-assertion, of glory, of intense localized energy and furious internecine rivalry, began to get exhausted, to decay, to become weaker and weaker, by degrees to disappear altogether. And in their place there sprang up everywhere the great princely houses—the Medici of Florence, the Visconti and the Sforza at Milan, the Este at Ferrara, the Bentivogli at Bologna, the Montefeltri at Urbino, the Baglioni at Perugia, the Malatesta at Rimini and Cesena, and the Gonzaghi at Mantua.[1]

These despots intrenched themselves in castles to overawe the cities which they ruled, continually threatened by the outward attacks of one another, and by attempts at poisoning or assassination from enemies within. Yet they maintained magnificent courts, surrounding themselves with scholars, poets, and painters.

[1] Selwyn Brinton: Renaissance in Italian Art.

HOW TO STUDY PICTURES

In the strange and frightful isolation in which the Italian despot often lived, ever plotting himself to keep his insecure throne, ever watching against plots within the city and without, this brilliant society of dependants became his solace and his highest pleasure. Traverse that wonderful palace of the house of Este—intact, surrounded by its moat, dominating with its insolent pride the old city of Ferrara. Into the upper galleries and banquet-halls the sunlight pours. We seem to hear the musical laughter, the rustle of the rich old cinque-cento costumes; the walls are hung with paintings by Dosso Dossi or Titian—naked wrestlers, figures running, and the radiant deities of the old reawakened mythology. And below, beneath even the moat, lies the other side of the picture: the horrible dungeons, dark, noisome, shadowy, where the political conspirator, the inconvenient relative, the too outspoken citizen, the suspected wife, were thrust, and—soon forgotten.

Yet within some such courts this life must often have been very brilliant and wonderful. At Mantua the marquis had brought from Padua the great Greek and Latin scholar, Vittorino da Feltre, to be tutor to his children. A villa was allotted to the household, and a system of education commenced which deserved the admiration and fame it soon gained. Besides the rich and noble youths who thronged to Vittorino, no less than sixty poor scholars were fed, clothed, and taught at his own expense. Plain living and high thinking were there the rule; diet and physical exercises—wrestling, fencing, swimming, riding—were carefully considered; the highest classic authors, Virgil and Homer, Cicero and Demosthenes, were revered as the supremest masters of style.[1]

Into this refined society of scholars and courtiers was Mantegna summoned, and in the service of this marquis and of three of his successors he remained, with the

[1] Selwyn Brinton, *op. cit.*

[32]

exception of two years spent in Rome, until the end of his life.

In the atmosphere of such a court he was completely at home, for here were focused into a brilliant epitome the great forces which, during this century, were leavening the whole of Italy and were also at work in Mantegna himself. These were, first of all, the moral qualities of self-assertion, belief in the dignity of man and in the grand possibilities of life, intense earnestness and eager seriousness; secondly, the mighty influence of the rediscovered Latin authors, and particularly of the Greek, the consequent admiration and worship of the antique, and the conviction that in it was to be found the key to unlock all the glorious possibilities of the modern life.

Mantegna, as we have seen, had been nourished upon antique sculpture; from his own standpoint as an artist, he was the equal of the classic scholars; they could learn from him, as he from them; he could share the effort of all to enlighten the present by the past. Therefore, if we turn again to this picture, still surviving on the wall of one of the rooms in the castle of Mantua, where all those people actually lived their proud, high-seeking, dignified, and, at times, terrible lives, we may be able perhaps to see it with truer eyes, and find it extraordinarily fascinating. We shall understand that it was with deliberation that Mantegna made the figures of the marquis and his sons particularly immobile, their draperies notably stiff. By thus emphasizing the resemblance of this portion of his picture to antique low-relief sculpture, he singled out these figures from the others for particular honor. That the whole group stretches across the composition with a general resemblance to an ancient bas-relief, is a tribute to the classic ideals which he and all those people worshiped. But that he was also a student of nature may be seen in the fine perspective of the landscape. A still finer example of perspective adorns the ceiling of this same room, which he decorated in such a way that one seems to be looking up at the sky through a circular opening, as we may see it actually through the eye of the Pantheon's dome. Around the circle is a balustrade, upon which stand a peacock and a basket of fruit; and leaning upon it are a girl with jeweled head-dress and a negress, who look down with laughing faces, while a band of winged boys play on the edge of the stone-work. Vasari relates what admiration this excited. Nothing so daring or so scientific had previously been accomplished in Italy.

The work, however, which seems to have pleased Mantegna himself best was his series of panels, painted on canvas, in all eighty feet long, representing the *Triumph of Cæsar*. Into this long procession he crowded the fruits of the study he most loved—as Vasari says:

the perfumes, the incense-bearers, the priests, the oxen crowned for sacrifice, the prisoners, the booty seized by the soldiers, the well-ordered squadrons, the elephants, the spoils of art, the victories, cities, and fortresses imitated on different cars, together with an infinitude of trophies, helmets, corselets, and arms of all kinds borne aloft on spears, with ornaments, vases, and rich vessels innumerable.

Of these paintings, marvelous exhibitions of knowledge, invention, and skill, Mantegna, who was most self-exacting and severe in the judgment of himself, said: "I really was not ashamed of having painted them." In 1628, two years before the sack of Mantua by the Austrians, they were sold to Charles I of England, and now are in Hampton Court Palace, irreparably damaged by "restoration." Fortunately they can still be studied in the magnificent series of engravings made from them by Andrea Andreani at the close of the sixteenth century. Of portions also of the *Triumph* Mantegna himself made engravings upon copper.

For this profound student of the antique, of nature, and of the scientific principles of drawing and painting, found time, in the midst of his work with the brush and pencil, to execute many engravings, among the most famous of which are an *Entombment of Christ* and a *Judith with the Head of Holofernes*. The prints of his engravings, traveling broadcast through Europe as well as Italy, helped to teach others and to draw many students to Mantua to build up their own knowledge by study of the great master's paintings.

I wish it were possible to illustrate here the two engravings mentioned above, for they throw a strong light upon Mantegna's genius. They prove, on the one hand his extraordinary intensity of feeling, on the other his extraordinarily dispassionate self-control, and also his power over line to make it express emotion. In the *Entombment* the lifeless, expressionless body of the Saviour is surrounded with dramatic energy: the bearers straining on the burden, the mourners weeping or tossing their hands in anguish, the Virgin in collapse, St. John standing erect with clenched hands and open mouth, shrieking in utter horror that such a thing should be! It is the work of a man whose imagination has been filled with the terribleness of suffering. Yet, when he draws Judith, he represents her as a beautiful Vestal virgin, a visionary, like Joan of Arc, dreamily and daintily passing her hand over the head of the murdered general who would have enslaved her nation. No sight of blood, nothing of sensationalism; he himself betrays no feeling, looks at the matter quite objectively, sees only in the horror of the situation a chance for most exquisite beauty of expressional line.

Could you compare it with our present picture, it would help you to understand that the severity of the latter was deliberate. Yet, even without the comparison, a study of the accompanying illustration will reveal how the intentional severity of the upright lines of figures, tree, and column has been counteracted and assuaged by the curving line, like a loop of links, formed by the tender figures in the group, the young ecclesiastic and the little children; and, further, by the diagonal lines of the beautiful landscape.

The stern old Paduan expressed the intense energy of his age, tempered only occasionally with the softer sense of beauty.

CHAPTER IV

FRA ANGELICO	JAN VAN EYCK
1387–1455	*1390(?)–1441*
Italian School of Florence	*Flemish School of Bruges*

BEFORE proceeding along the path which Masaccio and Mantegna have struck out, we must pause to consider a painter who, although a contemporary of theirs, belongs more to the past. He was the last inheritor of the Giottesque tradition, and the last of the painters whose work is thoroughly religious.

I invite you to turn aside into a little quiet garden, as it were, secluded within cloister walls, where Fra Angelico, painter and monk, a brother of the black-and-white order of the Dominicans, devoted his life to religious paintings. Choosing, as an example of his work, *The Annunciation,* I have placed it in comparison with *The Virgin and Donor* by Jan van Eyck, who shares with his brother Hubert the honor of founding the Flemish School.

One reason for this comparison is that we are trying to gain a bird's-eye view of the story of painting; not allowing ourselves to become absorbed in any one spot to the exclusion of others, but scanning the whole field and noting the great movements as they spring up, now here, now there, sometimes related to one another, some-

[37]

times separate, but all of them features in the general progress of European civilization. Surely it is interesting to realize that at the commencement of this fifteenth century, when Italy was waking up to its second and greatest activity, the Flemish also were waking up to art, the first among the Northern nations. Again, I have selected this comparison, because it was religious subjects that chiefly occupied the Flemish painters, and Fra Angelico is the most remarkable example in Italian art of a religious painter of religious subjects. Moreover, he worked in a beautiful seclusion, and secluded also was the art of Flanders, a choice garden in the northern wilderness. It was an art, too, of minute perfection of finish, and such was Fra Angelico's.

There is in both these pictures a minute finish of detail which suggests—what is indeed the case—that each artist owed something to the miniature-painters who decorated with tiny scenes the pages of the manuscripts. But in Fra Angelico's there is a greater simplicity and, as the artists call it, a greater breadth of style; for this picture was executed when he was about fifty years old; by which time he had been painting for thirty years and had come, as we shall see, under many influences that did not reach the Flemish artist.

So let us begin by studying the latter's picture. It was painted for presentation to a church, and the portrait of the donor, the Canon Rollin, was introduced. This was a common practice in the Renaissance days. The picture was intended to serve the double purpose of being " to the glory of God and in memory of the donor." Clad in a dark robe brocaded with flower-forms of a bronze hue that catch the light, now richly, now delicately, like the body and wings of a May-bug, the canon is kneeling in an attitude of prayer, but gazes upon the Virgin with a piercing look of scrutiny. In this strong face we feel sure that the artist has painted an extraordinarily faithful portrait; and from the fact that the expression of the face does not correspond with the humble and devout gesture of the hands, we learn that although Van Eyck painted religious pictures, he was not a religious painter in the way that Fra Angelico was.

Note also the greater elaboration of Van Eyck's picture. After he had secured a dignified composition, in which the principal figures should count as large and handsome spots and the background be broken up by contrast into a more complicated fretwork of decoration, he then set himself to carry each separate part to the finest possible degree of accurate and perfect workmanship. Here appears the Flemish spirit, with its patient, tireless pursuit of minute beauty, such as produced a nation of craftsmen, skilled in illumination, in miniature-painting, in jewelry and the working of gold and silver, in embroidery and the making of tapestries and stained-glass windows. But Jan van Eyck and his elder brother Hubert, although they had this love of minute perfection, had also large ideas, and never allowed the little details to detract from the grand general significance of the whole work.

We may examine, for example, the figure of the Christ; it is painted with the precise daintiness of a miniature and is very baby-like, yet it has also remarkable character, an air of seriousness, as if it were conscious of being more than its little form would indicate. The Virgin's robe is crimson; her face is not beautiful, being of the heavy, wholesome, practical type of the women of the country; but she has a wealth of golden hair, painted with wonderful realism, and over it a little angel holds a golden crown of exquisite workmanship decorated with pearls. Or you may study with interest the patterning of the marble floor; the elegant arcade of arches and columns, with the glimpse of a leaded window on each side; or the little garden beyond, where lilies are growing in the borders, magpies strut on the paths, peacocks sun themselves upon the balustrades, and two figures are looking out over the distant landscape. Here is a far-stretching scene in miniature: level country, characteristically Flemish, threaded by a river over which is a bridge connecting the town on the one bank with that on the other. People are passing over the bridge, or crossing the water in boats, or walking the streets, with an appearance of reality, although their stature is almost microscopic. Indeed, there is a great deal in the picture that it is impossible to discover in the black-and-white reproduction, which also gives little idea of the textures—that is to say, of the rendering of the different surfaces of marble, fabric, flesh, or metal and the rest, each according to its special quality—and none of the rich, full, firm coloring, brilliant as agate or precious stones.

This wonderful color is another reason of the fame of the Van Eycks. Artists came from Italy to study their pictures, to discover what they themselves must do in

THE ANNUNCIATION

VIRGIN AND DONOR   LOUVRE, PARIS   JAN VAN EYCK

order to paint so well, with such brilliance, such full and firm effect, as these two brothers. For the latter had found out the secret of using oil successfully as a medium. Before their day attempts had been made to mix colors in the medium of oil, but the oil was slow in drying, and the varnish added to remedy this had blackened the colors. The Van Eycks, however, had hit upon a transparent varnish which dried quickly and without injury to the tints. Though they guarded the secret jealously, it was discovered by the Italian Antonello da Messina, who was working in Bruges, and by him published to the world. The invention made possible the enormous development in the art of painting which ensued.

Little is known of the two brothers; even the dates of their birth being uncertain. Their most famous work, begun by Hubert and finished by Jan, is the altarpiece, *The Adoration of the Lamb*. Jan, as perhaps also Hubert, was for a time in the service of Philip the Good, Duke of Burgundy. He was entered in the household as " varlet and painter "; but acted at the same time as confidential friend, and for his services received an annual salary of one hundred livres (almost twenty-five dollars), two horses for his use, and a " varlet in livery " to attend on him. The greater part of his life was spent in Bruges.

In these two brothers the grand art of Flanders was born in a day. Like " the sudden flowering of the aloe, after sleeping through a century of suns," this art, rooted in the native soil, nurtured by the smaller arts of craftsmanship, reached its full ripeness, and expanded into blossom. Such further development as it experienced, we shall find, came from Italian influence; but the distinctly Flemish art, born out of local conditions in Flanders, was already full grown. The great French painter and critic, Fromentin, says of it: "Imagine a collection of the creations of the goldsmiths, executed in paint, in which one feels the handiwork of the enameler, the glass-worker, the graver, and the illuminator. Its sentiment is grave, for it is inspired by the sentiment of the monasteries; but it is under the patronage of princes, and its general character is resplendent."

And now let us turn back to Fra Angelico. Little is known of his early life except that he was born at Vicchio, in the broad fertile valley of the Mugello, not far from Florence, that his name was Guido, and that he passed his youth in Florence, probably in some *bottega,* for at twenty he was recognized as a painter. But he had already come under the influence of the great preacher and scholar, Giovanni Dominici, who traveled up and down the length and breadth of Italy, exhorting all men to the holier life practised by the order of Dominican monks. At the door of their convent on the slopes of Fiesole, just above Florence, Guido and his brother Benedetto, an illuminator, sought admittance. They were welcomed by the monks, and, after a year's novitiate, admitted to the brotherhood, Guido taking the name by which he was known in after life, Fra Giovanni da Fiesole; for the title of " Angelico," the " Angel," or " Il Beato," " The Blessed," was conferred on him after his death.

Henceforth he became an example of two personalities in one man: he was all in all a painter, all in all a devout monk; his subjects were ever religious ones and represented in a deeply religious spirit, yet his devotion as a monk was no greater than his absorption as an artist. Consequently, though his life was secluded within the walls of the monastery, he kept in touch with the art movements of his time and continually developed as a painter. His early work shows that he had learned of the illuminators who inherited the Byzantine traditions, and had been affected by the simple religious feeling of Giotto's work. Then he began to learn of that brilliant band of sculptors and architects who were enriching Florence by their genius. Ghiberti was executing his pictures in bronze upon the doors of the Baptistery; Donatello, his famous statue of *St. George* and the dancing children around the organ-gallery in the Cathedral; and Luca della Robbia also was at work upon his frieze of children, singing, dancing, and playing upon instruments. Moreover, Masaccio had revealed the dignity of form in painting. Through these artists the beauty of the human form and of its life and movement was being manifested to the Florentines and to the other cities, whither their fame spread.

Among the rest, Angelico catches the enthusiasm and gives increasing reality of life and movement to his figures. Furthermore, from the convent garden he could see the marvelous dome, designed by Brunelleschi, steadily rising above the Cathedral. What wonder that his imagination was fired and that he became, like other cultivated men of the day, an earnest student of architecture! At length, in the summer of 1435, the brethren moved into Florence and took up their abode in the monastery of San Marco. The original house was being added to, at the expense of Duke Cosimo de' Medici, by his favorite architect, Michelozzo. Can you not imagine with what joy Angelico must have watched the work, moved alike by the devout pride of a brother in his order and by an artist's sympathy with beauty? For he was to decorate the refectory and the corridors and cells; and close indeed must have been the bond between the painter and the architect.

If you turn again to the *Annunciation* that he painted later on the wall of the upper corridor, you will see how large a part the architecture plays in the composition of the picture.

The arcaded loggia is clearly inspired by the one down-stairs in the courtyard, and the two Ionic columns are careful copies of those which Michelozzo had just completed. Moreover, the vaulted ceilings, the round arch and slender columns with an adaptation of the Corinthian capital, are all characteristic of the elegant dignity of the arcades which this architect and Brunelleschi were introducing into the interior courts of their buildings, while leaving the outside grave and often stern and massive, like a fortress.

And from this we may glean two points of interest: first, how the different kinds of artists of this period learned from one another, working together in a newly awakened enthusiasm for beauty; and, secondly, that Angelico himself, by contact with these outside influences, had broadened and strengthened his own style. He was now about fifty years old, and this picture, representing his maturity, is far in advance of the earlier ones. They were apt to be crowded with figures and decorative details. This one is so open and spacious, freely letting in the quiet warmth of the twilight; and so simple in general plan and therefore decorative in a big way. Instead of a multiplicity of objects counteracting the effect of one another, a few leading features are enforced by repetition: the curved lines of the arches and ceilings, for example, and the upright ones of the columns and fence. And, in addition to the interlaced pattern formed by the contrast of these two sorts of lines, there is the massed contrast of the garden, interspersed as it is with little features, and of the broad, plain surfaces of the masonry, enlivened only by a few choicely selected details.

How this arrangement of beautiful simplicity, so elevated in its general design, so tender in its parts, accords with the character of the two figures and with the scene they are enacting! In the cool of the evening Mary has been surprised by God's messenger, Gabriel. He has but this moment alighted; his wings still glisten with the iridescence of the sky, and his body thrills yet with the rapidity of his flight, as he drops on one knee with bowed head and folded hands in adoration of her who is to be the mother of the Saviour. And at this apparition, flashing so suddenly across the quiet tenor of her days, Mary's face is troubled; but, as she harkens to the divine message, she too bows her head and folds her arms in adoration and in meek acceptance. "And Mary said, Behold the handmaid of the Lord; be it unto me according to thy word."

Fitly corresponding to the sentiment of the occasion is the tender purity of the color-scheme. The angel's robe is pale rose-color edged with gold; Madonna's robe is a paler pink, and her mantle deep blue; while, beyond the whiteness of the architecture, the grass is starred with daisies, and above the fence peep clusters of roses backed by dark-green cypresses.

And fitly corresponding too is the habitation of the picture. You pass out of the traffic of the streets into the quiet retreat of Michelozzo's court, some afternoon, perhaps, when the sloping sun plays lovingly over a few of the arches and columns, while the rest are drowsing in various gradations of shadow. A door in the cloisters leads into the chapter-house, adorned with Fra Angelico's *Crucifixion;* a second opens into the refectory, where the brethren took their meals in presence of another of their brother's pictures; and when you have mounted the stairs you pass along the corridor, out of which open the little private cells, where the black-and-white-habited monks worked and slept and meditated: in one of them Fra Bartolommeo—after Angelico's time, but, like him, a painter—and in another Savonarola, a later prior of the order, who stirred Florence to the depths by his denunciations of sin, and was hanged by his enemies, his body being burned and its ashes thrown into the Arno. You pass along beside the cells, each with its little window and its sacred painting on the wall done by Angelico, until at the end of the corridor you come face to face with this *Annunciation.*

Stilled is the busy life of the place, the monks are gone, their habitation now a show-place trod by the steps of visitors from all parts of the world. But the spirit of peace and piety still haunts the spot and finds its sweetest expression in this picture.

Compared with it, Van Eyck's *The Virgin and Donor* is mundane, of the world, worldly; it is the work of a great painter luxuriating in the opportunities which the sacred subject offered. Fra Angelico was no less ardent a painter, but his painting was saturated also with the feeling of devout religion. In the complete union of the artist and the devotee he stands alone in the history of painting. His gentle art and life represent, as I have said, a quiet back-water, secluded from the river of achievement that was gathering force and about to plunge on in full might through the fifteenth century.

CHAPTER V

ALESSANDRO BOTTICELLI
1444/7–1510
Italian School of Florence

HANS MEMLING
1430(?)–1494
Flemish School of Bruges

WE have seen that the revival of painting began with the study of the appearances of objects and an attempt to represent them as real to the senses of sight and touch; that the painters learned from the sculptors, who themselves had learned from the remains of antique sculpture; and that the result was a closer truth to nature, in the representation both of the human form and of its movement. We have also seen how in Flanders Jan van Eyck developed a grand school of painting out of the national skill of craftsmanship in the minor arts of decoration,—goldsmith's work, stained glass, embroidery, tapestry, and the like,—and that to the truth of natural form he added also a true appearance of textures. Further, we have seen how in Fra Angelico appeared the most perfect flower of that old religious feeling which for centuries had been a light in the darkness of the world.

We have now to consider the effect produced upon painting by the revival of the study of Greek, which revealed to Italy of the fifteenth century a new light, in the joy of which the older light was dimmed. Botticelli typifies this new inspiration. I have coupled with him the Flemish painter Memling, in order to continue our study of the Flemish School, and also because both these artists, though they worked apart and under very different conditions, had one quality in common. A certain *naïveté* of mind appears in each, an unaffected simplicity, frank and artless, fresh and tender like the child-mind or the opening buds of spring flowers. In Memling's case it is tinctured with gentle sentiment; in that of Botticelli, with a wistful yearning toward the light of old Hellas which was just beginning to dawn on the world of his time.

If you visit the Campo Santo at Pisa, you will see some frescoes which were painted in the fourteenth century, perhaps by Orcagna, or, as others think, by the brothers Lorenzetti. Their subjects are, *The Triumph of Death, The Judgment,* and *Hell.* They are terrible in their tragic intensity. A party of ladies and knights are going a-hawking; but their horses start back, sniffing at three open coffins in which half-decayed corpses are lying. For one of those awful plagues which periodically devastated Europe is stalking through the land. In another part of the picture appears a throng of youths and maidens dancing in a rose-garden, whom Death is mowing down with a scythe; elsewhere wretched creatures, mutilated by torture, are imploring Death in vain to ease them of their anguish; good and evil spirits struggle for the souls of men; and apart from these grisly horrors are hermits, living their lives of abnegation with the birds and beasts among the rocks.

These frescoes depict with horrible directness the dark turmoil of soul and body in the middle ages; the cruelty of man to man; the ever-present dread specter of death; the judgment of God, inexorable, inevitable; the solitude of the monkish life, as the only refuge from a sinful and doomed world; lurid fire, and blackness hanging like a thick pall above it, and no escape except in the renunciation of the world and of the joy of living.

But a glimmer of light was trembling on the horizon. The possibility of beauty in the living of this life was beginning to swallow up the horror of death; the soul of man, so long pent up and imprisoned in savage darkness, had been suddenly liberated; for what is called "The New Learning" had unlocked the dungeons of thought.

The newness consisted in two things: first, that the learning concerned itself with new subjects; secondly, that the knowledge of Greek was recovered by the western world.

Dante's poems were the swan-song of the middle ages. Seventeen years before his death, Petrarch was born; nine years later Boccaccio; and the poetry of both and the stories of the latter are the evangel of the modern world. Instead of speculating on the mysteries that lie beyond the grave, their theme is the present life and living humanity.

Moreover, both of them were inflamed with a longing to know all that was to be known of the older classic authors of Italy, and of the Greek classics upon which the Roman were founded. They ransacked Italy for manuscripts, and procured from a certain Leontius Pilatus, a native of Greece, a rude translation of Homer into Latin; for with the Greek tongue itself they had no acquaintance.

The introduction of this into Italian culture dates from 1396, when Manuel Chrysoloras, a Byzantine scholar, was appointed professor of Greek at Florence. From him and from his pupils the knowledge of Greek literature spread rapidly over Italy, accompanied by an extraordinary enthusiasm for the antique: for Roman and Greek art, and for Greek thought and Greek ideals. Hence the artist's devotion to the beauty of the human form, the scholar's admiration of Plato's philosophy. Artists and scholars thronged the court of Duke Lorenzo de' Medici—Lorenzo the Magnificent, patron of arts and letters; and among the brilliant throng none was more highly honored than Sandro Botticelli.

He was the son of a citizen in comfortable circumstances, and had been " instructed in all such things as children are usually taught before they choose a calling." But he refused to give his attention to reading, writing, and accounts, continues Vasari, so that his father, despairing of his ever becoming a scholar, apprenticed him to the goldsmith Botticello: whence the name by which the world remembers him. In those days, as we have noted before, men were masters of more than one craft. Among Sandro's contemporaries, for instance, Pollajuolo was painter as well as goldsmith, and Verrocchio goldsmith, painter, and sculptor. Botticello's Sandro, a stubborn-featured youth with large, quietly searching eyes and a shock of yellow hair,—he has left a portrait of himself on the right-hand side of his picture of the *Adoration of the Magi,*—would also fain become a painter, and to that end was placed with the Carmelite monk Fra Lippo Lippi.

Read for yourself Browning's poem "Fra Lippo Lippi," and discover the friar's discontent at being obliged to represent religious subjects according to the conventions prescribed by his patron, the church. For he was a realist, as the artists of his day had become, satisfied with the joy and skill of painting, and with the actual study of the beauty and character of the human subject. Sandro made rapid progress, loved his master, and later on extended his love to his master's son, Filippino Lippi, and taught him to paint. But the master's realism scarcely touched him, for Sandro was a dreamer and a poet.

You will feel this, if you refer to the two pictures and compare his *Madonna Enthroned* with Memling's. The latter's is much more realistic. It is true that it does not, as a whole, represent a real scene, for the Virgin's throne with its embroidered hanging or dossal, the canopy or baldachin above it, and the richly decorated arch which frames it in, are not what you would expect to see set up in a landscape. These are the conventional features, repeated with variations in so many Madonna pictures intended for altarpieces. But how very real are the two peeps of landscape, drawn, we may feel sure, from nature: a great man's castle and a water-mill, two widely separated phases of life, suggesting, perhaps, that the Christ came to save rich and poor alike. This would be a touch of symbolism; another may appear in the introduction of the apple, intended to remind us of the circumstances of the fall of man, which the Saviour

MADONNA ENTHRONED   ALESSANDRO BOTTICELLI

BERLIN GALLERY

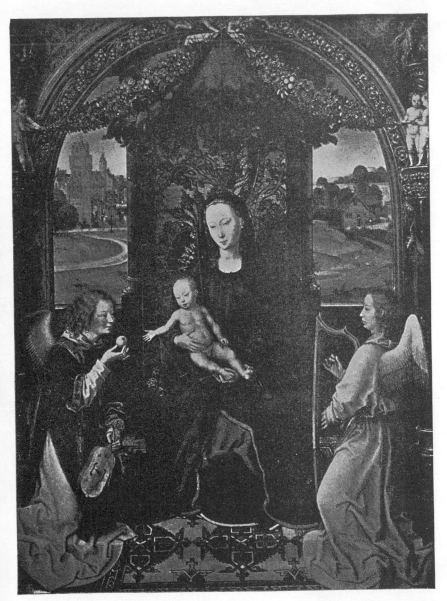

VIRGIN ENTHRONED   HANS MEMLING

UFFIZI GALLERY, FLORENCE

came into the world to redress. But Memling was satisfied merely to suggest the symbolism; and then devoted himself to rendering with characteristic *naïveté* a little scene of realism. The angel on the left is simply an older child, playfully attracting the baby's attention with an apple; the Christ is simply a baby attracted by the colored, shining object; and the pretty scene is watched intently by the other angel. On the Madonna's face, however, is an abstracted expression, as if her thoughts were far away; and indeed they are, yet not in pursuit of any mystical dream, but following that quiet, happy pathway along which a young mother's thoughts will roam. She is, in fact, only a girl-mother whom the artist has surprised, while she sits, unconscious of everything around her, wrapped up in the inward peace and joy of motherhood.

So we find in Memling's picture, despite the religious conception of its arrangement, a preoccupation with the natural appearances of persons and things, a close study of the way in which facts present themselves to the eye. This is apparent equally in the landscape, in the carved and embroidered ornament, in the character of the figures, and in the little story which they are enacting. As I have said, the spirit of the picture is realistic.

But turn to Botticelli's. Here the spirit is allegorical. He was fond of allegorical subjects, especially of mythological ones treated in a vein of allegory. His *Birth of Venus* and *Allegory of Spring* are the most famous examples. In the present case the subject is religious, but we may doubt if the Bible version of the story was in the artist's mind. He was commissioned to paint a Madonna and Child with attendant angels, and, poet and dreamer that he was, took the familiar theme and made it the framework of an imagery of his own. This imagery, it may be fairly safe to believe, had less to do with the old Gospel story than with the later gospel of the New Learning. In the figure of the Child-Christ there is a grave dignity, an assertion of authority; and not improbably the artist meant it to be symbolic of the wonderful new birth of classic culture. The only gesture of infancy is in the left arm and in the hand groping for the mother's breast. And she has the same kind of face, bowed in timid meekness, very sad in expression, which Botticelli gave to his *Venus*. Mother of love, mother of God,—he blends the Christian and the pagan worship to represent the mother of the " Desire of all nations." The cult of the Virgin, partly at least, had grown out of the ancient cult of Venus; and Botticelli, working in an age that was looking back to the classic past and trying to adjust the present to it, felt in Madonna and in Venus the twin expressions of a single sentiment—worship of the highest beauty in the person of woman. But beauty of face, as some may think, he does not give to his queen of love; she is meek and timid, as I have said, oppressed with gentle sadness; too frail as yet for a world still full of violence and confusion; sadly conscious that she is not yet at home in her new habitation. And in the faces of the angels also, the young, fair creatures that stand around the throne, there is a similar expression of wistful and unsatisfied yearning. It was so that Botticelli's own spirit peered through the still lingering darkness of the medieval times toward that light from Hellas which was beginning to dawn, but of which he himself never expected to see the noonday. Hence the strain of sadness in all his pictures; they have the note of infinite but ineffectual desire. So, when we understand this, we forget the homeliness of many of his faces, and find in them a spiritual significance which, we learn to feel, is a very touching and beautiful expression of the artist's own mind, of his particular way of looking at the world of his own time.

He looked at it as a poet, moved alike by the love of beauty and by the beauty of love; and out of the world's realities he fashioned himself dreams, and these he pictured. So his pictures, as I have said, are not records of fact, treated with a very pleasing fancifulness and reverence, as in this Madonna of Memling's; but visions, the beauty of which is rather spiritual than material. He tried, as it were, to paint not only the flower, but also its fragrance; and it was the fragrance that to him seemed the more precious quality.

So now, perhaps, we can begin to understand the difference between his technic—that is to say, his manner of setting down in paint what he desired to express—and Memling's. The latter, serene and happy, had all a child's delight in the appearances of things, attracted by them as the infant in this picture is attracted by the apple, and offering them to us with the same winning grace and certainty that they will please as the angel in the picture exhibits. So it is the facts, obvious to the senses of touch and sight, that he presents, with a loving, tender care to make them as obvious to us as possible, elaborating even the smallest parts. You have examined the beautiful workmanship in the ornamentation of the arch and in the garlands suspended by the charming little baby forms; but have you observed the tiny figures in the landscape? The castle drawbridge is down, and a lady on horseback passes over it, following a gentleman who may be riding forth to hunt, since a greyhound courses along behind him. From the mill is issuing a man with a sack of flour on his shoulders, which he will set upon the back of the donkey that waits patiently before the door; while a little way along the road stands a dog, all alert and impatient to start. These incidents illustrate Memling's fondness for detail and elaboration of finish, and his delight in the representation of facts as facts: traits which were characteristic of this early Flemish School. But observe that these minutely finished distant details illustrate also the *naïveté* of Memling. From where he stood to paint the foreground group, the figures in the background would appear simply as little spots of color. He did not paint the facts as they appeared to his eye, but as in his mind he knew them to be—the child's way of drawing.

By comparison with Memling, Botticelli is a painter not of facts, but of ideas; and his pictures are not so much a representation of certain objects as a pattern of forms. Nor is his coloring rich and lifelike, as Memling's: it is subordinated to form, and often rather a tinting than actual color. In fact, he is interested in the abstract possibilities of his art rather than in the concrete. For example, his compositions, as has just been said, are a pattern of forms; his figures do not actually occupy well-defined places in a well-defined area of space; they do not attract us by their suggestion of bulk, but as shapes of form, suggesting rather a flat pattern of decoration. Accordingly the lines which inclose the figures are chosen with the primary intention of being decorative. You will appreciate this if you will turn to the two pictures and compare the draperies of the angels. Those of Memling are commonplace in their prosy realism, compared with the fluttering grace of Botticelli's. But there is more in this flutter of draperies than mere beauty of line: it expresses a lively and graceful movement. These angels have alighted like birds, their garments still buoyed up with air and agitated by their speed of flight; each body being animated with its individual grace of movement. Compared with the spontaneousness and freedom of these figures, those of Memling seem heavy, stock-still, and posed for effect.

Now, therefore, you are in a position to appreciate the force of the remark that Botticelli, " though one of the worst anatomists, was one of the greatest draughtsmen of the Renaissance." As an example of false anatomy you may notice the impossible way in which the Madonna's head is attached to the neck, and other instances of faulty articulation and of incorrect form of limbs may be found in Botticelli's pictures. Yet he is recognized as one of the greatest draftsmen, because he gave to " line " not only intrinsic beauty but significance; that is to say, in mathematical language, he resolved the movement of the figure into its factors, its simplest forms of expression, and then combined these various forms into a pattern which, by its rhythmical and harmonious lines, produces an effect upon our imagination, corresponding to the sentiments of grave and tender poetry that filled the artist himself.

This power of making every line count both in significance and beauty distinguishes the great master-draftsmen from the vast majority of artists who use line mainly as a necessary means of representing concrete objects. To distinguish it from the latter use we may call it the *abstract* use of line.

Yet, although unique, Botticelli's art was but a link in the gradual development of Italian painting; whereas Memling's, like the Van Eycks', represented a growth complete in itself. Little is known of Memling's life. It is surmised that he was a German by descent and born in Mayence; but the definite fact of his life is that he painted at Bruges, sharing with the Van Eycks, who had also worked in that city, the honor of being the leading artists of the so-called " School of Bruges." He carried on their method of painting, and added to it a quality of gentle sentiment. In his case, as in theirs, the Flemish art, founded upon local conditions and embodying purely local ideals, reached its fullest expression.

His contemporary, Roger van der Weyden, who worked in Brussels and was the chief exponent of what is called the " School of Brabant," represented religious subjects with dramatic and emotional intensity; but his color was pale and thin, and his drawing angular and often extravagant in gesture. The sentiment of his pictures is Gothic: a term which sums up in a general way the religious feeling of the Northern races, more gloomy, intense, and painful than the Christianity of the South; producing the solemn, mysterious, intricate grandeur of the Gothic cathedral instead of the simpler, sunnier, and more elegant form of church built in the Romanesque style, which was a mingling of the Roman and the Byzantine methods of construction.

We shall have to say more about the Gothic feeling when we come to the consideration of the early German painting. Meanwhile the thing to note is that the Van Eycks and Memling, though living in an age that was influenced by this Gothic intensity, worked in an atmosphere of quiet and sunniness, cultivating, as it were, a little garden stocked with the simple flowers native to their country, and bringing it to perfection of development; so that this Flemish painting of the fifteenth century represents a little separate chapter in the history of art. At the beginning of the following century stands out the name of Quentin Massys (1466–1530?), but his work has already ceased to be distinctively Flemish, and shows the influence of Italy. For as commercial relations increased between the two countries, the artists of Flanders lost their national characteristics and became imitators, at a very great distance, of the Italian masters. As we are treating in this little book only of the vital periods and phases of art, the art of Flanders will disappear from our horizon for nearly a hundred years, to reappear in colossal shape, in the person of Rubens, at the beginning of the seventeenth century.

Italy's yearning toward the antique, to which Botticelli gave expression, we shall find satisfied in the work of Giovanni Bellini and of Raphael.

CHAPTER VI

PIETRO VANNUCCI (called PERUGINO)
1446–1523
Italian School of Umbria

GIOVANNI BELLINI
1430–1516
Italian School of Venice

AT the end of the previous chapter we touched on the Gothic intensity which characterized the art of the North, in the midst of which the Flemish art of the fifteenth century, that culminated in the Van Eycks and Memling, was like an oasis of repose and rich pleasantness. For these artists escaped the rigorous influences around them, chiefly through their pure delight in the actual presentation of objects, which made them first and chiefly painters, and only in a secondary way interpreters of the Christian dogma and religious zeal.

You will remember that a similar painter-like love of presentation distinguished the contemporaries of Botticelli in Florence, and we spoke of them as realists, while Botticelli, as we noticed, was a poet and a dreamer. The two artists who now demand our attention, Perugino and Giovanni Bellini, were also contemporaries of Botticelli; and in them too the painter-like point of view was pronounced, but tempered with—perhaps we should rather say, subordinated to—a very high purpose of sentiment.

They were among the first artists in Italy to perfect

[68]

the use of the oil medium, the secret of which had been discovered from the Van Eycks and brought into Italy by Antonello da Messina. It permitted a fullness and richness of color and a fusing of all the colors into an atmosphere of golden warmth—qualities that corre- sponded with the sentiments that each of them desired to express.

Let us try to understand the sentiment which is ex- hibited in these pictures. Perugino's is different from Bellini's, and yet both have something in common. In each of these two triptychs you will feel the presence of a wonderful calm. It has been said of Perugino that he is the painter " of solitude; of the isolated soul, alone, unaffected by any other, unlinked in any work, or feel- ing, or suffering with any other soul—nay, even with any physical thing." You will realize the truth of this, I think, if you study the Pavia altarpiece. Not only in the expression of each face, but also in the gesture and carriage of the body, there is an absolute uncon- sciousness of surroundings, a complete absorption in some inward spiritual ecstasy. The archangel Michael, the Virgin, and the archangel Raphael, who holds the young Tobit by the hand, are beings without sin or sor- row or even joy; filled with the " peace that passeth un- derstanding," that peace which comes of complete de- tachment from the world and of rapt communion with God. Nor is the type of the male figures masculine—it is said that Perugino's wife was the model for Raphael. Yet the pose of the Michael is not that of a woman; indeed, it would seem as if the artist's intention was to create a being who should be without thought or suggestion of sex; the embodiment, with as little bodily hindrance as possible, of a soul engaged in the beatitude of contemplation. His figures, then, do not represent Virgin, saints, and angels as such, but as personifications of intense soul-rapture. They are the souls and soul-saturated bodies which Perugino saw around him. For in the dying years of the fifteenth century Italy was torn with factions, a prey to sack and massacre at the hands of licentious bands of soldiers. Perugia itself, the little town on the hills of Umbria, where Perugino worked, was governed by treacherous and ferocious captains; its dark and precipitous streets were filled with broil and bloodshed, and its palaces with evil living. Yet it was one of the most pious cities in all Italy. Men and women sought refuge from the horrors of actual life in strange spiritual solitude, in life removed from all activities, steeped in devotion, passively contemplating a far-off ideal of purity and loveliness.

This was a very different thing from the active religious feeling of Fra Angelico: simple and childlike in its sunny faith; a product, as it were, of the open daylight; the lovable expression of a man who, as we have seen, entered humbly and intelligently into the activities around him. Yet Perugino's art, like Fra Angelico's, had its roots in the old Byzantine tradition of painting. You remember that the latter had departed farther and farther from any actual representation of the human form, until it became merely a symbol of religious ideas. Perugino, working under the influence of his time, restored body and substance to the figures, but still made them, as of old, primarily the symbols of an ideal. In him the Byzantine inspiration, so far as it was an expression of religion, reached its highest point of development.

It also reached a final development in Giovanni Bellini, though in another direction. This artist was the son of Jacopo Bellini, a Venetian painter, who, however, was settled in Padua during the time that Giovanni and his elder brother, Gentile, were in the period of studentship. Here, as we have seen, they came under the influence of Mantegna, who was also bound to them by the ties of relationship, since he married their sister. To his brother-in-law Bellini owed much of his knowledge of classical architecture and perspective, and his broad and sculptural treatment of draperies. Moreover, during these years Verrocchio was working on his equestrian statue of *Bartolommeo Colleoni,* "the most magnificent equestrian statue of all time"; and Giovanni's father had been a pupil of Mantegna's master, Squarcione, with opportunities of studying the remains of antique sculpture that he had collected.

So sculpture and the love of the antique played a large part in Giovanni's early impressions, and left their mark in the stately dignity of his later style. This developed slowly; indeed, during his long life of eighty-eight years he was continually developing; and the masterpiece, reproduced here, was executed when he was about sixty years old and Titian was one of his pupils.

The calm which pervades this picture is of a different kind from that which appears in Perugino's. Its suggestion is of stateliness, of the nobility of grand types of humanity. These figures have the ample quietude of strength in repose that belongs to those of Phidias upon the pediments of the Parthenon. Bellini, of course, knew nothing of these; but his study of such antique sculpture as had come within his observation, influenced by his own particular bent of mind, led him to a point of view very similar to that of the great Athenian. The latter's purpose had been to represent, not individuals, but types of humanity, ideally perfect, godlike beings, whose mental and physical powers were in complete poise. Hence his work is distinguished by grandeur of mass rather than by finish of detail. The successors of Phidias, on the other hand, showed an increasing tendency to individualize their figures by making them expressive of sentiment and emotion. A similar difference distinguishes Bellini from his successors in the Venetian School.

He is ranked as the greatest of the Venetian School of the fifteenth century—nay, more than that, as the greatest painter of the period—by no less an authority than Dürer, who, during his visit to Venice in 1494, wrote to a friend in a letter still preserved: "He is very old, but yet the best in painting." It must be remembered that at this date Titian was in his prime; so we may well ask upon what Dürer based his judgment. He knew his art theoretically and practically, so that he was able to appreciate the perfect mastery over the brush that was displayed alike by Titian and by Bellini; and, if he preferred the latter, it must have been because he himself was a very intellectual man and accordingly was in sympathy with the grave and elevated conceptions of

TRIPTYCH ALTAR-PIECE

GIOVANNI BELLINI

CHURCH OF THE FRARI, VENICE

Bellini rather than with the more sensuous and emotional art of Titian.

For this is the distinction between the two great Venetians. Bellini worked in a great calm, removed from passion. Swayed by intellectuality, serene and lofty and a little severe, he stands to the glowing, eager spirits that followed him as Phidias to Scopas and Praxiteles. In one respect, however, he shows the influence of his time. Observe the noble character in the heads of the four saints. He lived in an age when the portrayal of character was an important aim of art, and was himself a great portrait-painter—witness his noble portrait of Doge *Leonardo Loredano* in the National Gallery. During his long life he saw no fewer than eleven doges, and was state painter during the reigns of four.

To return to our picture. These bishops and monks have the bronzed, sunburned faces that may still be seen among the boatmen of Venice; the Virgin's complexion has the pure carnation tones of girls reared in a moist atmosphere; the cherubs, with their naked legs, recall the children that may still be seen fishing for crabs at sunset. In fact, the picture, as the French critic Taine remarked, " is full of local truth, and yet the apparition is one of a superior and august world. These personages do not move; their faces are in repose, and their eyes fixed like those of figures seen in a dream."

Here again is the symbol of an idea, as in the Byzantine paintings; but this time the symbol itself is founded on truth to actual local facts, and the idea is the elevation of these well-known facts into a lofty and ennobling type. It is not, as in Perugino's work, an escape from human nature into the abstract seclusion of the soul, but an assertion of the grandeur that may be inherent in humanity itself. Thus in Bellini's pictures the influence of the new learning of Greek culture and Platonic philosophy, toward which Botticelli groped tentatively, is seen in its highest and purest form.

And now let us try to discover something of the technical means by which Perugino and Bellini have expressed in these pictures their ideals. In one we have a notable example of Perugino's skill in combining figures with landscape; in the other, a hint of the dignity given to a composition by the introduction of architectural forms.

It was not until the seventeenth century that artists began to paint landscape for its own sake. By the Italians of the Renaissance it was treated as a background for figures; and while many artists—Perugino, for example, and the Venetians—made a close study of nature, they always kept inanimate nature subordinated to the human subject. The landscape in Perugino's triptych is a representation of Umbrian scenery, a beautiful vista of hills and river-threaded plain, stretching away to a low, distant horizon, with the delicate foliage of slender trees sprayed against the melting tenderness of the sky. To this beautiful effect of receding distance and of open sky, in the representation of which Perugino excelled, is largely due the impression that the picture produces. Just as the expression of the faces tells us that the thoughts of these beings are far away from the actual present, absorbed into infinite contemplation, so our gaze wanders on and on through the landscape, and

finally loses itself in the luminous infinitude of the sky.
The landscape, in fact, puts our own minds in tune with
those of the persons in the picture. If it were not there;
if, for example, the background were of gold, as in
the old Byzantine pictures, I suspect that we should
find these figures excessively sentimental; as, indeed,
many of Perugino's pictures are, for it is only occasionally that he rises to the spirituality of this one. But, as
it is, the sentiment of the figures is enlarged upon and
interpreted by the setting, just as in a Greek play the
emotions of the actors are explained by the chorus.

However, it is not only in interpreting such sentiment
as Perugino seeks to express that this union of landscape
and figures counts so much. One of the secrets of noble
composition is the balancing of what artists call the full
and empty spaces. A composition crowded with figures
is apt to produce a sensation of stuffiness and fatigue;
whereas the combination of a few figures with ample
open spaces gives one a sense of exhilaration and repose.
You may think there is a contradiction in the idea of
being at the same time rested and exhilarated, unless you
know the sensation of mountain-walking, when the zest
of the upper air fills you with desire to exert yourself,
and yet there is no fatigue in exertion; while the broad
sweeps of the sky above you and of plain and valley
below open lungs and imagination equally, and you feel
full of peace and, simultaneously, of eagerness. And
this illustration is not far-fetched, since it is a fact that
a picture reaches our imagination through our ordinary
experience of physical sensation. We know, for example, how soft and warm and caressing is the skin of a

little child; and if, in the picture of a child, the flesh is painted in such a way as to suggest this lovely texture, it will stimulate our imagination with pleasure. And it is in the degree that an artist stimulates our imagination through our physical experiences, that he seizes and holds our interest.

I have spoken of the effect produced by a combination of full and empty spaces, but this may be nothing more than a fine pattern. When, however, besides giving us a pattern of flat ornament in two dimensions, the artist can make us realize the third dimension of nature, —distance,—he so much the more kindles our imagination. For how many of us, as children, have looked at that hill which bounded the horizon of our home and longed to know what lay beyond it? And, in after years, the sight of the ocean, or of peak ranged beyond peak in the mountains, or of a summer sky at night, or of many other distant prospects, allures our imagination to travel on and on and lose itself in space. Now the mere suggestion of distance in a picture, secured by accurate perspective, will not affect us in this way; the artist himself must have this sort of ranging imagination, and then he will not only make you feel the distance, but the existence of every successive plane of intervening space, inviting your own imagination to range. Perugino preeminently had this feeling and the gift of expressing it: a mastery of what has been called by Mr. Bernard Berenson the art of "space-composition." There are many other technical points in the pictures that we might dwell on; but as our purpose in this little book is to proceed step by step, one thing at a time, we will limit our consideration to this one point,—the more so as some of the others will be met with later in the work of Perugino's most illustrious pupil, Raphael.

So, too, in the case of Bellini we will consider only a single technical point—the value of architectural accessories in adding dignity to the composition. These three panels are inclosed in a gilt frame which itself is a very handsome example of Renaissance design and craftsmanship. You will observe that the character of the design is architectural, and that the pilasters, the cornice, and the arch repeat, and therefore enforce, the architectural features of the picture. The general effect of this architectural setting is a mingling of force and grave distinction and of richness.

If you carefully compare this triptych with Perugino's, you will get an insight into the different effects produced, according as the background is landscape or architecture. In the former the lines are irregular, softly undulating, and distance melts into further distance; in Bellini's picture, however, the lines are firm and exact, the background has structural weight and stability. In one case the imagination spreads and finally loses itself in conjecture; in the other it is contracted and concentrated. Perugino's conception is very wooing; Bellini's, more monumentally impressive.

Let us pause for a moment on this word "monumental," since it expresses a quality which will constantly confront us in our study of art. In one sense it is the antithesis of nature: it belongs to a structure reared by the hand of man. Instead of being the result of natural laws working invisibly and over great periods of time, it is the result of formal laws invented by man (sometimes, perhaps, through a hint from nature) and compressed into a well-defined compass. A structure must necessarily be smaller than nature, yet it may impress us with a greater sense of dignity and grandeur. Nature's grandeur, as seen, for example, among the peaks and cañons of the mountains, fills us with awe; we are in the presence of stupendous forces uncontrolled by visible laws. Whereas a great building, as St. Peter's, for example, is a triumph of law over disorder; everything has been planned, calculated, regulated; in the presence of it man is not crushed down into awed insignificance, but, realizing that all this grandeur around him is the work of man's hand and brain, he is lifted up into glorious enthusiasm, filled with pride in the grandeur of humanity and in the consciousness of having a share in it. A building which can impress us in this way we call monumental. It is worth while to look a little more closely and discover by what means this impression is produced.

Architecture is the most original of the fine arts, not being an imitation of nature, as painting and sculpture are, but an invention of man's own, founded first of all upon necessity, and then made to contribute to the aspirations that filled his soul. Yet its principles are based upon qualities which man learned to admire in nature: stability, for example, height, and breadth, and spaciousness. The prophet Habakkuk, wishing to bring home to man the awful power of God, says that in his presence " the everlasting mountains were scattered, the perpetual hills did bow." He knew that it was the stability, the permanence of the mountains and hills which impressed his hearers. Again, man in all ages has lifted his eyes from the earth to the height and immensity of the sky; he piled stone on stone to reach this majesty of height, and spanned his columns with arches, and then assembled his arches into the mimic wonder of a dome. Trees taught him the aspiring grandeur of vertical lines; the level horizon, the quiet dignity of the horizontal; distance and space, the beauty of long vistas and of spaciousness. After much experimenting he discovered the proportion of height and breadth and length that would best produce a harmonious whole, and then added ornament which should enrich without impairing the structural dignity and stability of the mass.

Learning from architecture, the sculptors—who, as you remember, in early times were quite frequently architects as well—applied these principles, and sometimes so successfully that their compositions are monumental. Upon these principles also the painter based his compositions; but, as the lines of nature and of the human figure are not formal and rigid, he recognized how much his picture would gain in force and stability if he actually introduced some architectural features. This was a common practice with the artists of the Renaissance, and is one of the causes of the noble dignity of their pictures.

Bellini, in this one, has not only introduced architecture, but has adapted the character of the figures to it. How large and simple in mass are those of the bishops and monks, in which again appears the quiet grandeur of upright lines! Even in the figures of the Virgin and

Child there is a strongly sculptural suggestion: her pose is so firm and still, the cloak arranged in such simple and resolute folds. And the statuesque character of this figure in blue is enhanced by the open spaces around it of crimson and gold, which isolate it and increase its suggestion of everlasting stability and calm. Immobile and permanent as the everlasting hills, she sits there through the changes of time, guarded by men of the people ennobled into types of physical and mental grandeur, perpetual symbol of Bellini's intellectual elevation.

After filling the whole of the north of Italy with his influence and preparing the way for the giant colorists of the Venetian School, Giorgione, Titian, and Veronese, Bellini died of old age in his eighty-sixth year, and was buried, near his brother Gentile, in the Church of SS. Giovanni e Paulo. Outside, under the spacious vault of heaven, stands the *Bartolommeo Colleoni,* Verrocchio's monumental statue, which had been among the elevating influences of Bellini's life and art.

Verrocchio's influence must have been exerted also upon Perugino, if it is true, as Vasari asserts, that when he left Perugia to complete his education in Florence he was a fellow-pupil of Leonardo da Vinci in the sculptor's *bottega.* If he gained from the master something of the calm of sculpture, he certainly gained nothing of its force. It is as the painter of sentiment that he excelled; though this beautiful quality is confined mainly to his earlier works. For with popularity he became avaricious, turning out repetitions of his favorite types until they became more and more affected in sentiment.

CHAPTER VII

RAPHAEL SANZIO	MICHAEL WOLGEMUTH
1483–1520	*1434–1519*
Italian School of Umbria,	*German School of*
Florence, and Rome	*Nuremberg*

BY the beginning of the sixteenth century the Renaissance in Italy had ripened into a golden harvest. Leonardo da Vinci, Michelangelo, and Titian were in their prime, and within the long lives of these older men blossomed Raphael's comparatively brief life of thirty-seven years.

My reason for introducing him into our story a little before his chronological place is that now I wish to bring into comparison with Italian art the contemporary art of Germany. It seemed necessary to couple Leonardo and Dürer; therefore I took advantage of the fact that although Leonardo was older than Raphael he survived him, in order to join the latter with Wolgemuth, who was Dürer's master. For it is in Dürer, and later in Hans Holbein the Younger, that German art in the sixteenth century reached so high a point. Yet we may well study Wolgemuth, the better to appreciate the greatness of Dürer and Holbein, and also because his work is characteristic of the general art of Germany before these two great masters.

How it differs from Raphael's! The difference is

wide and high as the Alps which separated the two civilizations of which these two painters were, respectively, a product. At this point, when Italy is approaching the zenith of her Renaissance, and that of Germany is about to dawn, it is well to glance back over the history of the two countries, which for over a thousand years had been acting and reacting upon each other.

Since the days of Julius Cæsar the German tribes had been in conflict with Rome, but upon the outskirts of the Empire. In the fifth century they began to crowd down upon Italy itself.

In 410 Alaric, at the head of his Visigoths, penetrated to the gates of Rome, took it, and subjected it to a six days' pillage. Then Italy was ravaged successively by Attila and his Huns, by Ostrogoths and Lombards, until the genius of Charlemagne welded all the conflicting elements of the western world into the Holy Roman Empire (800 A.D.). But after his death the unwieldy structure succumbed to its own bulk; his descendants strove among themselves for supremacy, and the power of the feudal nobles was established. There followed a century and a half of domestic war, in which unhappy Italy was desolated by nobles and by invasions of Huns and Saracens, and filled with corruption and barbarism. At last, in 962, Otho the Great of Germany, having revived in his person the title of Emperor of the Holy Roman Empire, set himself to curb the power of the nobles and of the church by encouraging the growth of the cities and giving them free municipal authority. The result was a long period of fighting between the Papacy and the Empire, out of which arose the factions

of Guelphs and Ghibellines, who, under pretense of fa-
voring, respectively, the church or emperor, committed
every sort of atrocity. After two hundred years of
social chaos, the destruction of Milan by the Emperor
Frederick Barbarossa so enraged the Guelph cities of
the north that they formed a league, defeated his army,
and at the Peace of Constance (1183) secured their
recognition as free cities, each with its council and chief
magistrate, or *podestá*. But again the lull was only
brief. The maritime cities fought with one another for
the supremacy of the sea; while everywhere the lack of
military spirit in the cities and their domestic jealousies
made it possible for the leading family of the city, or
for the captains of fortune, to usurp the power of the
people and establish themselves as despots. We have
already noted how the Gonzaga family so established
itself at Mantua, and the Medici family at Florence,
glossing over their tyranny by the patronage of art and
letters. Italy, crushed, was again at the mercy of all
comers: of the rival despots, of the foreign mercenaries
that they hired, and of bands of condottieri who sold
their savagery to the highest bidders. Finally even her
commercial power was menaced and ruined. The capture of Constantinople by the Turks in 1453 cut off her
trade with the Orient; in 1497 the Portuguese Vasco da
Gama discovered the passage to India around the Cape
of Good Hope; five years previously the Genoese Co-
lumbus had opened up the New World; and the subsequent discoveries and conquests of Cortez, Pizarro, and
others diverted the stream of commerce, depriving Italy
of her supremacy and giving it to the western nations.

HOW TO STUDY PICTURES

In the sixteenth century nothing remained to Italy but the glory of arts, of letters, and of science, which in this period of national and civic humiliation reached its highest point of splendor: a terrible example, once more, of the truth that the finest culture will not save a nation, unless it is allied to the hardier virtues of manly courage and morality.

We have seen in previous chapters how people sought refuge from the turmoil in religion; how others turned from the horrors of the present to the beauties of the past, unearthing the remains of classic sculpture, recovering the manuscripts of the Roman authors, and drinking deep of the "New Learning" through the study of Greek literature. It is because the work of Raphael, apart from its technical skill and charm, combines so admirably the religious and the pagan feeling,—the personal intensity and reverence of the one and the impersonal serenity and happiness of the other,—that he holds a place distinct from any other artist. But, before pursuing this subject, let us turn to the conditions in Germany which produced a Wolgemuth as the forerunner of the greater Dürer and Holbein.

As each successive wave of Gothic invasion into Italy retired back behind the Alps, it carried with it some infusion of the civilization that it had destroyed. From this mingling of ancient culture with the untutored simplicity of the North sprang the modern world, with Christianity for its nurse. Art was the faithful handmaid of religion; and, as the northern world progressed toward civilization, the two worked together as mistress and servant. Germany, which at first was the country

THE ANSIDEI MADONNA   RAPHAEL SANZIO

NATIONAL GALLERY, LONDON

DEATH OF THE VIRGIN   MICHAEL WOLGEMUTH

MUSEUM OF FINE ARTS, BOSTON

now known as Bavaria, did not escape the rigors of war; it kept the Huns at bay and extended its rule to the shores of the Baltic. As the vast tracts of land were opened up, population increased, people began to congregate in towns and cultivate the arts of peace. A steady flow of commerce set in from south to north and back again; the main arteries of traffic being the Rhine and the Elbe, by which the products of eastern and southern countries were transported from Venice or Genoa to Bruges and Antwerp and the growing Hanse towns of the north. So, while the country at large was torn with strife, there grew up along the banks of the rivers or their connecting landways settlements of commercial people; towns, no longer centering round the castle of the local tyrant, but independent communities of peace-loving burghers, intent on their purses and ledgers rather than on swords and fighting. Midway in the path of commerce arose the famous cities of Nuremberg and Augsburg. Granted special favors by the emperors, they were free imperial cities, almost the only homes of liberty at that period; and they produced the two men who at that period rose to the highest rank in Germany as artists—Dürer and Holbein. Wolgemuth also was a native of Nuremberg.

This city was noted as early as the beginning of the fifteenth century for great mechanical activity and improvement in all kinds of machinery. She could boast the first German paper-mill and the celebrated printing-press of Antonius Koburger. In every branch of industry were men of skill and renown: watch- and clock-makers, metal-workers, and organ-builders, and

particularly workers in gold. Nuremberg had the reputation of being the best-governed city in Europe; her
merchants were nobles who extended their influence into
every country, until it was said of her that her "hand is
in every land." During the fifteenth century her progress in civilization was rapid; and the wealth of her
citizens began to be spent more and more on things of
beauty.

The German desire for the beautiful had first of all
expended itself in the architecture of the cathedrals
and churches. These differed from the ones of the
South, first of all, as the vertical line differs from the
horizontal; the aspiration of the eager, striving people
of the North finding expression in soaring towers
and spires, in high-pitched roofs supported upon lofty
pillars.

This departure from the lower and more level lines
of Southern architecture led to greater profusion and
intricacy of the parts; to the multiplication and elaboration of details; to long-drawn-out naves and the addition of side aisles, producing in every direction vistas
solemn and mysterious; to the enlargement of the
window-spaces and the dividing of them by elegant
traceries filled in with stained glass. These Gothic
cathedrals differ from the Italian somewhat as the forests of Germany differ from the broadly sweeping
plains and hills of Italy. And the German love of profusion and detail was exhibited also in the habit of decorating the exterior with sculpture and the interior with
wrought metal-work and carved wood. Even to this
day the dwellers in the Black Forest, like those who in-

habit the forest regions of Norway and Sweden, spend the long days of winter in carving objects in wood. Wood-carving was one of the earliest of the arts in Germany; gradually it was supplemented by the sculpture in stone of floral or foliage designs, or of figures to decorate the cathedrals and churches—figures of saints, lean and angular, or of terrible and grotesque creatures. For the ancient religion from which Christianity had weaned the Northern tribes was that of Asgard, savage and cruel, believing in giants and dragons, and blending the fierceness of a wild beast with the imagination and ignorance of a child. So the Christianity of medieval Germany inherited what was terrible and grotesque. This is reflected in the sculpture, and thence passed into painting; for, at first, the latter was only a helpmate to the architecture and learned its first lessons from the sculptors. The early painters represented in their pictures what they were familiar with in wood and stone; so that not only are the figures dry and hard, but in the groups they are packed one behind another, heads above heads, without really occupying space, in imitation of the method adopted in the carved relief.

And this unpainterlike way of painting continued even to the middle of the fourteenth century, by which time, however, the painters began to take a more prominent position. For people who wished to show their respect to the church and at the same time to perpetuate their own memory found they could get a more pleasing effect, and probably at a less cost, in paint than in wood or stone. So there grew up a demand for votive pictures, to be set up over the altar or hung upon a pillar, and these represented sacred scenes, often with portraits of the donor and his family introduced.

The principal pictures of this character executed at Nuremberg in the last thirty years of the fifteenth century issued from the workshop of Wolgemuth. At first he was in partnership with Hans Pleydenwurff, and upon the latter's death married the widow and carried on the business in his sole name. For a business it really was; the workshop being rather like a factory than a studio. A number of assistants were maintained, and they were apportioned certain specific parts of the same picture; it being the duty of one to fill in the architectural features, of another to paint the hands and heads, of others to put in the ornamental portions or the various objects introduced, and so on. The work, indeed, was carried on like any other commercial enterprise.

We have seen something of the same kind of thing in Perugino's *bottega:* assistants multiplying the master's types, and turning out a quantity of indifferent pictures, apparently for no higher purpose than to make money. Raphael, also, during his sojourn in Rome, when the demand upon his genius was taxed beyond his power of personally executing every commission, maintained his corps of assistants. But he never lost his high ideals as an artist; and, although a large portion of his famous decorations in the Vatican were actually painted by his pupils, the designs were his. Moreover, his genius for design was so extraordinary, inexhaustible in invention, always beautiful in plan, and the influence of his own elevated spirit so strong over his assistants, that even their work bears the impress of his creativeness.

The Madonna which illustrates this chapter is called "degli Ansidei," because it was painted for the Ansidei family, as an altarpiece to adorn the chapel dedicated to S. Nicholas of Bari in the church of S. Fiorenzo at Perugia. It is dated 1506, and belongs therefore to the end of the first of the three periods into which Raphael's life may be divided. For he worked successively in Perugia, Florence, and Rome, and is, in a measure, representative of the Umbrian, Florentine, and Roman schools.

The house in Urbino still stands where he was born in 1483. His father, Giovanni Santi (or Sanzio in the Italian form), was a painter of considerable merit; so Raphael's art education began in early childhood and was continued uninterruptedly through the remainder of his life, for to the very end he was learning, being possessed of an extraordinary capacity for absorbing and assimilating the ideas of others. He was only eight years old when his mother, Magia, died; but the father's second wife, Bernardina, cared for him as if he had been her own son; and her tenderness and his love for her may surely have helped to inspire the beautiful conception of motherhood which he portrayed in his Madonnas. In 1494 his father also died, leaving the boy, now eleven years old, to the care of an uncle, who, it is supposed, arranged for him to continue his studies under the painter Timoteo Vite, who was then living in Urbino. At about the age of sixteen he was sent to Perugia and entered in the renowned *bottega* of Perugino.

This *Madonna degli Ansidei,* painted in his twenty-third year, is full of recollection of the master's influence. We may note the low-lying landscape with the vault of sky above it, and the union with these of solemn architecture; moreover, the " sweet Umbrian sentiment " in the expression of the faces; and that each figure seems alone with itself in spiritual contemplation. Even the rather awkward and affected attitude of S. John betrays the influence of Perugino.

But already the pupil has outstripped the master. The figure of S. Nicholas is nobler than anything that Perugino painted, and more full of character. With what truth it depicts the pose and bearing of an absorbed reader, while the character of the head gives a foretaste of those portraits by Raphael in later years, which, it has been said, have no superiors as faithful renderings of soul and body.

But in another respect he has already outstripped his master; namely, in the noble serenity of the composition. Perugino, as we have seen, in combining the figure and architecture and landscape, was a master of space composition, but never with so firm an instinct for grouping and arrangement that the masses shall be not only dignified in themselves, but perfectly balanced. For this is Raphael's supreme distinction. The Venetians surpassed him in color, the Florentines in drawing, but few, if any, have equaled him in his mastery over the filling of a space, whether it be inside a frame or on the larger surface of a wall.

Let us briefly consider this matter of composition, which is the artist's way of building up his effects. Much of our previous study has been occupied with the gradual approach of artists toward a more truthful representation of nature; so at this point we do well to remember that, although nature is the basis of art, art is not nature. The latter is a vast field from which the artist selects certain items, afterward arranging them in a certain way, so as to produce a certain impression on the spectator's mind through his eyes. Selection and arrangement, therefore, are the principles of composition.

Now the method of arrangement may either follow nature's, as in the case, for example, of a landscape; or it may be an artificial arrangement, based upon conventions, such as in this picture of Raphael's. But even in the case of the landscape the artist must select. He must decide, in the first place, how much to include in his canvas, and then how he will place it according to the size and shape of his picture, leaving out, very likely, some of the objects of the natural landscape, since their introduction would interfere with the balance and unity of his picture.

If you stand a little distance from the open window and look out, it is improbable that what you see of the landscape will have either of these qualities. Probably the view will appear what it really is—a fragment of the landscape, its details, more than likely, confused or crowded. Or, if you approach nearer to the window, the view will widen out, but still you will feel that your gaze is hindered by the window-frame. On the other hand, you look through a picture-frame, and you should be able to feel that what you see is a scene complete in itself, that it has unity. Again, if you examine some particular tree,—say, for example, an elm, especially when the leaves are off,—you may note how the limbs and branches, for all their diversities, seem to compose together to make a balanced whole. Its parts are so bal-anced, and their relation to the whole mass so perfectly adjusted, that you exclaim, "What a beautiful tree!" This principle of organic unity, which appears in all nature's tree and plant forms, the artist borrows to give unity and balance to the artificial arrangement on his canvas.

This arrangement, in the language of the studios, is made up of full and empty spaces. In a landscape, for example, the sky would be an empty space, though a sheet of water in the foreground, or even a stretch of meadow or distant hills, might be treated so. For it is in the way an object is treated that it becomes a full or an empty space; the full ones being those which are in-tended to assert themselves most. Thus, in Raphael's picture which we are studying they consist of the figures and the throne; the arch, which under some circum-stances might be treated as a full space, here uniting with the sky and landscape to form the empty ones. And it is partly the equilibrium established between these and the full ones that makes the picture yield such a sugges-tion of wonderful composure. Another reason is the direction of the lines.

If you study them, you will find they present a con-trast of vertical, horizontal, and curved lines; and will grow to discover that it is the predominance of the ver-tical direction—aided somewhat, it is true, by the dignity of the arch—which produces such an impression of elevated grandeur. Do not fail to notice what a share the repetition of line plays in this effect. It was by repetition that the predominance of the vertical lines was built up. But there are repetitions of horizontal lines also; for example, in those of the steps and the canopy, the cornice of the arch, and S. John's arm, as well as of the broken level line of the landscape. Moreover, there are repetitions of the curved lines, especially in the moldings of the arch. But these are repeated also in a subtler way; for example, in the nimbus of the Virgin, and in the arched dome of each of the heads.

Lastly, observe that the unity of the composition is made additionally sure by everything being adjusted to one point. The book on the Virgin's lap is the focus of the whole. The diagonal lines of the canopy, those of the cornice and of the steps, lead toward this spot; so do the direction of the Virgin's head and the downward glance of her eyes, the Child's gaze, the bishop's book, and S. John's right arm and its index-finger. While all these are radiating lines, they are inclosed—locked in, as it were—by the arch, the continuation of which into a circle is suggested by the direction of S. John's left arm.

All this is the reverse of natural arrangement, being the result of a most carefully calculated plan, based upon the knowledge that the actual directions of lines, their contrasts and their repetitions, exert upon the mind certain definite influences. You will observe that the basis of this design is geometric, as are nearly all the compositions of the old masters and of most modern painters; a continual shuffling and reshuffling of vertical, horizontal, and curved lines; a building of them up, so as to approximate to various geometric figures, such as the circle, the angle, the triangle, and the various forms of the quadrilateral, or any or all in combination. For some psychological reason, perhaps because these forms are rudimentary and elemental, they are instantly satisfactory to the eye, and when played upon by such a master of composition as Raphael produce the highest kind of esthetic enjoyment.[1]

By this time it should be apparent that the beauty of Raphael's picture does not depend primarily upon the expression of the faces, which is the first thing that many people look at, nor, indeed, upon any or all of the figures, but upon what artists call the " architectonics " of the composition; that is to say, upon the way in which the parts of the composition are built up into a unified structural design. This, apart from anything to do with the subject or with the actors in it, moves our emotion in that abstract, impersonal way that the sight of mountains, skies, and valleys, or the roar of the ocean or the tinkle of a brook, may do. " The play 's the thing," said Hamlet; and so we may say of composition, that " composition is the thing." It is the framework, the anatomy, upon which the artist subsequently overlays his refinements and embellishments of color and expression.

If you will study the *Madonna degli Ansidei,* you will find that the tenderness of the Madonna's face, the

[1] The student would do well to study, in the light of what we have been considering, every illustration in this book, for the sole purpose of trying to discover in each case the part which composition plays in the impression of the whole picture.

rapture of S. John's, and the noble sweetness of S. Nicholas's are all of them echoes of the same qualities expressed in the whole composition; but that it is the actual direction of the lines, the shapes of the full and empty spaces, and their relation to one another, which make the chief impression, and that the expression of the faces is only a subsidiary detail, just as you are impressed by the total structure of some great building before you begin to apprehend its details.

Perhaps you will best understand the meaning and value of perfect composition by contrasting Raphael's picture with Wolgemuth's *Death of the Virgin*. In the latter there is no composition in the sense that we are using the word—that is to say, of an arrangement carefully planned to impress us by its abstract qualities. It presents only a crowd of figures more or less naturally disposed. Our attention is not engrossed by the whole, but scattered over the parts.

And this characteristic, we shall find, appears to a considerable degree in all German art. The German race has an instinctive appetite for detail. Its scholars and scientists are renowned for minute, patient, and thorough research; its artists, for accurate rendering of details. But this often leads to profuseness, in the intricacy and abundance of which the structural dignity of the whole is apt to be swallowed up. For you will find, as you continue your studies, that there is even more art in knowing what to leave out than in knowing what to put in; that simplification of the parts and unity of the whole are the characteristics of the greatest artists.

Among the various contrasts which are presented by

the two pictures, one may be singled out. Wolgemuth
has tried to represent the scene naturally, as it may have
happened, and has introduced around the Virgin figures,
studied from the actual men who walked the streets of
Nuremberg in his day; while Raphael's persons are
idealized types adapted from the real people to express
the idea which was in his mind. It is the same with his
arrangement of throne and arch and landscape. The
scene is not a real one; it is made up of things selected
in order to build up a structure of effect that would
suggest to our mind the idea which was in his. Here is
a sharp distinction in the way of seeing the facts of nature. One artist sees in them something to be rendered
as accurately as possible; the other extracts from them
a suggestion on which he may found some fabric of his
own imagination. From the one we get an impression
of reality which is apt to go no further than the mere
recognition of the facts; from the other, a stimulus to
our own imagination. One form of art chains us to
earth, the other aids us to take flight as far as our capacity permits us.

What helped to form Raphael's ideal? First of all,
the spirituality of Perugino's pictures. Then he visited
Florence: at first only for a short time, but before he
painted the *Madonna degli Ansidei*. During his second
and longer visit he became intimate with the work of
Leonardo da Vinci and Fra Bartolommeo. The influence of the former can be seen in the mysterious
beauty of the face in the *Madonna Gran Duca;* that
of the latter, in the supremely beautiful composition of
La Belle Jardinière; while he gained also a freedom and

greater naturalness in the drawing of his figures, and, through his friendship with the famous architect Bramante, a higher skill in the rendering of architectural forms and a deeper feeling for their grandeur. In fact, Raphael's capacity for being influenced by other artists was so remarkable that he has been called the " Prince of Plagiarists." But we must remember that the reproach which nowadays attaches to a man's making use of the motives of others cannot be extended to Raphael. The artists of the Renaissance freely borrowed from one another, and multiplied certain types of picture; the innumerable varieties, for example, of Madonna Enthroned having a family resemblance. Similarly in Japan, when an artist had mastered the rendering of a certain object, such as a bird's wing, other artists adopted his convention. Why should every one go back to the beginning and study for himself what had been already mastered? Much better to start with the accumulated capital of previous experience and knowledge, and, if the student has any originality of his own, draw from it a heightened dividend.

It was so with Raphael. To whatever he took from another he added something of himself; so that, though his borrowings were continuous and varied, he enriched the world with something personal and new. We have seen already how this present picture, while recalling Perugino, represents a distinct advance on that artist's capacity; and when he went to Rome, begged by Pope Julius II to decorate the *stanze,* or official chambers, of the Vatican, the composition of his first mural painting, the *Disputá,* is based upon a previous design of his master, yet surpasses in its completeness of decorative effect anything of Perugino's. In Rome, too, he had for models the ampler type of women which belongs to the south of Italy. Consequently his work becomes distinguished by still greater freedom and bigness of style. And, as he mixes with the world of great men who thronged the Eternal City, two other things are noticeable: his pictures become more human: the Madonnas embrace the infant Christ with the love of human motherhood; and, secondly, he is filled more and more with ardor for the antique.

He intersperses religious with classic subjects, and treats both in a classic spirit. It is as if Virgil had come to life again, but this time as a painter, whose aim was to link the later glories of the Renaissance with the early ones of Hellas; to make the legends of Hellas live again in the soul of the Renaissance; and to interpret the stories of the Hebrew Bible in Hellenic guise. The beautiful myths of Galatea, of Psyche and Venus, once more become realities visible to mortal eyes; Parnassus is again revealed; but now amid the constellation of Olympus appear the stars of Italian culture, Dante, Petrarch, and Boccaccio; and in silent companionship with them are the mighty ones of Athenian thought, Plato, Aristotle, Pythagoras, Socrates, and others, once more returned to earth and assembled beneath the arches of a noble building of the Renaissance. Through him the beauty of the antique world is recovered to the sight and soul of the modern.

But even more remarkable is what Raphael did with that other great volume of thought which had taken the place of the Hellenic. He not only started afresh the springs of Hellas, but that vast stream, derived from the Hebrews, which had flooded Christian Europe he conducted into Hellenic channels. He represented the Bible stories in Hellenic settings, retold them, as I have said, in the manner that a Virgil might.

When you remember that the New Learning was a revolt from the darkness and superstition of the middle ages; that in the beauty of pagan thought the beauty of the Christian was being neglected; and that, consequently, a clash between the two might have ensued in which one would have perished, you will understand the importance of what Raphael did. As a gardener will blend the pollen of two kinds of flowers and produce a third which unites the beauties of the two, so Raphael blended the Hellenic and the Christian in his religious pictures; and this new ideal so captivated the imagination of the world that for over three hundred years men pictured the religious story to their eyes and minds through the Hellenic atmosphere in which Raphael had placed it. It was not until painters had begun to value realism overmuch, to be more concerned with representing the appearance of things than the spirit enshrined in them, that they protested against the " incongruity " of clothing a Jewish fisherman in Hellenic draperies.

But Raphael himself and the people of his day felt no incongruity in this. They had become acquainted with the ideal beauty of antique sculpture, and of the serene elevation of Greek thought; crude ideas realistically represented were intolerable to them. Yet there was a beauty in this Christian thought at least as elevated and far more vital, because it touched the human heart of man in its relation both to this life and the future. How could it be made manifest?

We have noted already Raphael's method and its effect upon the world of his time, continuing to our own.

CHAPTER VIII

LEONARDO DA VINCI
1452–1519
Italian School of Florence

ALBRECHT DÜRER
1471–1528
German School of Nuremberg

HOW instantly these two masterpieces, Leonardo's *Virgin of the Rocks* and Dürer's *Adoration of the Magi,* seize our attention; yet how differently each claims our interest! In a general way, the difference consists in this, that the one is full of mystery, the other of clear statement. Leonardo has imagined a scene which appeals to our own imagination; Dürer has invented one that delights our understanding. The former's is a dream-picture, the latter's a wonderfully natural representation of an actual incident. In a word, while Dürer has tried to make everything plain to our eyes and understanding, Leonardo has used all his effort to make us forget the facts and realize the spirit that is embodied in them.

This contrast would alone make it worth while to compare the two pictures; but there are other reasons. These two men were contemporaries: Dürer, the greatest of German artists, most representative of the Teutonic mind; Leonardo, the most remarkable example of the intellect and imagination of the Italian Renaissance. It has been said of him that " he is the most thoughtful of all painters, unless it be Albrecht Dürer." So the fitness of comparing these two is evident.

Leonardo's early life was spent in Florence, his maturity in Milan, and the last three years of his life in France. Dürer, except for a visit of two years to Venice and of one year to the Netherlands, remained faithful to Nuremberg, the city of his birth.

Leonardo's teacher was Verrocchio—first a goldsmith, then a painter and sculptor: as a painter, representative of the very scientific school of draftsmanship; more famous as a sculptor, being the creator, as we remember, of the Colleoni statue at Venice. Dürer received his first lessons from his father, who was a master-goldsmith; his subsequent training, as an apprentice in the studio-workshop of Michael Wolgemuth.

Both Leonardo and Dürer were men of striking physical attractiveness, great charm of manner and conversation, and mental accomplishment, being well grounded in the sciences and mathematics of the day, while Leonardo was also a gifted musician. The skill of each in draftsmanship was extraordinary; shown in Leonardo's case by his numerous drawings as well as by his comparatively few paintings, while Dürer is even more celebrated for his engravings on wood and copper than for his paintings. With both, the skill of hand is at the service of most minute observation and analytical research into the character and structure of form. Dürer, however, had not the feeling for abstract beauty and ideal grace that Leonardo possessed; but instead, a profound earnestness, a closer interest in humanity, and a more dramatic invention.

This sums up the vital difference between them; and it is worth while to consider, first, some of the causes of this difference, and, secondly, the effects of it as illustrated in their work, in respect both of choice of subjects and method of representing them.

No doubt it is true that genius is born, not made. But while it is a mistake to try and discover reasons for a man being a genius, it is proper and most interesting to note how his genius has taken on a certain shape and direction as a result of his environment.

Now, Dürer was born a German; Leonardo an Italian. A great deal of the difference between the ways in which the genius of these two men manifested itself may be summed up in this statement. The Italian race, under its sunny skies, has an ingrained love of beauty. The German, in a sterner climate—" How I shall freeze after this sun," wrote Dürer during his stay in Italy to a friend in Nuremberg—retains to this day the energy that carved its way through the vast forests of his country, and some of the gloomy romance that haunted their dark shadows. The German spirit is characterized by a " combination of the wild and rugged with the homely and tender, by meditative depth, enigmatic gloom, sincerity and energy, by iron diligence and discipline." Very remarkable qualities these, and to be found in Dürer's work, which is the reason that we describe him as being so representative of the Teutonic race.

But it was not only the difference of race that helped to mold the genius of these two men differently; each was a manifestation of the Renaissance of art and learning which was spreading over Europe: Leonardo of that form of it which appeared in Italy, and Dürer of that which was beginning to appear in Germany. Had Dürer been born in Italy and reared up under Italian influences, and Leonardo's life been associated with Germany, who shall say what a difference would have resulted to the work of each? For the aim and character of these two branches of the Renaissance were very dissimilar.

The Italian, as we have seen, began by seeking a return to truth of natural form; but was soon influenced by the classic remains, which abounded in Italy and were so eagerly searched for and studied, that a worship of the antique, the Roman and Greek, absorbed men's minds. Raphael, as we have noted, clothed the story of the Bible in classic garb; classic myths, classic thought and literature, filled the imagination of the artists and thinkers; religion and a revived paganism skipped hand in hand. I use the word " skipped," because of the joy which possessed the Italians of the fifteenth and early sixteenth centuries in the new realization of their racial love of beauty. Painter after painter before Leonardo's time had tried to give expression to it; he was the heir of their endeavors and the contemporary of a number of gifted men, who gathered at Florence and under the patronage of the Medici made it a reflection of what Athens had been under Pericles.

The different character of the German Renaissance we shall best appreciate by noting that it was a part of the great movement which produced Luther and the Reformation. It was first and foremost an intellectual and moral revival; in time to be the parent of that civil

VIRGIN OF THE ROCKS   LEONARDO DA VINCI
LOUVRE, PARIS

ADORATION OF THE MAGI   ALBRECHT DÜRER

UFFIZI GALLERY, FLORENCE

and religious liberty which was to reshape a large portion of the world. And intimately identified with this movement was the printing-press.

Dürer was a great admirer of Luther; and in his own work is the equivalent of what was mighty in the Reformer. It is very serious and sincere; very human, and addressed to the hearts and understandings of the masses of the people. And he had a particular chance of reaching them, for Nuremberg under the enterprise of Koburger, a " prince of booksellers," as one of his contemporaries called him, had become a great center of printing and the chief distributer of books throughout Europe. Consequently the arts of engraving upon wood and copper, which may be called the pictorial branch of printing, were much encouraged. Of this opportunity Dürer took full advantage. He outdistanced all his predecessors in the art and brought it, at one bound, to such a pitch of perfection that his work was eagerly welcomed even in Italy, where pirated editions of his prints were published, and to-day he ranks first among wood-engravers and by the side of Rembrandt in engraving upon copper. Let us note the practical result of this upon his work as an artist.

Engraving as compared with painting is a popular art; many printings can be made from one plate or block and at comparatively slight cost, so that the artist's work reaches a great number of persons. It is easy to see how this might affect the character of his work: leading him to choose subjects with which the people were familiar; to treat them in a way that should secure their interest—that is to say, with simple directness and precision, and with dramatic earnestness that should appeal at once to the intelligence and the heart. That these qualities are characteristic of all Dürer's work, his paintings and engravings alike, may well have been due, in part at least, to his experience in the latter medium. But probably it would be more true to say that because these qualities were inherent in his personal character, they were reflected in his work and drew him particularly toward engraving.

It is quite possible, however, for pictures to be simple, precise, direct, and even dramatic, yet very commonplace. This Dürer's work never was; and that he contrived to make it so homely and natural and yet always dignified is because he was a genius, which is no more to be explained and accounted for in his case than in Shakspere's.

That he did not possess, as well, the gift of ideal beauty is due partly to the fact we have already noticed, —that the Renaissance in Germany was more a moral and intellectual than an artistic movement,—and partly to Northern conditions. For the feeling for ideal grace and beauty is fostered by the study of the human form; and this has been most flourishing in those Southern countries, such as Greece and Italy, where the climate favors a free, open-air life. In the Northern countries, clothes, being more necessary, assume a greater importance. They are a very important feature in this picture of Dürer's, and recall the elaborate costumes in those which we have examined by Van Eyck and Memling. Nuremberg, as we have remarked, was on one of the highways of travel between Italy and the cities of the

North Sea, but, while commerce was passing freely in both directions, the influence upon painting came to Germany chiefly from Flanders. As there, so in Germany, painting was closely allied with the decorative crafts, and the painters delighted in the portrayal of fabrics, metal, and woodwork. In this *Adoration of the Magi* we can detect at once the same fondness for depicting stuffs, embroidery, and objects of curious and beautiful workmanship as in Van Eyck's *Virgin and Donor;* and in the originals there is apparent, not only a similar skill in minute and elaborate details, but also a corresponding use of strong, rich coloring. But, while it was from Flanders that Dürer derived his style in painting, he passed beyond his exemplars in the variety and scope of his skill and in mental and moral force.

In the first place, no one has excelled him in delineating textures. You may see in this picture with what truth the different surfaces of wood, stone, hair, fur, feather, metal-work, embroidery, and so on are represented. This skill in textures is even more wonderfully exhibited in the black and white lines of his engravings. But the point particularly to be noted is that his genius does not stop short with the skill; back of it is a great force of intellectual and moral intention. He has the artist's love of the appearance of things, but he uses every object, not merely for its own sake and for the pleasure of representing it, but that it may enhance and intensify the main motive of his subject. On this occasion it is to contrast the splendor of the visitors from the East with the lowliness of the Mother and Child, and with the meanness of their surroundings; to contrast the harshness of the ruins with the dignity of the Mother, the innocent sweetness of the Babe, and the profound reverence of the Wise Men. He makes the scene impress us so deeply: in the first place, because he realized it himself so deeply, tenderly, reverentially, and powerfully in his own mind; and, secondly, because he has given to each figure and to every object its own quality and degree of character. He felt, and could convey to others, the significance of form; by which term I am trying to express two things.

First there is in the character of objects—their color, shape, hardness or softness, dullness or brilliance—a capacity to arouse our enjoyment. They excite especially what has been called our "tactile" sense; that is to say, the pleasure we get from actually handling things, or from having them represented to us in so real a way that we can imagine what would be the pleasurable sensation of touching them. But there is another way in which objects may be significant. For example, the things in our houses mean more to us than they would if we saw them set on a shelf in a shop window. In the latter case we enjoy only their appearance; in the other they are a part of our lives. Just in the same manner objects may be arranged in a painting so as to interest us only by their appearance, or in such a way that they are an actual part of the life of the picture.

This is a distinction that it is worth while to grasp, and no one can better help us to do so than Dürer. We know at once that this *Adoration of the Magi* impresses us, and, when we study it, we discover that the secret of its impressiveness is the extraordinary significance which the artist has given to external appearances.

Here is the point at which the genius of Dürer and that of Leonardo, similar in many respects, branch out like a Y into separate directions. It is not with the external significance of objects, but with their inward and spiritual significance, that Leonardo was occupied. A glance at the *Virgin of the Rocks* [1] is sufficient to make us feel that the artist is not trying to impress us with external appearances. The outlines of his figures are not emphasized as in Dürer's picture; the cavern curiously formed of basaltic rock, and the little peep beyond of a rocky landscape and a winding stream, the group of figures in the foreground by the side of a pool of water —all are seen as through a veil of shadowy mist. They may be real enough, but far removed from the touch of man; less visible to eye-sight than to soul-sight. It was the passion of Leonardo's existence to peer into the mysteries and secrets of nature and life. He was at once an artist and a man of science; turning aside, for a time, from painting to build canals, to contrive engines of war, to make mechanical birds which flew and animals which walked; while the range of his speculations included a foresight of the possibilities of steam and of balloons, a discovery of the law of gravitation, and a rediscovery of the principles of the lever and of hydraulics. Mathematician, chemist, machinist, and physiologist, geologist, geographer, and astronomer, he was also a supreme ar-

[1] This illustration is reproduced from the picture in the Louvre. There is another example of the subject in the National Gallery, which is regarded by the majority of critics as a replica of the Louvre picture executed by Leonardo's assistant, Ambrogio da Predis.

tist. And always it was the truth, just beyond the common experience of man, hidden in the bosom of nature or dimly discerned in the mind of man, that he strove to reach. Partly he grasped it, partly it eluded him; much of his life was spent in restless striving after the unattainable; so to him life presented itself as a compromise between certainty and uncertainty, between fact and conjecture; between truth that is clearly seen and truth that is only felt. And in his pictures it was this mingling of certainty and elusiveness that he sought to express.

The means he employed were, first, extreme delicacy and precision in the study and representation of form, and then a veiling of all in a gossamer web of chiaroscuro. He did not invent the principles of light and shade in painting, but he was the first to make them a source of poetical and emotional effect. Others had used chiaroscuro to secure the modeling of form by the contrast of light upon the raised parts with shadow on those farther from the eye; but Leonardo was the first to notice that in nature this contrast is not a violent one, but made up of most delicate gradations, so that the light slides into the dark and the dark creeps into the light, and even the darkest part is not opaque, but loose and penetrable. In making this discovery he discovered also that the general tint of an object—the "local" color, as the artists call it—gradually changes in tone as the object recedes from the eye, owing to the increase in the amount of intervening atmosphere. By representing in paint these delicate gradations of light and shade he succeeded in obtaining a subtlety of modeling that has never been surpassed; while, at the same time, the successive layers or planes of tone reproduce in his pictures the effect of nature's atmosphere.

Nature's, observe; because other artists of his time introduced an atmosphere of their own, bathing the figures, very often, in a golden glow which they obtained by washing a glaze over the whole or parts of the picture; very beautiful, but quite arbitrary and conventional. Leonardo, however, like Masaccio, imitated the effects of real atmosphere, in which he anticipated, as we shall see, the nature study of Velasquez.

How subtle Leonardo's effects were may be noted in this picture; for example, in the modeling and foreshortening of the limbs of the two infants, so exquisitely soft as well as firm, and in the lovely mystery of the faces of the Virgin and Angel. The latter belong to the same type as his portrait of *Mona Lisa:* oval faces with broad, high foreheads; dreamy eyes beneath drooping lids; a smile very sweet and a little sad, with a suggestion of conscious superiority. For as he searched nature for her mysteries, so he scanned the face of woman to discover the inward beauty that was mirrored in the outward. He made woman the symbol of what beauty and the search for beauty meant to himself, adding that infinitesimal touch of scornfulness, in acknowledgment that, after all his strivings to know and capture beauty, its deepest secret eluded him. Much of his life was spent in the search after what eluded him; he loved more to reflect and study than to put his ideas into actual shape.

So, while he and Dürer were alike in moral and intellectual greatness, in their eager study of nature and in the elevation of their art, each had a different ideal which led them very far apart in the final character of their work. Dürer's is full of the meaning of appearances, Leonardo's of the mystery that lies behind them; the former is vigorous, direct, and powerfully arresting, the latter sensitive, strangely alluring, but baffling and elusive.

CHAPTER IX

TIZIANO VECELLI (TITIAN)   HANS HOLBEIN THE YOUNGER
1477–1576   *1497–1543*
Italian School of Venice   German School of Augsburg

IT is because of the difference between these two
wonderful portraits—Titian's *Man with the Glove*
and *Portrait of Georg Gyze* by Hans Holbein the
Younger—that it is interesting to compare them. In
doing so we shall contrast not only the difference in the
personalities of these two artists, and the conditions
under which they worked, but also the difference of their
points of view and consequently of their methods. Let
us begin by studying the second difference, to an understanding of which the pictures themselves will direct us.

If we should try to sum up in one word the impression
produced by each, might we not say, "How *noble* the
Titian is; the Holbein how *intimate*"? Both the originals are young men: Titian's unmistakably an aristo-
crat, but with no clue given as to who or what he was;
Holbein's a German merchant resident in London,
whose name is recorded in the address of the letter in
his hand, and who is surrounded by the accompaniments
of his daily occupation. Presently we shall find out
something about the nature of his occupations; meanwhile we have surprised him in the privacy of his office,

and are already interested in him as an actual man, who lived and worked over three hundred years ago, and very interested also in the objects that surround him. We note already that the flowers in the vase are just like the carnations of our own day, but that the character of his correspondence is very different. Evidently he is a prosperous man, but compare the fewness of his letters with the packet which one morning's mail would bring to a modern merchant. Each is fastened with a band of paper, held in place by a seal; he has just broken the band of the newly arrived letter; his own seal is among the objects that lie on the table. But I interrupt the fascinating examination of these details to ask whether we do not feel already that we are growing intimate with the man.

Can we feel the same toward the *Man with the Glove?* Certainly, when we have once possessed ourselves of the appearance of this man's face, we shall not forget it. But that is a very different thing from knowing the man as a man. There is something, indeed, in the grave, almost sad, expression of the face which forbids, rather than invites, intimacy. He, too, seems to have been surprised in his privacy; but he is occupied, not with his affairs, as Georg Gyze is, but with his thoughts. It is not the man in his every-day character with whom we have become acquainted; indeed, it is not with the man himself that we grow familiar, but with some mood of a man, or, rather, with some reflection in him of the artist's mood at the time he painted him.

For Titian found in the original of this portrait a suggestion to himself of something stately and aloof from common things; he made his picture interpret this mood of feeling; he may have been more interested in this than in preserving a likeness of the man; we may even doubt whether the man was actually like this. Certainly, this could not have been his every-day aspect, in which he appeared while going about whatever his occupation in life may have been; it is one abstracted from the usual, an altogether very choice aspect, in which what is noblest in his nature is revealed without the disturbance of any other condition.

It is, in fact, an idealized portrait, in which everything is made to contribute to the wonderful calm and dignity of the mood. The name of the original has not been handed down; there is no clue to who or what this man was—only this wonderful expression of feeling; and, as that itself is so abstract, exalted, idealized, baffling description, posterity has distinguished this picture from others by the vague title, *Man with the Glove.*

Here, then, is another distinction between these pictures of Titian's and Holbein's. The treatment of the former is idealistic, of the other realistic. Both these artists were students of nature, seeking their inspiration from the world of men and things that passed before their eyes. But Holbein painted the thing as it appealed to his eye, Titian as it appealed to his mind; Holbein found sufficient enjoyment in the truth of facts as they were, Titian in the suggestion that they gave him for creating visions of his own imagination; the one viewed the world objectively and was a realist, the other subjectively and idealized.

This, of course, is a distinction not confined to these

two artists. Indeed, all the comparison we have been making between their respective points of view is of general application. The distinction between the subjective, universal, and idealistic on the one hand, and the objective, particular, and realistic on the other, repeatedly confronts us in the study of art. In fact, every artist illustrates either one or other of these points of view, or, more usually, a combination of the two: hence, to appreciate the work of various men, it is necessary to grow to a clear understanding of these contrasts and of the innumerable degrees to which they may shade into each other. So large a subject cannot be exhausted by the comparison of any two pictures; yet from these by Titian and Holbein a considerable insight may be gained.

In what respect was Holbein a realist? In our study of art we should be very distrustful of words. We cannot do without them, but must remember that they have no value of themselves; that they are only valuable as far as they provide a shorthand expression of some idea. The idea, and not the word in which it is clothed, is the important thing; but unfortunately a word cannot have the completeness and finality of a mathematical formula. In arithmetic, for instance, $2 \times 2 = 4$ is universally true; but in the world of ideas there are so many "ifs and ans" that the exact statement is impossible. So beware of words, and, instead of being satisfied with phrases, try to think into and all around the thought that is behind the phrase.

What, then, is a realist? Naturally, one who represents things as they really are. But can anybody do that? If ten men the equals of Holbein in observation and skill of hand had sat down beside him to paint the portrait of Georg Gyze and his surroundings, would their pictures have been identical ? Could even any two men, working independently, have painted the ink-pot alone so that the two representations would be identical ? Have any two men exactly similar capacity of eyesight ; and, if they have, will they also have exactly identical minds? The fact is, a man can draw an ink-stand only as its appearance physically affects his eye and makes a mental impression on his brain. In other words, objects, so far as we are concerned, have no independent reality; you cannot say, " This is what an apple really looks like," but only, " This is how it presents itself real to me." The personal equation intervenes; that is to say, the personal limitation of each individual.

So, in the strict sense of representing an object as it really is, no painter can be a realist; while, in the general sense of representing an object as it seems real to his eye and brain, every painter may be called a realist. Then how shall we discover the meaning of the word " realist " as used in painting? Let us look for an explanation in the two pictures.

Both painters represented what seemed real to them; but do we not observe that, while Titian was chiefly occupied with the impression produced upon his *mind,* it was the impression made upon the *eye* which gave greater delight to Holbein? No man who did not love the appearances of things would have painted them with so loving a patience. While to Titian the thing which appeared most real about this man, the thing most worth his while to paint, was the impression made upon his mind, so that what he painted is to a very large extent a reflection of himself, a mood of his own subjectivity, Holbein concentrated the whole of himself upon the objects before him. His attitude of mind was objective. His intention was simply to paint Georg Gyze as he was known to his contemporaries—a merchant at his office table, with all the things about him that other visitors to the room would observe and grow to associate with the personality of Gyze himself.

We may gather, therefore, that realism is an attitude of mind; one that makes the painter subordinate himself and his own personal feelings to the study of what is presented to his eye; which makes him rejoice in the appearances of things and discover in each its peculiar quality of beauty; which makes him content to paint life simply as it manifests itself to his eye, to be indeed a faithful mirror of the world outside himself.

It is not because Holbein was a realist that he is celebrated, but because of the kind of realist he was. You will find that realism often runs to commonplace; a man may see chiefly with his eye because he has little mind to see with; may take a delight in the obviousness of facts because he has no imagination; the material appeals to him more than the spiritual. But Holbein was a man of mind, who attracted the friendship of Erasmus, the greatest scholar of his age; and he brought this power of mind to the enforcing of his eye. The result is that the number and diversity of the objects in this portrait do not distract our attention from the man, but rather seem to increase our acquaintance with his character and disposition. We recognize the order and refinement which surround him, and find a reflection of them in his face. On the other hand, when we examine the details, we find each in its way exquisitely rendered; for, as I have said, Holbein loved things of delicate and skilful workmanship, and left many designs for sword-scabbards, dagger-sheaths, goblets, and goldsmith's work.

Yet compared with the elaborated detail of Holbein's portrait, how large, simple, and grand is the composition of Titian's! The aim of the one artist was to *put in* everything that was possible *without injury to the total effect;* of the other to *leave out* everything but what was *essential.* Holbein's picture is a triumph of well-controlled elaboration; Titian's of simplification. I hope to show further that this distinction is characteristic of the personality of these two men; but, for the present, let us notice how completely each method suits the character of the subject: the man of affairs, calm and collected amid a quantity of detail, the man of contemplation, aloof from every distraction.

That Holbein painted all these details because he felt them to be really part of the personality of Gyze may be inferred from the fact that, though he loves to introduce little objects of choice workmanship, his treatment of the portrait of a scholar like Erasmus is very large and simple. Yet even then there is a minuteness of finish in the modeling of the flesh and in the painting of the hair and costume, which might easily be niggling and trivial, but that in Holbein's case it is only part of the singular penetration of his observation and extraordinary manual delicacy, brought to the rendering of something which he has studied with all the strength of his manhood.

Yet the breadth and simplification of Holbein are not like Titian's, being simply and sweetly dignified, where Titian's are majestically grand. Turn again to the *Man with the Glove*. Shut out with your fingers, first one of the hands, then the other, and then the sweep of shirt, and notice each time how the balance and dignity of the composition are thereby destroyed; for its magic consists in the exact placing of the lighter spots against the general darkness of the whole. By this time we realize that the fascination of this portrait is not only in the expression of the face and in the wonderful eyes, but also in the actual pattern of light and dark in the composition. Then, taking the face as the source and nucleus of the impression which the picture makes, we note how the slit of the open doublet echoes the piercing directness of the gaze; how the expression of the right hand repeats its acute concentration, while the left has an ease and elegance of gesture which correspond with the grand and gracious poise of the whole picture.

Grand and gracious poise! Not altogether an unapt characterization of Titian himself. At once a genius and a favorite of fortune, he moved through his long life of pomp and splendor serene and self-contained. He was of old family, born at Pieve in the mountain district of Cadore. By the time that he was eleven years old his father, Gregorio di Conte Vecelli, recognized that he was destined to be a painter and sent him to Venice, where he became the pupil, first of Gentile Bellini, and later of the latter's brother, Giovanni. Then he worked

MAN WITH THE GLOVE   TITIAN

LOUVRE, PARIS

PORTRAIT OF GEORG GYZE   HOLBEIN THE YOUNGER

BERLIN GALLERY

with the great artist Giorgione. From the first, indeed, he enjoyed every privilege that an artist of his time could desire. The Doge and Council of Venice recognized his ability; the Dukes of Ferrara and Mantua followed suit; and, as the years went on, kings, popes, and emperors were his friends and patrons. In his home at Biri, a suburb of Venice, from which in one direction the snow-clad Alps are visible and in the other the soft luxuriance of the Venetian Lagoon, he maintained a princely household, associating with the greatest and most accomplished men of Venice, working on until he had reached within a year of a century of life. Even then it was no ordinary ailment, but the visitation of the plague, that carried him off; and such was the honor in which he was held, that the law against the burial of the plague-stricken in a church was overruled in his case and he was laid in the tomb which he had prepared for himself in the great Church of the Frari.

No artist's life was so completely and sustainedly superb; and such, too, is the character of his work. He was great in portraiture, in landscape, in the painting of religious and mythological subjects. In any *one* of these departments others have rivaled him, but his glory is that he attained to an eminence in all; he was an artist of universal gifts,—an all-embracing genius, equable, serene, majestic.

The genius of Holbein also blossomed early. His native city of Augsburg was then at the zenith of its greatness; on the highroad between Italy and the North, the richest commercial city in Germany, the frequent halting-place of the Emperor Maximilian. His father,

Hans Holbein the Elder, was himself a painter of merit, and took the son into his studio. A book of sketches made during this period by the young Hans, preserved in the Berlin Museum, shows that he was already a better draftsman than his father. In 1515, when he was eighteen years old, he moved to Basel, the center of learning, whose boast was that every house in it contained at least one learned man. Here he won the friendship and patronage of the great printer Froben and the burgomaster Jacob Meyer. For the former's books he designed woodcuts; for the latter he painted a portrait, and, later, the famous *Meyer Madonna*. In this the Virgin is represented as standing, and the Meyer family kneeling: the father and his two sons on the right, and opposite to them his deceased first wife and his then living second wife and only daughter. In 1520, the year of Luther's excommunication, he was admitted to citizenship at Basel and to membership in the painters' guild: sufficient testimony, as he was only twenty-three, to his unusual ability.

In that same year Erasmus returned to Basel, and accepted the post of editor and publisher's reader to his friend Froben. Erasmus spoke no modern language except his native Dutch, and Holbein seems to have been ignorant of Latin, yet a friendship sprang up between the two, and the artist designed the woodcuts for the scholar's satirical book, "The Praise of Folly," and painted his portrait. About this time he made the famous series of designs of the *Dance of Death;* the drawings of which were so minute and full of detail that when Hans Lützelberger, their engraver, died in 1527, it was ten years before another wood-engraver could be found sufficiently skilled to render the action and expression of the tiny figures.

But book illustration was poorly paid and the times were lean ones for the painter, since the spread of the Reformation had cut off the demand for church pictures. Holbein found himself in need of money, and accordingly, by the advice of Erasmus, set out for London with a letter of introduction from the scholar to Sir Thomas More, the King's Chancellor.

"Master Haunce," as the English called him, arrived in England toward the close of 1526. The London of that day presented some crude contrasts. Side by side with buildings of Gothic architecture had arisen later ones of Renaissance design, but the average houses were still of wood and mud, huddled together in very narrow streets, the rooms small and the flooring of the lowest story merely the beaten earth. The houses of the upper class lined the bank of the Thames, and it was in one of these, situated in what was then the village of Chelsea, that Sir Thomas More lived. Here Holbein was welcomed, and made his home during this first visit to England. He painted portraits of many of the leading men of the day, and executed drawings for a picture of the family of his patron, which, however, was never painted; for, two years later, in consequence of an outbreak of the plague, he returned to Basel.

But Basel was no longer what it had been: Froben was dead; Erasmus, Meyer, and others of the cultivated class had abandoned the city, which was in the clutches of the Reformers, who showed their zeal for religion by a crusade against art. Consequently, in 1531, Holbein returned to England. But here, too, had been changes; More was in disgrace, so that Holbein, cut off from court patronage, attached himself to the merchants of the Steelyard.

These were the London representatives of the Hanseatic League, a combination of commercial cities, at the head of which were Lübeck and Hamburg. It had been formed as early as the thirteenth century, for mutual protection against piracy and to promote the general interests of trade, and had established factories, or branches, in various places, as far removed as London and Novgorod. These, under special privileges derived from the respective governments, gradually absorbed the main business of the import and export trade. Georg Gyze was a member of the London factory, a merchant of the Steelyard, and in his portrait the steelyard or scale for the weighing of money, the symbol also of the merchant guild, hangs from the shelf behind his head.

By 1537 Holbein had come to the notice of Henry VIII, and was established as court painter, a position which he held until his death. This seems to have occurred during another visitation of the plague in 1543; for at this date knowledge of the great artist ceases. When he died or where he was buried is not known.

What a contrast between his life and Titian's! One the favorite, the other the sport, of fortune. For though the greatness of both was recognized by their contemporaries, Titian lived a life of sumptuous ease in the beautiful surroundings of Venice, while Holbein, often straitened for money, never wealthy, experienced the rigor of existence; more or less a victim to the religious convulsions of the time, forced by need and circumstances to become an alien in a strange land, dying unnoticed and unhonored. The world to Titian was a pageant, to Holbein a scene of toil and pilgrimage.

Titian viewed the splendor of the world in a big, healthful, ample way; and represented it with the glowing brush of a supreme colorist. On the other hand, Holbein is eminent in German art because he finally emancipated it from Gothic thraldom. He was the foremost artist of the German Renaissance, beside whom Dürer seems to belong to the middle ages. Yet the latter's art must be joined with his to produce a complete representation of the genius of the race. In both are manifested the decorative feeling, the eager curiosity, the love of elaborate detail that distinguish German art. But, while Holbein reflected the conscientiously earnest, matter-of-fact spirit, Dürer reflected also the romantic temperament that underlies it. After these two, if we except Lucas Cranach, no painter in German art demands the student's attention until the nineteenth century.

CHAPTER X

ANTONIO ALLEGRI (called   MICHELANGELO BUONARROTI
       CORREGGIO)
      1494–1534   1475–1564
Italian School of Parma   Italian School of Florence

I
T would be impossible to imagine a greater contrast
than the one presented by these two pictures—Correggio's *Mystic Marriage of Saint Catherine* and
the *Jeremiah* by Michelangelo. And the difference is
all the more worth studying because these artists are the
most typical representatives of two very different phases
of that wonderful outburst of energy which we call the
Renaissance.

We have seen how two currents of striving united in
Raphael's work; how he satisfied the old religious yearning as well as the newly aroused passion for the antique;
how he reclothed the Bible story in classic guise. We
have seen, too, that in Leonardo da Vinci were revealed
the subtlety of his time, its eagerness for perfection, the
dawn of the spirit of scientific inquiry, which, reawakened by the study of Aristotle and Plato, was
searching into the mystery of the universe and man's
relation to it; and that in this peering forward Leonardo
anticipated some of the facts of science rediscovered
and established by later philosophers and scientists.

We can now study in Correggio that element in the

[142]

Renaissance conveniently called " pagan "; which, for the present, may be briefly summarized as a tendency to look back further than the beginning of the Christian religion, further, even, than the classic times, to that dream of a golden age, of perfect peace and happiness and innocence, when men and women lived a natural life, and shared the woods and streams, the mountains and the fields, with satyrs, nymphs, and fauns. Correggio has been called the " Faun of the Renaissance."

But in those splendid yet terrible days of the Renaissance peace was continually disturbed by wars and civil strife; innocence crept to shelter from the wickedness which shamelessly prevailed; and happiness went hand in hand with anguish. Italy of that day was like a huge caldron into which all the human passions, good and evil, had been flung, while underneath it was the fire of an impetuous race, that after long smoldering had now leaped up with volcanic force. The seething tumult of these contending passions is reflected in the work of Michelangelo.

While Correggio represents the exquisite fancifulness of that period, Michelangelo is an embodiment of its soul.

Compare again these two pictures. Correggio has here taken for his subject one of the beautiful legends of the church. Catherine was a lady of Alexandria who, living about 300 A.D., dared to be a Christian, and eventually died for her faith by the torment of the wheel, which latter appears as an emblem in many of her pictures. She had a vision in which it was made known to her that she should consider herself the bride of Christ;

and the theme of this mystic marriage was a favorite one in the turbid times of the Renaissance, when women sought the cloister as a refuge from the wickedness and tyranny of the world.

But how has Correggio treated this subject? Does he make you feel the sacrifice of Catherine; or suggest to you anything of the religious fervor and devotion with which the vision must have inspired herself? In the background are little figures, scarcely to be seen in the illustration, which, if you search into them, tell of suffering; but they do not really count in the impression which the picture makes upon us. What we get from it as a whole is a lovely, dreamy suggestion, as of very sweet people engaged in some graceful pleasantry. The mother is absorbed in love of her child, wrapped up in the consciousness, common to young mothers, that her child is more than ordinarily precious. The baby itself is a little, roguish love, a brother of the little Cupids and *putti* that abound in Correggio's pictures, eying with the watchful playfulness of a kitten the hand of Catherine. The latter plays her part in the ceremony with little more feeling than that of any other child-worshiper; while the St. Sebastian, with his bunched locks reminding us of ivy and vine leaves, has the look of the youthful Dionysos, the arrow recalling the thyrsus which the young god used to carry.

There is not a trace of religious feeling in the picture, or of mystic ecstasy—only the gentle, happy peace of innocence. There may be violence out in the world, but far away; no echo of it disturbs the serenity of this little group, wrapped around in warm, melting, golden atmosphere. Elsewhere may be hearts that throb with passion, consciences sorely eager to do right or stricken with the memory of sin; but not in this group. These beings are no more troubled with conscience than the lambs and fawns; their hearts reflect only the lovableness of their sunny existence, as the placid pool reflects the sunlight. They are the creatures of a poet's golden dream.

Compare with them the *Jeremiah*. Here, instead of delicate gracefulness, are colossal strength, ponderous mass, profound impressiveness; back and legs that have carried the burden, hands that have labored, head bowed in vast depth of thought. And what of the thought?

More than two thousand years had passed since Jeremiah hurled his denunciations against the follies and iniquity of Judah, and in his Lamentations uttered a prophetic dirge over Jerusalem, hastening to become the prey of foreign enemies. And to the mind of Michelangelo, as he painted this figure of *Jeremiah,* sometime between 1508 and 1512,—that is to say, between his thirty-fourth and thirty-eighth years,—there was present a similar spectacle of his own beloved Italy reeling to ruin under the weight of her sins and the rivalries of foreign armies, and perhaps also a prophetic vision of how it would end. As Jeremiah lived to see the fall of Jerusalem, so Michelangelo lived to see the sacred city of Rome sacked in 1527 by the German soldiery under the French renegade Constable Bourbon.

It is the profundity of Michelangelo's own thoughts that fills this figure of *Jeremiah*. Like the Hebrew prophet's life, his own was a protest against the world. Jeremiah fled to Egypt; Michelangelo into the deepest recess of his own soul. In this figure of *Jeremiah* he has typified himself.

Whether consciously or unconsciously, who shall say? Always the artist puts into his work a portion of himself, and of this feeling in himself that he is striving to express he is of course conscious. But this feeling is the sediment left in him from many experiences, some—the most of them, probably—forgotten; so, as he labors to express it in his painting or statue, he very likely is not conscious of its personal application to himself, being absorbed by the work before him. And still more likely is this unconsciousness in the case of great artists; for in them there is more than memory and experience, more even than knowledge and imagination: something inexplicable to us, not to be understood by themselves; what we vaguely call soul, and the ancients, more vaguely still, but with nearer approach to truth, called " afflatus " —divine inspiration.

The French philosopher Taine wrote: " There are four men in the world of art and literature so exalted above all others as to seem to belong to another race— namely, Dante, Shakspeare, Beethoven, and Michelangelo."

They are of the race of the Titans, the giant progeny of heaven and earth. The old race warred with heaven, but was finally subdued and sent down to Tartarus. Three, at least, of these modern Titans, Dante, Beethoven, and Michelangelo, were at continual war in their souls with conditions that environed them, and found hell on earth. Not that the world treated Michelangelo worse than many others; but, as Taine says, " suffering must be measured by inward emotion, and not by outward circumstances; and, if ever a spirit existed which was capable of transports of enthusiasm and passionate indignation, it was his." Such a man as Michelangelo could not escape from the tempest of the world by wrapping himself up in dreams of a " golden age," as Correggio did.

Once more compare the two pictures, to observe the difference of their technic. One reason of difference is that Correggio's is painted in oil on canvas, Michelangelo's in fresco on the plaster of the ceiling. The meaning of the word " fresco " is " fresh," and the peculiarity of the method consisted in painting on the plaster while it was still damp, so that the colors, which were mixed with water, in the process of drying became incorporated with the plaster. The wall or ceiling to be so decorated was coated with the rough-cast plaster and allowed to dry thoroughly; after which a thin layer of smooth finish was spread over as large a portion of the surface as the artist could finish in one day. Meanwhile he had prepared his drawing, and, laying this against the surface, went over the lines of it with a blunt instrument, so that, when the drawing or cartoon was removed, the outline of the figures appeared, incised in the damp plaster. Then he applied the color, working rapidly, with a full assurance of the effect which he wished to produce, since correction, or working over what had already been painted, was not easy.

On the contrary, with oil paints the artist can work at his leisure, allowing his canvas time to dry, working over it again and again, and finally toning it all together by brushing over it thin layers of transparent colors, called glazes. It was by the use of these latter that Correggio obtained the warm, melting atmosphere in which his figures are bathed, and which is one of the distinguishing characteristics of his style. We can realize at once how this method was suited to the dreamy luxuriance of his imagination; while, on the contrary, more in harmony with the genius of Michelangelo was the immediate, smiting method of the fresco. For in the strict sense of the word he was not a painter; that is to say, he was not skilled in, and probably was impatient of, the slower, tenderer way in which a painter reaches his results. He was not a colorist, nor skilled in the rendering of light and atmosphere; but a great draftsman, a great sculptor, and a profound thinker. He labored with his subject in his brain, and then expressed it immediately with pencil or charcoal, or more gradually by blows of the mallet upon the chisel. But in either case it was the thought, straight out from himself in all the heat of kindled imagination, that he set upon the paper, or struck out with forceful action of the tool.

He used to say that he had sucked the desire to be a sculptor from his foster-mother, the wife of a stone-cutter; and in his later life, when sore oppressed, he would retreat to the marble-quarries of Carrara under color of searching for material. To him each block of marble, rugged, hard, and jagged, held a secret, needing only the genius of his chisel to liberate it; and in the same way his own soul was imprisoned in a personality eternally at odds with the world, that to the seven popes whom he successively served during his long life of eighty-nine years seemed very hard and unyielding.

MYSTIC MARRIAGE OF ST. CATHERINE   CORREGGIO

LOUVRE, PARIS

JEREMIAH   MICHELANGELO

SISTINE CHAPEL, ROME

CORREGGIO—MICHELANGELO

It is the feeling of the sculptor that we recognize in this painting of *Jeremiah;* the feeling for solidity and weight of mass, for stability of pose; a preference for simple lines and bold surfaces, arranged in a few planes. To appreciate this distinction, compare Correggio's picture: its intricacy of lines, the distance of its receding planes, but more particularly the character of its composition, consisting of so many varieties of lighted and shadowed parts, and the absence of suggestion that the figures are firmly planted. While Correggio has relied upon beautiful drawing, upon exquisite expression of hands and faces, and on color, light, and shade, and his golden atmosphere that envelops the whole, Michelangelo relied solely upon form—the form of the figure and of the draperies. This is to admit that, judged from the standpoint of painting, he was not a great painter. He himself told Pope Julius II, when the latter requested him to paint this ceiling of the Sistine Chapel at Rome, that he was not a painter, but a sculptor; yet, after he had shut himself up for four years, and the scaffold was removed, a result had been achieved which is without parallel in the world.

Very wonderful is the profusion of invention spread over this vast area of ten thousand square feet. The fact that there are three hundred and forty-three principal figures, many of colossal size, besides a great number of subsidiary ones introduced for decorative effect, and that the creator of this vast scheme was only thirty-four when he began his work—all this is wonderful, prodigious, but not so wonderful as the variety of expression in the figures.

[153]

HOW TO STUDY PICTURES

If there is one point more than another in which Michelangelo displayed his genius it is in this, that he discovered the capability of the human form to express mental emotions. While the ancient Greeks sought, in their rendering of the human form, an ideal of physical perfection, and the later Greeks, as in the group of Laocoon and his sons attacked by serpents, sought to express the tortures of physical suffering, Michelangelo was the first to make the human form express a variety of mental emotions. In his hands it became an instrument, upon which he played, like a musician on his organ, extracting themes and harmonies of infinite variety. And just as it is within the power of music to call up sensations, which we feel deeply and yet cannot exactly put into words, which elude us and merge themselves in the abstract and the universal, so Michelangelo's figures carry our imagination far beyond the personal meaning of the names attached to them. We know, for example, who Jeremiah was, and what he did; but this figure, buried in thought, of what is he thinking? To each one of us, thoughtfully considering the picture, it has a separate meaning.

On the other hand, we could come very near to a mutual understanding of the emotions aroused by Correggio's picture; although he too, as we have seen, was intent upon representing, not the concrete fact of a marriage, but the abstract ideas of peace, happiness, and innocence. Therefore, the difference between the ways in which these two pictures affect us is not one of kind, but of degree. Both detach our thoughts from the concrete and carry our imagination away into the world of abstract emotions; but while Correggio's appeals to us like a pastoral theme by Haydn, Michelangelo's is to be compared to the grandeur and soul-searching impressiveness of Beethoven.

Michelangelo, therefore, compels us to enlarge our conception of what is beautiful. To the Greeks it was physical perfection; to Correggio physical loveliness joined to loveliness of sentiment; but Michelangelo, except in a few instances, such as his painting of *Adam* on the Sistine vault, and his sculptures of the *Pietà* and of the figure of the *Thinker* over the tomb of Lorenzo de' Medici, cared little for physical beauty. As far as we know, he reached the age of sixty-four years without ever being attracted by the love of woman; then he met the beautiful Vittoria Colonna, widow of the Marquis of Pescara. They were mutually drawn together by the bond of intellectual and spiritual sympathy; their communion was of soul with soul; and Michelangelo, now moved by love to be a poet, expressed his soul in sonnets, as beforetime he had done in sculpture and painting.

The beauty, therefore, of his sculpture and paintings consists finally in the elevation of soul which they embody and the power they have to elevate our own souls. Their beauty is elemental; for example, the picture we are studying is not so much a representation of Jeremiah, as a typal expression of a great soul in labor with heavy thoughts. Accordingly, in Michelangelo's figures, lines of grace are for the most part replaced by lines of power—the power of vast repose or of tremendous energy, even of torment, either suppressed or desperate. Though a master of anatomy and of the laws of composition, he dared to disregard both if it were necessary to express his conception: to exaggerate the muscles of his figures, and even put them in positions which the human body could not assume. In his latest painting, that of the *Last Judgment* on the end wall of the Sistine, he poured out his soul like a torrent. What were laws in comparison with the pain within himself which must out? Well might the Italians of his day speak of the *terribilità* of his style: that it was, terrible!

In a brief study of so great a man it is possible to allude to only one more feature of the picture—namely, its architectural details. These, real as they look, are painted on the level surface of the vault. It is characteristic of Michelangelo that, having this vast space to decorate, he should begin by subdividing it into architectural spaces, since he was architect as well as sculptor, painter, and poet. For a time the building of St. Peter's was intrusted to his care, and in the last years of his life he prepared plans for it and made a model of its wonderful dome. There was much dispute as to whether the ground-plan of the building should be of the design of a Greek or of a Roman cross. Bramante had urged the former and Michelangelo adhered to it, intending the dome to be its crowning feature. Unfortunately, in the beginning of the seventeenth century the nave was lengthened, and this change from the Greek to the Roman cross has interfered with the view of the dome from nearby and otherwise diminished its effect.

Michelangelo died in Rome, February 18, 1564, after dictating this brief will: " I commit my soul to God, my

body to the earth, and my property to my nearest relations." His remains were conveyed to Florence, and
given a public funeral in the Church of Santa Croce.

Compared with this long and arduous life, Correggio's seems simple indeed. Little is known of it, which
would argue that he was of a retiring disposition. He
was born in the little town of Correggio, twenty-four
miles from Parma. In the latter city he was educated,
but in his seventeenth year an outbreak of the plague
drove his family to Mantua, where the young painter
had an opportunity of studying the pictures of Mantegna and the collection of works of art accumulated
originally by the Gonzaga family and later by Isabella
d'Este. In 1514 he was back at Parma, where his talents
met with ample recognition; and for some years the
story of his life is the record of his work, culminating
in that wonderful creation of light and shade, *The Adoration of the Shepherds*, now in the Dresden Gallery,
and the masterpiece of the Parma Gallery, *Madonna
and Child with St. Jerome and the Magdalene*.

It was not, however, a record of undisturbed quiet,
for the decoration which he made for the dome of the
cathedral was severely criticized. Choosing the subject
of the *Resurrection,* he projected upon the ceiling a
great number of ascending figures, which, viewed from
below, necessarily involved a multitude of legs, giving
rise to the *bon mot* that the painting resembled a " fry
of frogs." It may have been the trouble which now ensued with the chapter of the cathedral, or depression
caused by the death of his young wife, but at the age of
thirty-six, indifferent to fame and fortune, he retired to

the comparative obscurity of his native place, where for
four years he devoted himself to the painting of mythological subjects: scenes of fabled beings removed from
the real world and set in a golden arcady of dreams.
All that is known regarding his death is the date, March
5, 1534.

CHAPTER XI

*PAOLO CALIARI (called
VERONESE)
1528–1588
Italian School of Venice*

*JACOPO ROBUSTI (called
TINTORETTO)
1518–1594
Italian School of Venice*

THE art of Venice, it has been said, "was late in
its appearance, the last to come, the last to die,
of all the great Italian schools." It reached its
culmination in Titian, whom we have already considered, and in Paul Veronese and Tintoretto, his contemporaries. Most characteristically, perhaps, in the last
two.

For the grandeur of Venetian art does not consist in
its representation of the motives which exercised the
other schools of Italian art. It was not saturated with
the religious motive, or with the classical; nor intent on
realistic representation. It combined something of each,
but only as a means to its purpose of making art con-
tributory to the joy and pageantry of life. While the
searching spirit of the Renaissance was reflected in Da
Vinci, its soul in Michelangelo, and the Christian faith
and classical lore united in Raphael, the motive of the
Venetians was the pride of life: pride particularly in the
communal life of Venice, in her institutions, in her un-
surpassed beauty, in her royal magnificence as the
Queen City of the East and West.

HOW TO STUDY PICTURES

Eleven hundred years before the birth of Paul Veronese, A.D. 421, a handful of Roman Christians, driven out of Aquileia by the Lombards, had taken refuge upon Torcello, one of the sandy islands amid the lagoons. In time they spread to other islands, Malamocco and Rivalto, from which they repelled an attack made by Pepin, the son of Charlemagne, thus throwing off the yoke of the Eastern emperors. Rivalto was then selected as the seat of government; Venice was founded, and in A.D. 819 the doge took up his residence on the spot still occupied by the Ducal Palace. Nine years later a Venetian fleet brought from Alexandria the body of St. Mark; he was adopted as the city's patron saint; his emblem, the lion, became the symbol of the Venetian government; and a church was erected in his honor, where now stands the great cathedral, adjoining the palace of the doges.

Henceforth these two structures became the embodiment of the city's spiritual and temporal life; the assertions of her proud independence and superb ambitions; the visible expressions of her strongly personal religion and intense patriotism. From the first she set her face to the sea, and by her geographical position became the entrance-port through which the wealth of the East poured into Europe. So, when she planned her great church of St. Mark's in the eleventh century, it was to Byzantium that she turned for craftsmen and artificers, and the edifice, which rose through this and the following centuries, was Oriental both in style and in the lavishness of its decoration. It came to be like a colossal casket, the outside and inside of which was being embellished con-

tinually with more precious and sumptuous display.
Some architects will tell you it is a monstrosity, because
it lacks the dignity of form, the harmony between the
whole and its parts, that are essential to a great composition.

It is not, however, on the score of form that it challenges the admiration of the world, but as an example,
the most superb in Europe, of applied decoration. Its
exterior is incrusted with carven work, brilliant with
gold, sumptuous with columns of most precious marbles:
with costly marbles, also, its interior is veneered; its
vaultings covered with glass mosaics, its windows filled
with colored glass—the glass-work fabricated on the
island of Murano, originally by Byzantine artists. The
interior is a miracle of color, seen under every conceiva-
ble variety of lights and shadows; by turns gorgeous,
tender, stupendous, or mysteriously lustrous, impreg-
nated everywhere with an atmosphere of infinite subtlety. Not form, as I have said, but color, light and
shade, and atmosphere; and these are the qualities that
prevail in Venetian painting. They are a heritage from
the Byzantine influence, reinspired continually by the
waters and skies of Venice; and they were the only ade-
quate means of representing pictorially the variegated
opulence of Venetian life.

Let us glance for a moment at the growth of the
power of Venice. In the thirteenth century,—namely,
1204,—under her Doge Dandolo, she took Constantinople and planted her colonies on the shores of the
peninsula of Greece and on the adjacent islands. During the fourteenth century she waged war with her naval

rival, Genoa, conquered her, and extended her own power over the neighboring cities of Vicenza, Verona, and Padua, until the whole district of Venezia was under her sway, while her colonies extended along the shores of the Adriatic and Mediterranean as far as Trebizond, on the northeast coast of Asia Minor. By the commencement of the fifteenth century her glory was in its zenith. The French ambassador, De Commynes, writing to his sovereign, describes Venice as the " most triumphant city I have ever seen, and one which does most honor to ambassadors and strangers; which is most wisely governed, and in which the service of God is most solemnly performed."

But the wave, having reached its summit, was already beginning to decline. In 1453 the conquest of Constantinople by the Turks began the undermining of the commerce of Venice with the Levant; and, following the voyage of Vasco da Gama round the Cape of Good Hope, the trade with India gradually passed into the hands of the Portuguese. Then, in 1508, the Pope, the German Emperor, and the King of France conspired against Venice in the League of Cambrai; and although she " remained herself untouched upon the waters of the Lagoons, she lost her possessions on the mainland "; while through the years which followed, almost singlehanded, she held the Turks at bay. Yet it was in the long-drawn-out decline of her power that her art reached its supreme height. With Titian, whose long life bridged the fifteenth and sixteenth centuries, it is still magnificently poised; with Tintoretto and Paul Veronese, both of whom belonged entirely to the latter century, it is an art of display and some exaggeration.

VERONESE—TINTORETTO

Peculiarly characteristic of Venetian art was the pageant picture representing some great religious or state function redounding to the glory of Venice. The most beautiful city in the world, her own external life was a continual pageant, but on frequent occasions her canals and piazza were the scenes of officially regulated ceremonials. The arrival and departure of ambassadors were events of particular magnificence; the church's processions, such as those of Corpus Christi, were conducted with a splendor that was only surpassed in the great state pageant wherein Venice was annually wedded to the Adriatic.

The Doge's Palace, embodiment of her power as a state, under the rule of its doge and Council of Ten, was five times damaged by fire, and after each catastrophe repaired with greater magnificence. In the fire of 1576 the paintings by Bellini, Alvise Vivarini, and Carpaccio which had adorned the interior were consumed; and those which now decorate its walls and ceilings are the work of the later artists, notably of Titian, Tintoretto, and Veronese. With very few exceptions, the subjects of the pictures set forth the glory and power of Venice, which find their highest expression in the Hall of the Great Council, that body of one hundred nobles, nominally the government, but actually superseded by the inner Council of Ten. The walls are covered with large mural paintings, representing triumphal incidents of war and diplomacy. Around the frieze are portraits by Tintoretto of seventy-six doges, a black tablet with the inscription *Hic est locus Marini Falethri decapitati pro criminibus* hanging where should be the portrait of Doge Marino Faliero, a traitor to the terrible Council of Ten.

The splendor of the whole culminates in the center of the eastern ceiling, in the *Glory of Venice* by Paul Veronese.

The illustration of it here reproduced should be held above the head, in order that the angle of vision may correspond with that at which the original is viewed. Then it becomes apparent with what wonderful skill the architecture and the figures have been made to conform to the conditions of seeing the picture. High up against the magnificent architectural setting, of that imposing kind with which the architect Palladio was delighting his contemporaries, between pillars of Oriental design, such as adorn the *Beautiful Gate of the Temple* in Raphael's cartoon of Peter and John curing the lame man, Venezia sits enthroned. She is robed in ermine and blue silk, gold embroidered, and above her fair-haired head a winged figure, poised in air, suspends a crown, while another, higher up upon a cloud, blows through a trumpet. Grouped at the foot of the throne, and resting upon clouds, are five female figures, symbolizing, from the right, Justice, Agriculture, Peace, Commerce, and Victory, and beside the last sits the male figure of a soldier, holding a branch of laurel. From a balcony beneath them men and women in beautiful attire look up with faces of radiant happiness and devotion, while down below, two horsemen appear among a crowd of persons.

" This picture," writes the artist E. H. Blashfield, " is so rich and so silvery in its color "—the latter appearing in the architectural parts—" that it may be called magnificent in its technic as in its motive. As a subject, it is exactly what Veronese loved best to treat, and among

THE GLORY OF VENICE   PAOLO VERONESE

HALL OF THE GREAT COUNCIL, DUCAL PALACE, VENIÇE

THE MIRACLE OF ST. MARK   ACADEMY, VENICE   TINTORETTO

his works only *The Marriage at Cana* and *The Family of Darius* can rival it. . . . No picture shows a more masterly arrangement: a style at once so sumptuous yet elevated, figures whose somewhat exuberant loveliness is saved from vulgarity by an air of pride and energy, magnificent material treated with such ease and sincerity."

We should particularly remark the last words, "ease and sincerity." As to the ease of Veronese, I quote from various sources: "His facility of execution has never been equaled." "Every one of his canvases, replete with life and movement, is a feast for the eye." "Veronese was supreme in representing, without huddling or confusion, numerous figures in a luminous and diffused atmosphere, while in richness of draperies and transparency of shadows he surpassed all other Venetians or Italians." "He is of all painters, without a single exception, the one whose work shows most unity."

As to his sincerity, it arose from the fact that he was simply what he was—a painter. He does not appeal to our intelligence, as Titian, or to our sense of dramatic poetry, as Tintoretto. His is the Kingdom of the World, the pride of strong and beautiful bodies, the splendor of external appearances; and he gave himself to it with the single purpose of representing what appealed to the eye. "Joyous, free, proud, full of health and vigor, Veronese is the very incarnation of the Italian Renaissance, that happy time when under smiling and propitious skies painters produced works of art with as little effort as trees put forth their blossoms and bear their fruit."

" These being the prominent features of his style, it remains to be said that what is really great in Veronese is the sobriety of his imagination and the solidity of his workmanship. Amid so much that is distracting, he never loses command over his subject, nor does he degenerate into fulsome rhetoric." In the exuberance of his fancy and the facility of his brush, moreover in the skill with which he " places crowds of figures in an atmospheric envelope, bathing them, so to speak, in light," he resembles Rubens. " But he does not, like Rubens, strike us as gross, sensual, fleshly; he remains proud, powerful, and frigidly materialistic. He raises neither repulsion nor desire, but displays with the calm strength of art the empire of the mundane spirit." Equally in this quality of sober restraint he differs from Tintoretto. " Where Tintoretto is dramatic, Veronese is scenic."

This distinction is well worth analyzing. It may seem for a moment as if the two ideas were identical; but " scenic " has to do with the things apparent to the eye, " dramatic " with the unseen workings of the mind, as expressed in word or gesture. A pageant is scenic; but the attempt to reproduce the thought, which moves each individual to separate expression of his feelings, would bring it into the category of dramatic. The distinction is made clear by a comparison of the *Glory of Venice* with Tintoretto's *Miracle of St. Mark.* We feel a desire to know the story represented in the latter. This in itself is to admit a difference. Veronese being, as I have said, simply what he was—a painter—needs no commentary. The purport of his picture is at once self-evident. You will be told by some that this self-evidentness is the proper scope of painting; that "art for art's sake" should be the sole object of the painter; that the representation of anything else but what is apparent to the eye is going outside the province of the art; and that the preference which so many people have for a picture which makes an appeal not only to the eye, but to the intellect or the poetic and dramatic sense, is a proof of vulgar taste which confuses painting with illustration. The best answer to this is that not alone laymen, but artists also in all periods,—artists of such personality that they cannot be ignored,—have tried to reinforce the grandeur of mere appearances with something that shall appeal to the mind and soul of men.

Tintoretto was one of them; not by overt intention, but because the poetic and dramatic fervor was in him and it had to find utterance. The points of main importance are the value of the story that he represents and his manner of representing it. Now, to the Venetians, any incident connected with their patron saint was of extreme interest, recognized at once and enjoyed. The one pictured here has reference to the legend, that a Christian slave of a pagan nobleman had persisted in worshiping at the shrine of St. Mark; whereupon his master haled him before the judge, who condemned him to be tortured. But as the executioner raised his hammer, St. Mark himself descended from heaven and the weapon was shattered. We see the saint, hovering above the crowd; the executioner in his turban, turning to the judge to show the broken hammer; the judge leaning forward in his seat, and the various individuals in the crowd pressing round with different expressions of amazement. Following a custom of the time, Tintoretto has introduced the portrait of himself three times: in the bearded man who leans forward between the columns on the left, in the figure immediately to the right of the executioner, and again in the face that appears beneath the judge on the extreme right of the picture. No Venetian of Tintoretto's time could be unresponsive to such a theme, so realized; any more than an American of to-day could fail to be impressed, were there an artist capable of representing some incident in the life of Washington in such a way as to involve all that the idea of Washington presents to the American imagination.

Now as to the manner of presentment: Tintoretto, when a youth, wrote upon the wall of his studio as an ideal to be reached: " The drawing of Michelangelo, the coloring of Titian." His father being a dyer of silk (*tintore*), the lad at first assisted in the work, hence his nickname, " Il Tintoretto," "The Little Dyer." However, as he showed an aptitude for drawing and painting, the father obtained permission for him to work in Titian's studio; but for some reason his stay with the great master lasted only a few days. For the rest, he was his own teacher, studying and copying the works of Titian in the churches and palaces; and, having obtained casts of Michelangelo's figures upon the Medicean tombs, drawing them from every possible point of view. It is said that he also made little figures in clay, and suspended them by a string from the rafters in his studio, that he might learn how to represent them in mid-air, and as they appeared when viewed from underneath.

It was very difficult even in Venice for a young untried painter to obtain recognition; but at last an opportunity occurred. In the Church of Santa Maria del Orto there were two bare spaces nearly fifty feet high and twenty broad; he offered to paint them for nothing but the price of the materials; and, the offer being accepted, produced *The Last Judgment* and *The Golden Calf*. He was now about twenty-eight years old. So great was the impression produced by these works that he was shortly after invited to paint four pictures for the Scuola di San Rocco, one of which was the picture we are studying. There were many of these schools in Venice, and they vied with one another in securing the services of painters to decorate their walls. The brothers of the Confraternity of San Rocco gave Tintoretto a commission for two pictures in their church, and then invited him to enter a competition with Veronese and others for the decoration of the ceiling in the hall of their school. When the day arrived, the other painters presented their sketches, but Tintoretto, being asked for his, removed a screen from the ceiling and showed it already painted. "We asked for sketches," they said. "That is the way," he replied, "I make my sketches." They still demurred, so he made them a present of the picture, and by the rules of their order they could not refuse a gift. In the end they promised him the painting of all the pictures they required, and during his lifetime he covered their walls with sixty large compositions. After the fire of 1577 in the Ducal Palace he shared with Veronese the larger part of the new decorations.

Among his pictures there is the *Marriage of Bacchus and Ariadne,* described by John Addington Symonds as " that perfect lyric of the sensuous fancy "; with which the same writer couples his *Martyrdom of St. Agnes,* " that lamb-like maiden with her snow-white lamb among the soldiers and priests of Rome," as an illustration " that it is not only in the region of the vast, the tempestuous, and the tragic, that Tintoretto finds himself at home; but that he has proved beyond all question that the fiery genius of Titanic artists can pierce and irradiate the placid and the tender secrets of the soul, with more consummate mastery than falls to the lot of those who make tranquillity their special province."

Yet it is his phenomenal energy and the impetuous force of his work that are particularly characteristic of Tintoretto and earned for him the sobriquet among his contemporaries, " Il Furioso." He painted so many pictures, and on so vast a scale, that some show the effects of over-haste and extravagance, which caused Annibale Carracci to say that, " while Tintoretto was the equal of Titian, he was often inferior to Tintoretto."

But the *Miracle of St. Mark* is one of his grandest pictures; admirable alike in the dramatic movement of the figures, the beauty of the coloring, and the emotional use that has been made of light and shadow. If we compare it with Veronese's we shall discover the difference between the dramatic and the scenic. The figures in the latter have a sumptuous repose, finely adjusted to the general strain of triumph that resounds from the whole picture; but in Tintoretto's the wonderfully foreshortened body of St. Mark plunges through the air with the impetuosity of an eagle. " There is not a figure in the picture that does not act, and act all over; not a fold of drapery nor a tone of flesh that does not add to the universal dash and brilliancy." The coloring of the costumes includes saffron, blue, gold, and deep crimson; the sky is of greenish hue passing to a golden haze over the horizon; while the body of the slave is a center of luminousness. For the chief characteristic of the picture is Tintoretto's use of light and shade.

He uses it with dramatic and emotional effect; " with him," as has been said, " it is the first and most powerful of dramatic accessories; he makes light an actor in his vast compositions." We shall see how Rubens, fresh from Italy, used light and shadow in this emotional way in his *Descent from the Cross;* but usually, like Veronese, he enveloped his figures in clear full light; while Tintoretto makes his emerge into light from darkness. Some of his pictures, whether from effects of time or the manner of their painting, are to-day black and coarse-looking; but in the best and well-preserved ones, as in our present example, the shadows themselves are luminous with color.

While his life was a tranquil one, spent for the most part in his studio, his mind teemed with ideas; his conceptions came to him in lightning bursts of inspiration, the whole scene vividly clear; rapidly and without hesitation transferred to the canvas. Hence some of his work is exaggerated in force and confused in composition. Such, at least in its present condition, is the vast canvas of *Paradise* in the Ducal Palace, the largest oil-painting in the world, measuring thirty by seventy-four feet, upon which he painted during the last six years of his life. He lies buried in Santa Maria del Orto, the church in which his first important work was done forty-eight years before. Veronese, the younger man, had been dead six years.

With these men died the last of the giants of the Italian Renaissance. That mighty movement had run its course, and was succeeded by decline. The vital force of painting now reappeared in other lands.

CHAPTER XII

DOMENICO THEOTOCOPULI
(called EL GRECO)
1545–1614
Spanish School

FRANCISCO DE ZURBARÁN
1598–1662
Spanish School

THE student of art, when he reaches the period of the seventeenth century, turns a sharp corner. He has been traveling for three centuries in Italy, with brief visits at long intervals to Flanders and Germany, the second of his trips to the latter including a visit to England. But, as he turns the corner of the seventeenth century, Italy is left behind, Spain attracts his attention to the west, while far to the north Holland and, a second time, Flanders beckon him.

For in Italy the last of the great artists passed away with Tintoretto. The country itself had become the prey of despots who were in the hire of foreign rulers; and the loss of political liberty was accompanied by lower social standards, by intellectual and artistic decline. There were still clever painters, but they were little men, without originality, content to reproduce the manner of their great predecessors; copying chiefly their weaknesses; trying by extravagances to disguise the absence of originality in themselves.

At this period, to find something vital in art—something, that is to say, which grows and ripens because of the independent force of life within itself—we must turn to Spain and to the north. For the present Spain shall detain us.

Spanish painting during the sixteenth century had been nourished on the example of the Great Italians. It was the period of the so-called "Mannerists," who imitated the manner of Leonardo da Vinci, Raphael, and Michelangelo. Yet, even while they did so the painters exhibited what has always been the characteristic of Spanish art—a love of Naturalism. They learned from the Italians the secrets of drawing, foreshortening and perspective, the principles of composition and the art of expressing emotion; but the figures which they introduced had not the ideal abstraction that the Italians gave to theirs. While the Italians made their figures more stately or beautiful than life, and arranged their gestures, poses, and groupings so as to build up grandiose compositions, the Spanish artists represented actual types of local character and disposed the figures with more regard for the probabilities of the action in which they were engaged. They also carried their love of naturalism to an extreme in the delineation of scenes of suffering; blood, wounds, and evidences of disease being often represented with revolting insistence. This is particularly noticeable in the religious pictures, which form the chief branch of Spanish painting, the next in importance being that of portraiture. For in Spain painting was scarcely an independent art. It relied upon the patronage of the Church and of the King, whose proudest heritage was the title of "Catholic Sovereign." In consequence, it was not only the religious subject that was imposed upon the artists by the Church, but its treatment also. The latter had to conform to the rules and regulations, extending even to the colors of the saintly garments, which ecclesiastical authority enforced.

There were three great centers of painting, each of which produced its school of artists. Valencia, on the east coast of the Peninsula, produced the School of Valencia, of which the leading figure was José Ribera, who, however, lived the greater part of his life in Naples, where he was known as "Lo Spagnoletto," "The Little Spaniard." Closely allied with this school was the School of Andalusia, with headquarters in Seville. Meanwhile, in the north, centered in Madrid, the seat of monarchical government, was the School of Castile.

To the last named belonged El Greco, while the Andalusian School claimed Zurbarán. The latter's professional life began about the time of the other's death, so that the coupling of these two artists in this chapter may seem to be rather arbitrary. Its convenience, however, is justified, because both were ardent exponents of different phases of the religious life of the time, and the differences which appear in their art are as interesting as their similarities. Moreover, both have shared a common fate. El Greco was forgotten soon after his death in the rising greatness of Velasquez, and Zurbarán's reputation in his own lifetime was superseded by that of Murillo. Both were overlooked during the eighteenth century, and it was not until the end of the nineteenth that an interest in their art revived. To-day Zurbarán is esteemed at least as highly as Murillo, while

El Greco is recognized not only as a strikingly individual genius, but also as one who had a great influence upon the genius of Velasquez.

The pictures selected for comparison are the master-works of their authors; altar-pieces of monumental size and probably the finest ceremonial pictures in Spain. For all their dissimilarity they have much in common. Each has a row of figures at the base, which represent the union of the Church and the laity in a common faith on earth, while above their heads is revealed a vision of heaven. Each, too, as we shall see presently, is a grand example of arrangement of masses so as to produce not only a handsome pattern of decoration, but also one that we may describe as firmly planted on the ground and growing upward to a culminating focus of interest.

We note, however, a great difference. In the Zurbarán the naturalness which characterizes the figures at the foot is continued throughout the whole of the composition, exhibited both in the figures and the clouds of glory, the only deviation from naturalness being that the clouds have sufficient solidity to support the figures. On the other hand, in El Greco's canvas the clouds have no resemblance to natural ones; indeed, they are more like draperies, as if some great tableaux-curtains had been drawn apart to reveal the mystery above. Moreover, the figures of the Virgin and of the nude man are not in proportion to the sizes of their heads. The figures have been unnaturally elongated, and, further, the nude figure is, from the point of view of natural representation and anatomical correctness, "badly drawn." Were a student in an art school to draw a nude in this way, his instructor would criticize it sharply, and, as a matter of fact, many critics condemn severely this figure of El Greco's, and, indeed, his whole treatment of the upper part of the design. They say that the lower part is very fine, but that the rest justifies the opinion of many of the artist's own contemporaries, King Philip II among them, that El Greco was eccentric to the verge of madness. We shall try to enter into El Greco's intention presently, but meanwhile may observe that while he has treated the lower part realistically, he has chosen to distinguish the heavenly vision from the earthly by treating the former symbolically.

As a preparation to understanding this intention, let us briefly study the personality of El Greco and his particular relation to the spirit of his times, as it was expressed in the city of his adoption, Toledo. For he was not a Spaniard, but was born of Greek parentage in the Island of Crete. Hence the sobriquet by which he was known, El Greco, The Greek, his real name being Domenico Theotocopuli. The date of his birth is in doubt, and we have no particulars of his life before he came to Spain, except that he had studied with Titian and spent some time in Rome. Our first knowledge of his having settled in Toledo comes from the date 1577, appended to his signature on an altar-piece, *The Assumption of the Virgin,* which was painted for the church of San Domingo el Antigua in Toledo, and is now in the Art Museum in Chicago.

The picture immediately recalls Titian's masterpiece and at the same time challenges comparison with it.

El Greco has abandoned the three-tier character of his master's composition. The figure of the Father is left out and the Virgin lifted to the top. As in Titian's canvas, she is supported by angels and cherubs, and soars above a group of the faithful. Here, however, the latter are ranged around an empty sarcophagus, into which some gaze, while others are looking up. El Greco's canvas lacks the majestic upward impetus of Titian's, but is more intimate, reverential, spiritual. For the types are not generalized idealizations; they are personalities—types that through his pictures we come to recognize as Toledan, and each displays the reverence and adoration of a personal living faith. A corresponding feeling appears in the treatment of the draperies and color scheme. The former, especially in the case of the Virgin, are not voluminous and swirling, as in Titian's. They present simple, broad surfaces beneath which the movement of the figure is more apparent, and the rich hues of crimson and blue have been subtilized, etherealized. Instead of the mundane splendor suitable to Venice, the picture breathes the intense spirituality of Toledo.

For Toledo, which had once been the center of Moorish civilization, was now the living heart of Catholicism, which nowhere burned so intensely as in Spain. In Italy it had been all but overwhelmed by the "New Learning"; elsewhere it had been assailed by the attacks of Protestantism. But against Protestantism and Humanism alike the Spaniards had pitted their inveterate conservatism, and the dangers to Catholicism elsewhere had quickened the fervor of their faith. To-

BURIAL OF COUNT ORGAZ   EL GRECO

CHURCH OF SAN TOMÉ, TOLEDO

APOTHEOSIS OF ST. THOMAS AQUINAS   FRANCISCO DE ZURBARÁN

MUSEUM, SEVILLE

ledo, with its cathedral famous throughout Spain for
the wealth and grandeur of its ceremonial, was the
stronghold of what was called the "Counter-Reforma-
tion." El Greco, himself a devout Catholic, became the
exponent of the pomp and glory of the faith as well
as an interpreter of the religious ecstasy of the faithful.
In old days the Toledans had been Knights of the Cross
against the Crescent, and the devotion, fired by many a
fight and intensified in lonely vigils, still burned in them
as a fierce spiritual flame. El Greco was a contemporary of Cervantes, and, while the latter depicted
with the exaggeration of satire the excess of the chiv-
alric spirit, the painter expressed with the exaggeration
of the ecstatic believer the spirituality of religious
mysticism.

Now, in a sense all high expression in art, and equally
in life, is based upon exaggeration—the word means
literally the selection of some one thing and the heaping
up of its importance. It was so that a Wilberforce,
harping upon the abolition of slavery in season and out
of season, making it for himself the one object of his
efforts, and treating it as if it were of sole and supreme
importance, converted an indifferent world to his reform. Even temporal success in life is not obtained by
the jack-of-all-trades, but by the master of one, the
specialist who is almost bound to exaggerate the importance of his own speciality. Still more in matters spiritual, to stir the souls of men and lift them to high
thought and conduct, there is needed the exaggeration
of the zealot.

In the case of art, we have already seen how Michelangelo dared to ignore the facts of anatomical construction in order to increase the expression of his figures. We shall see later that Rembrandt sought the same aid by different means—namely, by suppressing parts of the figure beneath the obscurity of shadow, and concentrating the light on those parts which would most help the expression. In consequence of this, critics who did not understand his motive have said that he was "slovenly" in his drawing.

Now, what is to be understood by drawing? It is, of course, the rendering of an object by outline or by means of color. But to what end? Is the artist satisfied to secure a resemblance to the object such as any one can immediately recognize; or is he intent upon interpreting the significance of the object, of suggesting the emotion with which the object inspires him, or of making his rendering of the object convey to the imagination of others something that has kindled his own imagination? In the one case it is representation that is his motive, in the other expression; and the artist who feels that the value of expression far transcends that of representation will dare to *misrepresent* by exaggeration or otherwise, if he believes that by so doing he can increase the volume and the intensity of expressional suggestion.

Perhaps we are now in a position to enter into the motive of El Greco's *Burial of Count Orgaz*. It decorates the little church of San Tomé, the founder of which, Count Orgaz, died in 1323. Legend relates that when the leading men of Toledo gathered round the grave, Saints Augustine and Stephen came down from heaven and lowered the revered form into its tomb. It is this miracle that El Greco was commissioned to paint. In the lower part of the picture he has represented the burial, not as a legend, but as a fact, accepted by the faithful, in proof of which he gives the row of mourners the faces of some of his own contemporaries. As he wished to make the fact of the miracle visible to the eye, he is careful to make the representation as real as possible and true to the appearances of the scene.

Meanwhile, there is involved in the occasion more than the physical eye can see, a spiritual fact visible only to the eye of faith. He would suggest to the imagination what was in the thoughts of the mourners and was still cherished in the thoughts of himself and the rest of the faithful. He would render a vision which no eye had seen except the eye of the spirit; wherefore he no longer relies upon physical representation, but upon spiritual expression. Below, he had depicted the fact; above, he would suggest the soul of the fact. The Count appears at the feet of the Redeemer, while the Blessed Virgin and St. John the Baptist intercede on his behalf, and the concourse of saints and angels and of Toledans who have joined the hosts of heaven await the issue. While, below, there is a solemn resignation to the facts of life, above, there is joy in heaven, intense, vibrant, that surges upward in rhythmic waves of praise and prayer to the throne of the Redeemer.

In order to secure attention to the Redeemer's figure and prevent it from being "skied," as artists say of a picture hung too high, the figures of the Virgin and St. John were exaggerated in size, so that they might be sure to catch the eye and lift it to the figure above. The trio of forms thus serve to make an emphatic spot, balancing the mass of figures at the base. The latter form a handsome design of black and white, relieved by the pale flesh tones, while proper importance is given to the dead in his black Toledan armor by the gorgeous vestments of the saints. The coloring of the Heavenly Vision is fainter, more rarefied, more spiritualized, the clouds being grayish, tinged with faint blue and green; the Virgin's draperies, pale soft blue and diaphanous rose, the general coloring being subdued, but frequently rent with flashes of brighter tone.

Indeed, in the upper part, it is not so much upon color that the composition depends as upon tone—that is to say, the relative quantity of light and less light in the various hues; and even from the photograph it can be seen that the light—pulsating here, there gleaming like the edge of a scimitar in motion—is applied less to produce the modeling of the forms than to suggest the vibration and energy of movement. While the lower part of the composition expresses power, stable and self-contained, the other expresses power in movement. It is, as a scientist would say, dynamic, while the former is static.

It is this distribution of light that makes some people condemn the upper part, because it is, they say, unnatural and interferes with the natural appearance of the forms. But in this part, as we have seen, El Greco was less concerned with representation than with expression. Meanwhile, it may not be so unnatural as some artists who draw from stationary models would have us believe, for light on a moving form assumes a series of apparently fantastic surprises; and, as you watch them, you very likely lose consciousness of the forms and see only the play of light, which you recognize as evidence of movement. I well remember a remarkable illustration of this in one of Miss Isadora Duncan's bare-legged dances. At one point she came down the stage, lifting her knees alternately somewhat like the stepping of a doe; and, as her legs moved, the light from the sides, from above, and from the footlights flashed upon them, distracting the eye from their contours and form and leaving only an impression of a rhythmic play of light. Her natural pose took on just such surprises of illumination as El Greco over and over again introduced into the composition of his figures for the purpose of suggesting expression.

It is because he was so notable a master of expression that the modern world, tired of so much preoccupation with representation, has "discovered" him. He was in his own day an exception and the forerunner of a much later motive in art, so that perhaps it is difficult to appreciate him properly at this point of our story. The student, therefore, after finishing the story, might do well to return to this chapter, and would find in it, I believe, a clearer meaning and a deeper interest.

But now to consider Zurbarán. In him there appears nothing of mysticism or ectasy. He lived in a less strenuous atmosphere of religious thought; partly because his lines were laid in the South, and partly because by his time a change had passed over the national religion. The rigors of the Inquisition had been superseded by an era of peace and happiness, of gentle reverence for the beauty of religion and of kindly emulation in good works. It is this aspect of religion, viewed through the quiet and orderly routine of the monastic life, that chiefly occupied Zurbarán. Fond of seeking the seclusion of the cloister and of identifying himself with the simple, frugal lives of the brothers, he became, as it were, painter-in-ordinary to the white-frocked order of the Carthusians and the black-and-white Dominicans. No painter has ever treated with more technical dignity the ample folds and broad surfaces of black and white draperies. Zurbarán made them eloquent of the qualities of order, simplicity, and restraint which were elements in his own temperament. While his attitude was closely sympathetic, it was entirely free from the tendency to excessive sentiment that was apt to mark the southern painter. It was in characterization that he excelled.

All these qualities are finely represented in his masterpiece, the *Apotheosis of St. Thomas Aquinas,* executed when he was only twenty-seven years old. It now hangs in the Provincial Museum of Seville, but was originally painted as an altar-piece for the church of the College of St. Thomas, whose founder, Archbishop Diego de Deza, is represented at the foot of the composition, kneeling opposite to the Emperor Charles V, who had been a patron of the foundation. All the heads are clearly portraits, that of "The Angelic Doctor," as St. Thomas was affectionately called, being, tradition says, a portrait of the Prebendary of Seville in Zurbarán's own day. The saint belonged to the Dominican order, so that the central feature of the composition is the black-and-white of the habit. The same colors are echoed in the three ecclesiastics below, headed by the archbishop in white alb and rosy crimson cape and cassock. The emperor's mantle is of cloth of gold, while gold-embroidered "orphreys" embellish the sumptuous copes of Saints Gregory, Ambrose, and Augustine, three of the doctors of the Church who support the saint, and a cardinal's crimson hat and cape distinguish the fourth, St. Jerome. Above, on the left, are seated the Christ and Virgin, and on the right St. Paul and St. Dominic, the last in black-and-white. The glory that surrounds these figures is dappled with cherub heads, and its open space is echoed below in a glimpse of a street, showing presumably a part of the church of the college. The effect of this opening is to carry down the upper open space into the lower part of the composition, thus helping to counteract the division of the composition into three tiers and to draw the whole into a unity.

For now that we have created in imagination the general color scheme of the composition, we can study in the photograph its lines and masses and spacing. Its distinguishing characteristic is its organic construction; every part, that is to say, has a distinct function to perform, and all are so related that nothing is superfluous and everything works together to make the whole an effective unit. Moreover, as in the case of El Greco's masterpiece, the whole represents not merely an organized pattern, but an organic growth. Note, for example, how the sweeping line of the emperor's mantle and, in a less degree, the hands and upturned face of the archbishop carry the eye upward to the saint, the lines of whose habit receive and respond to the directions of the lines below, while his right hand diverts some of the attention from himself to the distant figures of the Christ and Virgin. Observe also how the line of the book in his left hand merges with the general convex curve formed by the masses of the four doctors, and again how this curve is balanced down below by the concave curve, formed by the kneeling figures and the table.

Thus, if you chose to make a skeleton pattern of the design, you would set in the center an isosceles triangle, drawn from the lower corners—where it is strongly anchored on each side by a mass—and leading up to its apex in the saint's head. Then, across this triangle, you would draw a concave arc and above it a convex one. By this time the rectangular space of the canvas has been opposed by a triangular mass, which in its turn has been relieved by a circular. Such, reduced to its simplest terms, is the organic construction of the composition; based, as all the great Renaissance compositions were, on the principle of the opposition of geometrical forms. Its individual distinction depends upon the broad and simple way in which the principle has been applied. The composition has what mechanicians would call " functional simplicity," for they will tell you that naval engines can stand a harder and more prolonged strain than any other form of machinery, and

that the reason is their organic simplicity. The parts
have been reduced to as few as possible, and the capacity of each to perform its function has been raised
to the highest efficiency. So it is interesting to note
that the principle which makes for superior usefulness
in mechanical construction also conduces to the dignity
of artistic composition.

But, while the dignity and grandeur of Zurbarán's
composition result from the organic simplicity of its
masses and lines and spaces, the eye is not only impressed by the largeness of the design, but can find
pleasure in the parts; in the variety of the details,
sometimes broadly handsome, elsewhere sumptuously
elaborated, and also in the characterization of the heads.
These, you will note, group themselves into types. In
one corner are variations of the type of the courtier and
man of affairs; in the other different phases of piety
and asceticism, while in the doctors there is the contrast
of profound scholarship and spiritual preëminence.

Zurbarán's reputation in Seville caused Philip IV to
invite him to Madrid, where he was chiefly occupied
with portraits, especially of ladies. These possess distinction, for the draperies are handled with simple effec-
tiveness and the color schemes have much sober richness
and subtlety of tone. Yet in these society portraits
he failed to exhibit the sympathy with and grasp of
character which came so spontaneously to him when
employed upon religious and monastic pictures.

El Greco, in *The Burial,* as we have seen, and indeed
in all his subject-pictures, introduced portraiture. He
was also a great master of the portrait pure and sim-

ple; as, for example, in the portrait of *Don Fernando Niño de Guevara,* which was evidently in the memory of Velasquez when he painted his portrait of *Innocent X.* For Velasquez, so little disposed to be influenced by any other artist, however great, did not disdain to learn of El Greco. He occasionally borrowed from the latter's compositions, and meanwhile was permanently affected by El Greco's use of color—his superb blacks and whites and his subtle tones of rose and blue. For this pupil of Titian refined upon his master's mundane splendor of crimson, blue, and golden yellow and rich green, translating them into rarefied hues, and, so to say, spiritualizing them by the subtlety of the tones. It was in this preference for simplicity and sensitiveness of color and for rare qualities of tone that El Greco influenced Velasquez. For the same reason, and also because of his gift of expression, El Greco is rousing the enthusiasm of the modern world.

CHAPTER XIII

PETER PAUL RUBENS

1577–1640

Flemish School

*DIEGO RODRIGUEZ DE
SILVA Y VELASQUEZ*

1599–1660

Spanish School

AS we noted in the last chapter, leadership has passed from Italy to Spain and to its vassal, Flanders. The pictures selected as a basis for the study of these two giants are *The Descent from the Cross* by Rubens and *The Maids of Honor* (*Las Meñinas* in the Spanish) by Velasquez. The former was painted when Rubens was thirty-five. He had completed his education by a sojourn of eight years in Italy, where, in the service of the Duke of Mantua, he had had special opportunities of study, being employed during part of the time in making copies of masterpieces for his patron.

He was now returned to Antwerp, and one of the first works in which he declared himself to be a master was *The Descent from the Cross*. It shows him to be under the Italian influence, and not yet the original artist that he became. *The Maids of Honor,* on the contrary, was painted by Velasquez only four years before he died, and represents the finest flower of his maturity.

Possibly our first impression of the Rubens picture will be, "How beautiful!"—of the Velasquez, "How curious!" In the one case the figures almost fill the can-

[197]

vas and are grouped so as to decorate it with an imposing mass of light and shade and a beautiful arrangement of lines; whereas in the other the figures are all at
the bottom of the canvas, and do not present a similarly
beautiful pattern of lines and masses. The one looks
like a magnificent picture; the other seems to be rather
a real scene, as indeed it was.

The story of *Las Meñinas* is that Velasquez was painting a portrait of the king and queen, who sat where the
spectator is as he looks at the picture, and their little
daughter, the infanta Margarita, came in with her maids
of honor, her dog, and her dwarfs, accompanied by her
duenna and a courtier. The little princess asks for a
drink of water; the maids of honor hand it to her with
the elaborate etiquette prescribed by the formalities of
the most rigidly ceremonious court in Europe. The
scene presented so charming a picture that the king desired Velasquez to paint it. The artist has included
himself in the group at work upon a large canvas, on
which it is supposed he was painting the portraits of the
king and queen when the interruption occurred. Their
reflection appears in the mirror at the end of the room,
and the chamberlain, Don José Nieto, stands outside the
door, drawing a curtain. The scene is indeed represented with such extraordinary realism that the French
critic Gautier writes, "So complete is the illusion that,
standing in front of *Las Meñinas,* one is tempted to ask,
'Where is the picture?'"

It is the mature work of a painter whose motto was,
"Verdad no pintura" ("Truth, not painting"). By
comparison, the principle which Rubens followed is

"Painting and truth." Let us see how the two ideas are illustrated in the respective pictures.

The Descent from the Cross arouses one's feeling of awe and pity to an extraordinary degree. This is partly due to the actual moment in the great tragedy of the Redemption which the artist has seized. The terrible anguish of the Crucifixion is past; to it has succeeded the pathetic nothingness of death; the poor, limp body is being tenderly cared for by the faithful few who have come, under the cover of night, to render the last office to the Dead. Joseph of Arimathæa is superintending the lowering of the precious burden; young John, the beloved disciple, supports its weight; Peter has mounted the ladder with characteristic eagerness, but the memory of his denial is with him, and, fixed in contemplation of the divine face, he lends no hand; and the three Marys are there, the one stretching out her arms with a mother's yearning for embrace, the Magdalene grasping the foot that she had once bathed with her tears. Each attendant figure, though so different in its individual expression of feeling, joins with the others to complete a unity of deepest reverential tenderness. Then in contrast to these strong forms, so full of life and feeling, is the relaxed, nerveless body of the Dead. I wonder if ever the pitiful helplessness of death, or the reverent awe that the living feel in the presence of their beloved dead, has been more beautifully expressed.

Let us try to discover by what actual resources of the painter's art Rubens has achieved this result. We have mentioned the contrast between the bodies of the Dead and the living figures. It is an illustration of the painter's power to stimulate what has been called the "tactile imagination"; that is to say, to suggest the physical sense of touch and the feelings in the mind aroused by it. A lesser artist might have conceived this way of presenting the scene and drawn all the figures in the same positions, making, in fact, the same appeal to our eye, and yet not affected us in the same way, because he would make no appeal to that other sense of *touch,* which really in most people is the more easily roused. For people more readily appreciate hard and soft, rough and smooth, stiff and limp, hot and cold, than the colors and shapes and grouping of objects. It is this sense of touch which Rubens had so wonderful a skill in suggesting. Look, for example, at the modeling of the shoulders and head of Peter. What strength and bulk and sudden tightening of the muscles, as he turns and holds himself still! The line of the shoulders and the direction of the eyes point us to the Saviour's head. It has dropped of its own weight, as the hand of the man above let go of it. The left arm is still grasped by the other man—at the elbow, observe, so that his hand not only helps to sustain the weight of the body, but keeps the forearm stiff. We feel that, when he lets go, it too will fall lifelessly. Compare also the huddled, actionless position of the Saviour's form with the strong body of John, braced so firmly by the legs. So, one by one, we might examine the figures, feeling in our imagination the physical firmness and muscular movement that each would present to the touch, coming back again and again to the feeling, How limp and flaccid is the dead body!

This last feeling might produce in us either disgust
or pity. Rubens has insured the latter, partly by depicting in the living figures a reverence and tenderness in
which we instantly participate; also, by the persuasive
beauty of the composition.

Let us study the latter, first in its arrangement of line,
secondly in its arrangement of light and shade, though
the two are really blended. Every figure in the composition has either the beauty of grace or that of character;
and the most beautiful is the Saviour's, which has the
elongated, pliant grace of the stem and tendrils of a
vine. And the drooping flower upon it is the head, to
which all the principal lines of the composition lead.
Start where you will and follow along the direction of
the figures, your eye finally centers upon the Saviour's
head. It is the focus-point. And note that on the edges
of the group the lines begin by being firm and strong in
character, gradually increasing in suppleness and grace
as they draw near the sacred figure, until finally all the
dignity and sweetness of the picture come to an intensity in the Head. Lest the central figure should be lack-
ing in impressiveness as a mass, its effect has been broadened by the winding-sheet, against the opaque white of
which its own whiteness of flesh is limpid and ashy in
tone. Apart from the flesh-tints, the other hues in the
picture are black, almost black-green, and dull red.
Thus by its color as well as by the lines the figure of
the Saviour is made the prominent spot in the composition. Moreover, placed as it is upon the most brilliantly
lighted part of the picture, its own tenderer lighting is
made more emphatic.

The figure is being lowered, as it were, down a cataract of light which leaps up in a wave at the bottom, and scatters flakes of foam around it. These alight on the faces, hands, and sometimes on an arm or foot, in every case just those parts of the composition which are important in the expression of gesture or sentiment.

In this distribution of light, as well as in the arrangement of the lines, there has been a careful building up of effect, everything calculated to arouse the emotion and make at once a magnificent spectacle and a profound impression. Painted as an altar-piece to be viewed from a distance, it is an example of the "grand style," belonging to that "high-bred" family of pictures represented most nobly in Italian art. Compared with it, *The Maids of Honor* may appear to have little grandeur.

While the Rubens presents a beautiful pattern of decoration, the Velasquez seems barren, more than half the canvas being given up to empty space. The figures in the former have a grand flow of line, those in the latter seem stiff and awkwardly grouped. The Rubens excites our emotion, the Velasquez our curiosity.

Before studying closely *The Maids of Honor,* we must recall the fact that in 1628 Rubens visited the court of Spain for nine months; that Velasquez watched him paint and came under the fascination of his personality; that he saw Ruben's admiration for the great Italian pictures which hung in the king's gallery; that by the advice of Rubens he shortly afterward visited Italy, and studied in Venice, Milan, and Rome. In fact, Velasquez was well acquainted with the grandeur of Italian painting; and in the middle period of his life, between

1645 and 1648, had an opportunity to execute a grand example of decorative painting. The king commissioned him to decorate the walls of the new summer palace, Buen Retiro, whereupon Velasquez painted the famous *Surrender of Breda*. It represents Justin of Nassau handing the keys of the city to his conqueror, Spinola, the last of the great Spanish generals. It is a noble decoration and at the same time one of the finest historical paintings in the world, contradicting the assertion made by some painters that the two ideas are incompatible.

Some years before it was painted Rubens had completed a series of historical decorations, which are now in the Louvre, to celebrate events in the life of Marie de Medici, queen of Henri IV of France, and mother of Louis XIII. Here again is shown the difference between Rubens and Velasquez; for these pictures by Rubens present a blaze of color, a profusion of sumptuousness, a pageant of imagination in which gods and goddesses and allegorical figures mingle with the actual personages. Velasquez, on the contrary, while keeping in mind the decorative necessities of the canvas, kept himself also to the simple and very touching circumstances of the incident. Even in the enthusiasm of painting a great decoration, he preserved his regard for "truth."

So it was not because of ignorance of what other great painters had done, or of what he himself could do to rival them on their own ground,—for *The Surrender of Breda* could hang without loss of dignity beside a Titian, —that he turned his back upon all traditions of the Italian grand style, and in the years of his maturity produced *The Maids of Honor,* a new kind of picture. It was new because it was the product of a new kind of artist's eyesight; of a new conception of realism.

We have seen in Holbein's *Portrait of George Gyze* an example of that kind of realism which is solely occupied in giving a faithful representation of the figure and its surrounding objects. But if you compare that portrait with Velasquez's picture, you will feel, I think, that the attention is scattered over Holbein's picture, while in the case of Velasquez's the eye immediately takes it in as a whole. The little princess is the center of the scene, the light being concentrated on her, as it is around the principal figure in Rubens's picture; but, though our attention is centered on the child, it revolves all round her and immediately embraces the scene as a whole. The realism of this picture is a realism of unity. Moreover, it gives us a single vivid impression of the scene, such as the king received; so we may call it also a realism of impression.

To illustrate what is meant by realism of impression let us contrast an example of the extreme opposite: *1807 —Friedland,* by Meissonier, in the Metropolitan Museum, New York. It is not necessary to have seen it to appreciate the difference; enough to know that it represents a regiment of cavalry galloping past Napoleon, saluting him as they charge the enemy; and that the armor and weapons and accoutrements of all these men are painted with the finish and exactness of a miniature. No eye in the world could have seen the bridles and bits and spurs and buttons, and the thousand other sharply

DESCENT FROM THE CROSS   RUBENS

ANTWERP CATHEDRAL

MAIDS OF HONOR   VELASQUEZ

PRADO GALLERY, MADRID

defined details, as those soldiers galloped by. While each detail represents realism, their sum total is, from the point of view of the painter or of the spectator, false. The reason is that Meissonier has painted, not what he could see, but what his mind informed him must be there.[1] And what is the result? The picture does not affect us as a whole; but people study over it, moving their eyes, as if from word to word or from line to line on the page of a book; and then, because every item looks so real, they exclaim, "How wonderful!"

Velasquez's picture, on the other hand, makes an instant and complete impression, because he has included in it only as much of detail as the eye could embrace at one glance; more, however, than a less gifted and an untrained vision could encompass. But it was Velasquez's distinction that he had a marvelous power of receiving a full impression and of vividly retaining it in his mind until he had rendered it vivid upon the canvas.

If we turn back again to a comparison of *The Descent from the Cross* and *The Maids of Honor,* do we not realize a much more instantaneous and vivid impression in the Velasquez? The Rubens, also, is a noble example of unity, but it is a unity of effect produced chiefly by the balance of the dark and light parts; yet the method adopted is arbitrary, as compared with the Velasquez. To state it briefly: Rubens has put the light where he needed it for his composition; Velasquez has taken it as he found it. Streaming through the window, it permeates the whole room, not striking the figures simply on one side and leaving the other dark, but en-

[1] See the chapter on Memling, page 64.

veloping them and penetrating to the remotest corners of the ceiling. Even in the reproductions, you can see how much more real the light is in the Velasquez; how it is bright on the parts of the figures that lie in its direct path; less bright in the half-lights, where it strikes the figure less directly; reflected back, as for example from the dress of the little princess on to that of the maid on her left; how it steals round everything and penetrates everywhere. For Velasquez recognized that light is elastic and illuminates the air. Also he noticed that the light was whiter on objects near the eye, grayer and grayer on objects farther and farther back, owing to the intervening planes of atmosphere hanging between like veils.

Hence he was the first to discover a new kind of perspective. Men long ago had learned to make the lines vanish from the eye; to make the figures diminish in size and shape as they recede from the front; and to explain the distance by contrasts of light and shade. But he perfected what had been anticipated by Leonardo—the perspective of light. By the most delicate and accurate rendering of the quantity of light reflected from each and every part of the room and the figures and objects in it, and by recognizing the veils of atmosphere, he gave to the figures the reality of form and to the room its hollowness and distance.

Painters distinguish between the color of an object and its color as acted upon by light. Thus, in the case of a white dress, they would say that white was its "local color." But it is not white like a sheet of paper; it varies in degrees of whiteness according to the quantity of light reflected from its various parts. And these varying quantities of light reflected from the various planes of the objects, they call "values." Velasquez excelled in the rendering of "values."

This attention to values, or the truthful rendering of light, involved other truths: for example, that the outlines of objects are not, except in special cases, sharply defined,—the light plays round their edges and thereby softens and melts them; and the objects themselves do not appear as if they were cut out in paper and pasted on the canvas, but are masses of more or less illuminated color, merged in the surrounding atmosphere. Consequently, Velasquez gave to the contour-lines of his figures an elusiveness; sometimes they are strong and assertive, at other times they melt into the atmosphere. And as light shows itself to our eyes by being reflected from the infinite molecules of the air, so Velasquez's rendering of light introduced an appearance of real atmosphere into his pictures. You have only to compare this one of his with Rubens's to be sure this is so.

Having thus briefly (and therefore inadequately, I am afraid, for it is a large and difficult subject) glanced at the things that Velasquez tried for, we are in a better position to understand how his realism was a realism of impression. Firstly, he saw his subject at a single glance, eye and hand instantaneously coöperating; and he confined his impression to what a less keen eye, assisted by him, could also take in as a single impression. Secondly, by his marvelous penetration into the action of light, and his skill in rendering it, he set upon the canvas the scene as he had received the impression of it, with such subtle fidelity that our own observation is stimulated, and we receive the impression vividly.

By this time the picture should no longer appear to be empty; nor the figures crowded at the bottom. We should feel that the background and ceiling are connected, by that vertical strip of light up the edge of the canvas, with the figures in the foreground, so as to make a unified composition of balanced masses of light and less light. In the wonderful truth to life of the figures —the exquisite daintiness of the little princess, the affectionate reverence of the maids, the grotesqueness of the dwarfs, and the courtly sensitiveness of the artist's figure —we should have entered into the intimate human feeling of the whole group and ceased to be troubled by the curious style of the costumes.

These costumes, more than likely, and the fact that Velasquez lived in the palace painting courtly scenes and portraits, had much to do with his striking out a new style. How could he introduce such hooped skirts into a picture in the grand manner of Italian painting? His great genius was therefore compelled to find another outlet, and did so in directions which were new and permanent additions to the art of painting.

Rubens, on the other hand, not less original, took from the Italian style what could be of use to him, and then built upon it a style of his own. It is distinguished by a wonderful mastery of the human form and an amazing wealth of splendidly lighted color. He was a man of as much intellectual poise as Velasquez, and, like the latter, was accustomed to court life. But while Velasquez, bound to the most punctilious, ascetic, and superstitious court in Europe, was driven in upon himself, and became more and more acutely sensitive, — Rubens, traveling from court to court with pomp as a trusted envoy, had the exuberance of his nature more and more developed. As an artist, he had the wonderful faculty of being habitually in a white heat of imagination, while perfectly cool and calculating in the control of his hand. Hence the enormous output of his brush. It might be said that he was as prolific in the representation of the joy and exuberance of life as Michelangelo was in the representation of the life of the emotions.

Velasquez, for nearly two centuries, was forgotten outside of Spain. Italian art continued to be the model to imitate; and even when a return to the truth of nature was made at the beginning of the nineteenth century, sixty years passed before this great example of "Truth, not painting" was "discovered." Then a few painters visited the museum of the Prado at Madrid, which contains most of his pictures; others followed, and the world became gradually conscious that in these pictures of Velasquez, especially in the wonderful series of portraits of the king and members of the court, which he made during forty years of royal intimacy, there was revealed a great and solitary genius. Since then he has exercised, as we shall see, such an influence upon modern painting that he has been called "the First of the Moderns."

CHAPTER XIV

ANTONY VAN DYCK
1599–1641
Flemish School

FRANS HALS
1580/4–1666
Dutch School

THE commencement of the seventeenth century witnessed the birth of a new nation and of a new art—the Dutch. When the emperor Charles V abdicated in 1555, he allotted Austria and Germany to Ferdinand I, Spain and the Netherlands to his son Philip II. The rule of Spain was in one way beneficial to the Netherlands, or Low Countries (Holland and Belgium), since it opened to them the trade with the New World and the West Indies. Antwerp rose to greatness. "No city except Paris," says Mr. Motley, "surpassed it in population or in commercial splendor. The city itself was the most beautiful in Europe. Placed upon a plain along the bank of the Scheldt, shaped like a bent bow with the river for its string, it inclosed within its walls some of the most splendid edifices in Christendom. The world-renowned Church of Nôtre Dame, the stately Exchange, where five thousand merchants daily congregated—prototype of all similar establishments throughout the world—the capacious mole and port—were all establishments which it would have been difficult to rival in any other part of the globe."

Such it was before the "Spanish Fury." In 1567 the Duke of Alva arrived with ten thousand veterans for the purpose of stamping out the Reformed faith; established his "Council of Blood"; beheaded the Counts of Egmont and Horn after a mock trial; and commenced a reign of terror and bloodshed. In the six years of his governorship he boasted that he had put to death eighteen thousand persons besides those killed in battle; for the people had risen under William the Silent, and the war for independence was begun. In 1579, by an agreement at Utrecht, the seven northern provinces united for mutual defense; the southern holding back, because they adhered to the Roman Catholic form of faith. Antwerp, however, though not in the League of United Provinces, became a focus-point of the struggle, and in 1585 capitulated to the Duke of Parma.

Thirty-one years later the English ambassador paid a visit to the place, and wrote home to a friend:

This great city is a great desert, for in ye whole time we spent there I could never sett my eyes in the whole length of the streete uppon 40 persons at once; I never mett coach nor saw man on horseback; none of our own companie (though both were workie dayes) saw one pennieworth of ware either in shops or in streetes bought or solde. Two walking pedlars and one ballad-seller will carry as much on their backs at once, as was in that royall exchange either above or below,—and the whole countrey of Brabant was suitable to this towne; faire and miserable.

When Philip II died in 1598, Spain was exhausted almost to prostration, and his successor was glad to conclude an armistice of twelve years with the United

Provinces. But at its conclusion war was resumed, and it was not until 1648 that by the peace of Westphalia the independence of the northern provinces of Holland was finally assured.

Meanwhile, during those seventy years of conflict in which a new nation was in the forming, a new art had been born. While the northern provinces were fighting for their liberties, a number of painters came to manhood, whose work was of such originality as to constitute a new school of painting—the Dutch School; "the last," as Fromentin says, "of the great schools, perhaps the most original, certainly the most local."

It was original because it was local. Across the Scheldt in Antwerp, Rubens was in the prime of his powers (among his retinue of pupils was Van Dyck); but, though his fame must have crossed to the Dutch, his influence did not. That people, stubborn against foreign domination, was stubbornly fashioning a kind of art of its own. Its artists were independent of Rubens, of the great Italian traditions, of everything but what concerned themselves. By their religious views they were separated from the chance of painting altarpieces or mythological subjects, and by their revolt they were cut off from viceregal patronage, such as the Flemish enjoyed. A nation of burghers, busy with war and commerce, they developed, out of their own lives, their love of country, and pride in themselves, a new art.

In one word, the Dutch art was an art of portraiture. It began with the painting of portraits of persons, and then proceeded to the painting of landscapes and of the outdoor and indoor occupations of the people, and to the painting of still-life,—all with such simple intention to represent the things as they appeared, and with such fidelity to the truth, that the whole range of subjects may be classed as portraiture. It was not "grand art," but it was intimate and sincere.

The first of the great men, chronologically, was Frans Hals, whose *Portrait of a Woman* we are comparing with Van Dyck's *Marie Louise von Tassis*. There is a story related by Houbraken, which may or may not be true, that Van Dyck passing through Haarlem, where Hals lived,[1] desired to see the painter; but, though he called several times, he could not find him at home. So he sent a messenger to seek him out and tell him that a stranger wished to see him; and, on Hals putting in an appearance, asked him to paint his portrait, adding, however, that he had only two hours to spare for the sitting. Hals finished the portrait in that time; whereupon his sitter, observing that it seemed an easy matter to paint a portrait, requested that he be allowed to try and paint the artist. Hals soon recognized that "his visitor was well skilled in the materials he was using; great, however, was his surprise when he beheld the performance; he immediately embraced the stranger, at the same time crying out, 'You are Van Dyck; no person but he could do as you have now done.'"

Assuming the story to be true, how interesting it would be if the two portraits existed, that one might see what Frans Hals, accustomed to the heavier type of the

---

[1] He was born in Antwerp, whither his family moved for a time in consequence of the war. They seem to have returned to Haarlem about 1607.

Dutch burghers, made of the delicately refined features of Van Dyck, and how the latter, who always gave an air of aristocratic elegance to his portraits, acquitted himself with the bluff, jovial Hals, who was as much at home in a tavern as in a studio! For no two men could be more different, both in point of view and method, though they were alike in one particular, that each was a most facile and skilful painter.

Let us turn to the two portraits, which are very characteristic examples of these two masters. First of all, examine the hands. You have recognized, no doubt, that hands are very expressive of character. In good portraits there is always a correspondence of feeling and character between the hands and the head. Hals was a master in this respect. There is also an absolute unanimity between the expression of the hand and that of the face in the Van Dyck, even to the curl of the forefinger, which echoes with extraordinary subtlety the curious slanting glance of the eyes.

But when we learn that this artist kept servants in his employment whose hands he used as models for the hands of his sitters, we begin to wonder where this idealizing of nature stopped, and whether the face and carriage of the figure also may not have come in for a share of it. As we know, too, that it was his habit to make a rapid study of his sitters in black and white chalk upon gray paper, and to hand it to his assistants for them to paint the figure in its clothes, which were sent to the studio for that purpose, after which he retouched their work and painted in the head and hands, we feel a suspicion that Van Dyck was as much interested in illustrat-

MARIE LOUISE VON TASSIS   ANTHONY VAN DYCK

LIECHTENSTEIN GALLERY, VIENNA

PORTRAIT OF A WOMAN   FRANS HALS

NATIONAL GALLERY, LONDON

ing his own ideas of elegance and refinement as in reproducing the actual characteristics of his sitters.

We shall hardly feel this in the *Portrait of a Woman* by Hals. Of the fact that the woman looked in the flesh just as he has represented her on the canvas, we are as sure, as if we had looked over his shoulder and watched her grow to shape beneath his brush. He has put in nothing but what he saw, left out nothing that could complete the veracity of the record.

We turn back to the Van Dyck, and have ceased to wonder if Marie Louise were really like this. Her portrait is an exquisitely beautiful picture—let it go at that; and then again we turn to the Hals, and again we have forgotten that it is a portrait. It is a real woman that we face, one of stout and wholesome stock, whose husband may have had a hand in the shaping of the new republic, who may have been the mother of sons who fought in the long struggle for freedom. Those hands! —one loves them; strong hands, coarsened by their share in the work of life, now folded so unaffectedly in the calm and peace of living, which right good doing has won. When you look at them, and, still more, when you read their fuller story in that high, broad forehead, with the strong, big skull beneath it, as indicative of steadiness of purpose as the wide-apart eyes; in that resolute nose, with its lift of energy in the nostril; and in the firm, kindly, wise mouth, you realize how it was that Holland, having by its energy and patience set a barrier to the ocean, could keep at bay the power of Spain, and achieve for itself, after long waiting, liberty of life and thought.

This portrait, while self-sufficient as a record of a woman who actually lived, is more than that: it is a type of the race to which she belonged. It is a type, too, of the whole school of Dutch painting; so straightforward, intimate, and sincere. Moreover, such a marvel of painting!

The Dutchmen of the seventeenth century, having abandoned the large field of decorative composition, settled down in the small space of their canvases to a perfection of craftsmanship that has never been surpassed in modern art. From the standpoint of pure painting, they formed a school of great painters; differing among themselves in motives and manner, but alike in being consummate masters of the brush.

Hals set his figures in clear light, so that the modeling is not accomplished by shadows, but by the degree of light which each surface of the flesh or costume reflected. In this respect he worked like Velasquez, but in a broader way. He distributed the lights and painted in the colors in great masses, each mass containing its exact quantity of light; and so great was his skill in the rendering of values that he could make a flat tone give the suggestion of modeling. Thus in the almost uninterrupted flat white tone of this woman's ruff we do not miss the absence of many lines to indicate the folds of muslin.

Compare the treatment of the ruff in Van Dyck's portrait; indeed, the explicit way in which the whole of the elaborate costume is rendered. Nothing is left to the imagination. Everything is told with rhetorical elaboration. The contrast of the Hals portrait offers an in-

structive example of what painters mean by the word
"breadth," and a lesson also in the effect of breadth on
our imagination; for we get from the broad simplicity
of this portrait a strong invigoration, whereas from Van
Dyck's a pleasant intoxication. Yet, while we miss the
breadth in the Van Dyck, do not let us overlook the
freedom with which it is painted, so that there is nothing
small or niggling in all these details; they are drawn together, like the drops of water of a fountain, into one
splendid burst of elegance.

In the latter, however, the character of the woman is
considerably smothered. Perhaps it was the case that
she had little character, that she was simply a fine lady
of fashion; or it may be that that aspect of her was the
one which chiefly interested the artist. He seems to have
been particularly impressed with her eyes, which indicate
at least a trait of character; and in a very subtle way
he has made the attitude of the figure and the gesture of
the hands and head correspond to it. So in a limited way
the picture is representative of a type.

Hals, on the other hand, did not fix upon any particular trait or feature: he broadly surveyed all the externals of his sitter, and represented them as a whole;
and with such clear seeing that, although he never penetrates into the mind of his subject,—as we shall find
Rembrandt did,—he does get at the heart of it, and, in
his straightforward characterization of what he sees,
suggests that character lies beneath it.

In this respect his work is very like the man himself.
He must have had fine qualities of mind; else how could
he have seen things so simply and completely, and ren-

dered them with such force and expression, inventing for the purpose a method of his own, which, as we have seen, was distinguished by placing his subject in the clear light and by working largely in flat tones? To get at the essential facts of a subject, and to set them down rapidly and precisely, so that all may understand them and be impressed by them, represent great mental power, and place Hals in the front rank of painters. Yet, as a man, he allowed himself to appear to the world an idle fellow, over-given to jollification, and so shiftless that in his old age he was dependent upon the city government for support. That he received it, however, and that his creditors were lenient with him, seem to show that his contemporaries recognized a greatness behind his intemperance and improvidence; and, when in his eighty-second year he died, he was buried beneath the choir of the Church of St. Bavon in Haarlem.

In great contrast to Hals's mode of living was Van Dyck's. He was early accustomed to Rubens's sumptuous establishment; and, when he visited Italy with letters of introduction from his master, lived in the palaces of his patrons, himself adopting such an elegant ostentation that he was spoken of as "the Cavalier Painter." After his return to Antwerp his patrons belonged to the rich and noble class, and his own style of living was modeled on theirs; so that, when at length in 1632 he received the appointment of court painter to Charles I of England, he maintained an almost princely establishment, and his house at Blackfriars was the resort of fashion. The last two years of his life were spent in traveling on the Continent with his young wife, the daughter of Lord Gowry, Lord Ruthven's son. His health, however, had been broken by excess of work, and he returned to London to die. He was buried in St. Paul's Cathedral.

He painted, in his younger days, many altarpieces, "full of a touching religious feeling and enthusiasm"; but his fame rests mainly upon his portraits. In these he invented a style of elegance and refinement which became a model for the artists of the seventeenth and eighteenth centuries, corresponding, as it did, to the genteel luxuriousness of the court life of the period.

On the other hand, during the latter century Hals was thought little of, even in Holland, whose artists forsook the traditions of their own school and went astray after other gods—to wit, those of the Italian " grand style." It was not until well on in the nineteenth century that artists, returning to the truth of nature, discovered that Hals had been one of the greatest seers of the truth and one of its most virile interpreters. To-day he is honored for these qualities, and also for the fact that, out of all the Dutch pictures of the seventeenth century now so much admired, his are the most characteristic of the Dutch race and of the art which it produced.

CHAPTER XV

REMBRANDT VAN RIJN　　　*BARTOLOMÉ ESTÉBAN MURILLO*
1606–1669　　　　　　　　*1617–1682*
Dutch School　　　　　　　Spanish School of Andalusia

AS remarkable as the sudden uprising of a native art in Holland is the fact that it almost immediately reached its maturity, and, in the person of Rembrandt, produced one of the foremost artists of the world. He is one of the few great original men who stand alone. You cannot trace his genius to the influence of his time or to the work of other men who preceded him; nor, although he had followers, could any of them do what he did. He shines out in solitary bigness.

So it is not so much for comparison as for convenience in continuing our method of study, that I couple his name with Murillo's. Yet, having done so, we may find that they have something in common; a common center round which Murillo makes a small circle, Rembrandt an infinitely larger one. Each was a realist as well as an idealist; both painted light, and both translated religious themes into the dialect of the common people.

In his *Children of the Shell,* Murillo chose for subject the infancy of the Christ and St. John; the latter represented with a staff-like cross in token of his future career as preacher and pilgrim, while the application of the legend upon the scroll, " Ecce Agnus Dei," to the little Saviour is further illustrated by the introduction of a lamb. These symbols were prescribed by the church's tradition; Murillo put them in partly because his patrons demanded them, and partly because he himself was a devout Christian; but in other respects he is influenced by a man's love of little children and an artist's desire to create a beautiful picture. He takes for his type the warm-skinned, supple, brown-eyed children that played half-naked in the bright sunshine of Seville; their beauty of limb and grace of movement being characteristic of their free, open-air life. This part of the picture is real enough; a bit of nature translated into paint. But the act in which they are engaged, and the way in which it is represented, suggest an idealization of the facts; and this ideal feeling is increased by the soft vaporous light in which the little bodies are bathed; a kind of light "that never was on sea or land," a product of the artist's imagination.

The people of Murillo's own day loved his work because they could enter into it and understand it, for it portrayed in its virgins, children, and saints the type of figures with which they were familiar, with the sweet gentleness of sentiment that reflected the dispositions of this Southern race. For by that time the darkness of the Inquisition had cleared away; the Jesuits were winning the devotion of the people by beautifying the churches; monks and nuns had abandoned the rigor of self-inflicted torture, and were seeking by lives of kindliness and by holy contemplation to have visions of the divine love. Pictures were demanded that should represent this happier change. Elizabeth, the saintly Queen of Hungary, engaged in doing acts of mercy to the sick and poor; St. Anthony of Padua, the holy Franciscan monk, blessed with an ecstatic vision of the Child-Christ in the midst of a choir of infant angels; the Holy Family, poor peasant folk, but radiant with heavenly light and love—these, and the like, Murillo painted, and in such a way that the people of his day could recognize the counterparts of themselves, men and women and children, familiar to their daily experience, and yet lifted up above them in a light far lovelier than that of their own beautiful sunshine—a spiritual light. So they loved his work; and for the same reason—that it is of earth and yet above it, humanly natural and yet spiritually ideal—it has continued to be loved.

Rembrandt's picture, on the other hand, *The Sortie of the Banning Cock Company*, did not satisfy the men for whom it was painted. It is one of the kind known as a "corporation picture": an aggregation of portraits. Sometimes it was the council of one of the trade guilds; sometimes the governing body or the surgical force of a hospital; very often one of the numerous militia companies, that wished to be commemorated. Frans Hals painted many of these pictures; so also did another popular Dutch painter, Bartholomeus van der Helst. Both these artists gave great satisfaction to their patrons; for they took care that each member, who had paid his quota toward the expense of the picture, should have his portrait clearly delineated. It was, after all, a correct concession to a quite reasonable vanity. Besides, the whole tendency of Dutch art, as we have seen, was toward direct and intimate portraiture, and the racial tendency of the Dutch mind toward straightforwardness and clarity and precision in all things. The people, on the one hand fighting against the encroachments of the ocean and the invasion of the Spaniard, and on the other extending their trade over the world, were living very real lives, and their artists as a body were realists.

Rembrandt had proved himself a realist when he painted, in his twenty-sixth year, *The Anatomy Lesson,* in which the famous Dr. Tulp is represented conducting a lecture in dissection before a class of surgeons. It was a work of marvelous realism, and immediately secured for the young painter a number of commissions from those who wished to have their portraits painted, and caused his studio to be sought by students eager to learn from him. It made him famous.

Ten years later he was asked to paint this picture of Captain Banning Cock's company of musketeers. With the assurance of genius, he dared to depart from the usual way of representing such a subject. Instead of grouping the company in their guild-house, he represents them issuing from it, as if the occasion were a shooting-match. The captain, dressed in black with a red scarf, is giving directions to his lieutenant, whose costume is yellow with a white scarf around his waist; the drummer is sounding the call, which arouses the barking of a dog; the ensign shakes loose the big flag; a sergeant stretches out his arm as he gives an order; picket-men are hurrying out, a musketeer is loading his gun, a boy running beside him with the powder-horn;

and in the midst of the group, "as if," says Mr. John La Farge, "to give a look of chance and suddenness to the scene, is the figure of a little girl, strangely enough with a dead fowl strung from her waist." She appears to be engaged in some form of play with a boy, who has a leaf-crowned helmet on his head and is turning his back so that it is his leg which is chiefly visible.

Rembrandt, in fact, chose an instant of sudden and general animation, and by his genius made it thrill with the appearance of actual life. The picture, as originally painted, was larger than at present; but when it was removed to the Amsterdam town hall it did not fit the space on the wall and was cut down in size, a slice being taken off the right side and the bottom. This barbarous treatment has particularly interfered with the relation of the two front figures to the rest of the group, giving them too much an appearance of stepping out of the picture, whereas in its original size we may be sure the balance of the composition was complete.

To draw its various parts into one supreme impression Rembrandt abandoned the custom of setting all the figures in a clear, even light, and welded the whole together in an elaborate pattern of light and shade. This had become darkened by dirt and smoke, so that the picture was taken by French writers of the eighteenth century for a night scene, and styled *Patrouille de Nuit,* and Sir Joshua Reynolds followed their error by calling it *The Night Watch.* Subsequent cleaning, however, has proved that, notwithstanding some darkening of the color as the result of time, the picture represents a daylight scene. The company streams out of the dark door-

way into bright sunlight, which plays upon it with innumerable accidental effects.

In such action of light, with its glints of surprise and
manifold variations, there is joy to the artist, especially
to one whose mind was so alive to what is momentary
and unusual as Rembrandt's; a mystery, also, and abundance of mental and artistic suggestion, in the varying
depths of shadow. Moreover, it may have seemed to
him the most effectual way of securing the unity and
momentariness of the impression. If every part had
been shown with equal distinctness, it would have been
impossible for the spectator to receive from it the instantaneous shock of wonder and surprise that he now experiences. His attention, instead of being immediately
focused, would have been scattered over a hundred details. As it is, he sees the picture as a whole, and, before he begins to consider the parts, receives a single,
profound impression.

This original treatment, so entirely at variance with
traditions of corporation pictures, cost Rembrandt the
patronage of the civic guards, and his commissions fell
off from that time forward.

That Rembrandt was wrong to paint this particular
picture in this way is also the opinion of the great
French critic and artist, Eugène Fromentin, because the
occasion was not a suitable one for putting into practice
this peculiar method of lighting. Fromentin's argument, briefly summarized, is as follows:

Rembrandt was compact of two natures: one, the realist; the other, the idealist. At times he was impressed
with the facts of things—the main, essential facts of a

landscape or of a human personality; and, whether he is painting with the brush or drawing on copper with the etching-needle, the result is a wonderful synthesis or summary of the truth of actual appearance. At other times it is the truth beneath the surface, the invisible truth, that fascinates him; and in his attempts to express this he discovered for himself a new treatment of light. It was something different from the chiaroscuro, or arrangement of light and shade, which other artists used for the threefold purpose of giving substance to form, of producing an effect of aërial perspective, and of making the picture brilliant and impressive in pattern. He, too, used this method of chiaroscuro, but he carried it much farther than any other artist before or since, so that it is called, after his name, the Rembrandtesque treatment. He immersed everything in a bath of shadow, plunging into it even the light itself; he surrounded centers of light with waves of darkness. The darkness itself in his pictures is transparent; you can peer into it and discover half-concealed forms; everything provokes curiosity; there is mystery; and it acts upon the mind, so that the real and the imaginary become mingled. It is at once reality and a dream.

Rembrandt discovered for himself this power of making chiaroscuro a source of emotional feeling; but he went even farther. Light exists independent of the objects it shines upon, and he tried to paint only with the help of light, to draw only with light, to make the light itself express ideas and emotions. To succeed it was necessary to make great sacrifices; to relinquish much that was dear to his other self, the realist: the strong drawing and firm modeling, the magnificent certainty of effect. These are qualities that might be looked for in a picture of citizen-soldiers, such as *The Sortie of the Banning Cock Company,* but are absent from it. It was required of him by the circumstances that he should paint a reality; what he produced was a vision of light glimmering like phosphorescence on darkness.

This picture was Rembrandt's first big effort to embody his new conception of the possibilities of painting, and his whole after life was a struggle to reconcile the two sides of his nature, culminating in 1661, eight years before his death, in that triumph of mingled realism and idealism, *The Syndics of the Cloth-workers' Guild.* And in many single portraits are revealed the wonderful resources of this treatment of light and shade for the purpose of expression. The heads are enveloped in darkness, out of which emerge the features, the eyes especially arresting the attention. Through the depth and poignancy of their gaze one seems to look into the very soul of the subject. This faculty of profound suggestion, the power of a man who sees into the heart of things and makes others partake of his imagination, appears also in his etchings.

Rembrandt is recognized as the Prince of Etchers, by reason both of the range and quality of his prints, which include landscapes, portraits, Biblical subjects, and studies of beggars and of other picturesque specimens of poverty. Sometimes they are executed with extraordinary economy of means, a few lines in opposition to the spaces of paper giving the impression of a far-reaching landscape flooded with sunshine; sometimes they are worked up into richness of texture, or again are elaborate creations of light and shade.

Etching being an art which demands certainty of brain and hand and yet admits of so much illusion, we may understand why throughout his life Rembrandt, realist and idealist, was so fond of it. The method is briefly this. A polished copper plate is covered with a film of melted wax, which is then blackened with smoke by holding it over a lamp or candle. The artist with a needle, or any correspondingly sharp-pointed instrument, draws his design in the wax; thus baring the copper where the lines appear. He then plunges his plate into a bath of nitric acid, which bites into the parts exposed, the surfaces still covered with the wax resisting the eating in of the acid. When the plate has been bitten and the wax removed, a roller, covered with printing-ink, is passed over it, that the ink may settle into the channels. The surface is then cleaned, and dampened paper is laid over it and pressed down in a printing-press, so that the paper sucks up the ink from the hollows of the lines. This actual process of printing is the same as is used in the case of steel-engravings; but in the latter the lines have been dug out by a sharp instrument in the hard metal; whereas in the case of etching the hand moves freely and easily through the soft wax; and, further, instead of the groove in the metal being sharp and hard from the tool, it is soft and furred by the insinuating tooth of the acid. An etching, therefore, is richer in its blacks, with a more generous contrast of light and shade, and at the same time, if the artist

CHILDREN OF THE SHELL   THE PRADO, MADRID

MURILLO

chooses to make it so, more delicate. It is, of all the methods of art, the one which responds most immediately to the volition of the artist; it is preëminently the artist's art. That Rembrandt should have practised it throughout his life, and have attained in it a proficiency which no other artist has surpassed, is of itself sufficient to place him in the foremost rank of art. The artist who has most nearly approached him in scope and excellence as an etcher is Whistler.

We started with a comparison of Murillo and Rembrandt, and have discovered, if I have told the story right, that the smaller thing, which Murillo attempted, he did to the satisfaction of his contemporaries and of posterity; whereas Rembrandt, striving for something infinitely greater, had his successes and his failures, was misunderstood by the people of his day, and during the century which followed, when the influence of Italian painting, spreading over Europe, had penetrated even into Holland, was neglected. The story of their work corresponds with the story of their lives.

Murillo's proceeded smoothly and pleasantly. He was born in Seville, the birthplace also of Velasquez. At the age of eleven he was apprenticed to an uncle who was a painter, and his gentle nature and diligence soon made him a favorite with his master and his fellow-students. He managed to live by painting little pictures of sacred subjects on linen; offering them for sale at the *feria,* or weekly market. It was the custom to bring paints and brushes to the fair, so that patrons could have the pictures altered to suit their taste; and, as he sat among the stalls, he had plenty of opportunity of studying and sketching the city urchins and beggar boys that lay or frolicked in the sunshine. He afterward painted many of these, and they are among his best work, so true to life and vigorously executed. In this way two years passed.

Then there returned to Seville a fellow-student of Murillo's, who had exchanged painting for soldiering and been with the army in Flanders. But the sight of the works of Rubens and Van Dyck had revived his love of painting, and he had visited London to study under the latter artist. He was now back in Seville with some copies of Van Dyck's work, and with so many stories of what he had seen, that Murillo was stirred with the ambition to go to Rome. He trudged on foot to Madrid, and called on his fellow-townsman, Velasquez, to secure letters of introduction. The great artist received him kindly, and, being struck with his earnestness, invited him to stay in his own house. Velasquez was called away in attendance on the king, and during his absence Murillo made copies of paintings in the royal galleries by Ribera, Van Dyck, and Velasquez himself. The latter, on his return, was so pleased with the progress the young man had made, that he advised him to go to Rome; but by this time Murillo had no desire to leave his country. He stayed in Madrid for further study, and then returned to Seville after three years' absence.

One of the mendicant brothers of the little Franciscan monastery had collected a sum of money, which the friars determined to expend upon some paintings for their cloister. The amount was too small to attract the well-known artists of the city, so with much compunction they gave the commission to the young, untried Murillo. It was the opportunity he wanted; and he made such good use of it that his reputation was at once established. Henceforth his time was fully occupied in decorating churches and in painting for private individuals; he was admitted into the best society, made a rich marriage, became the head of the School of Seville, and all the time was beloved of the people.

A fall from a painter's scaffold cut short his activity. Incapacitated from work, he lingered for two years, spending much of his time in prayer in the church of Santa Cruz, beneath Campana's painting of *The Descent from the Cross;* and beneath this, by his request, he was buried.

The date of Rembrandt's birth has been subject to question, but 1606 is now usually accepted. His father, Harmen van Rijn (Harmen of the Rhine), owned a mill on the banks of the Rhine at Leyden. When quite young the boy was sent to the Latin school in order that, as Orless, a good authority upon his early life, puts it, "he might in the fullness of time be able to serve his native city and the Republic with his knowledge." However, his inclination toward drawing was so marked that his father placed him with Jacob van Swanenburch. Three years later he went to Amsterdam to study under Lastman, who had spent many years in Rome. But with him Rembrandt stayed only six months, and then returned to Leyden, "resolved," as Orless says, "to study and practise painting alone in his own fashion." He stayed at home six years, working much from the members of his family, and frequently etching his own head, with various kinds of facial expression. In 1630 he moved to Amsterdam, which henceforth was to be the scene of his life. The city at that time had recovered from the shock of war and was rapidly growing in commercial prosperity and liberally encouraging the fine arts. For a time all went well with Rembrandt. *The Anatomy Lesson,* painted in 1632, had made him famous; commissions poured in and students flocked to his studio. Two years later he married a young lady of property, Saskia van Uylenborch, to whom he was deeply attached, and whose portrait he painted or etched eighteen times, besides using her as a model in various pictures. He was able now to indulge his taste for beautiful things; was a generous buyer of other artists' work, and filled his handsome house in the Breedstraat with treasures. Ten years of domestic happiness and magnificent production followed his marriage, and then, in 1642, the clouds gathered.

In that year he was involved in disputes, as we have seen, over *The Sortie of the Banning Cock Company;* but, worse than that, his beloved Saskia died, leaving an infant son, Titus. In the emptiness of his home and heart, the great artist buried himself with ever deeper purpose and grander energy in his work. It is characteristic of this sad time that his portraits of himself cease for six years. Then appears an etching, in which he no longer represents himself in splendid clothes, with fierce mustache and flowing hair; but as a simple citizen. His hair and mustache are trimmed; a large hat covers his head, his tunic is unadorned; he is seated at a window, drawing, but lifts his head and gazes full at the spectator with his piercing eyes. During this time he owed much to the sympathy of the burgomaster Jan Six, a scholar and connoisseur; and the burgomaster's mansion, the celebrated Six Gallery at Amsterdam, owed much of its fame to the examples which it contained by Rembrandt.

In 1656 he was overtaken by financial troubles, due to legal disputes with the trustees of his wife's will, to his liberality toward his family in Leyden, and to his own love of buying works of art and his lack of business ability. He was declared a bankrupt, his house was sold, and his treasures were dispersed at auction; and, by the time that his creditors were satisfied, there was nothing left for him. But his devotion to his art was unabated; the years which followed were distinguished by a series of noble paintings and etchings, among them *The Syndics*. It is good to know that he had friends, and that his last years, though contracted in means, were comfortable. In the last portrait of himself, painted a year before his death, he has depicted his face wrinkled by time and care, but laughing heartily. It sums up the triumph of the man and the artist over evil fortune.

After his death he was soon forgotten. Through the eighteenth century Dutch painters, like those of other countries, turned to Italy for inspiration; Rembrandt's homely naturalism, representing, for example, the Bible scenes, peopled with rude peasants instead of fine men and graceful women in classic robes, was scorned as vulgar; his marvels of light, condemned for the " slovenly conduct of his pencil "; his portraits, that search into the souls of his subjects, despised for their "laborious, igno-rant diligence." He was neglected, while Murillo con-tinued to be abundantly admired.

Now, however, when painting has shaken itself free from conventional traditions and once more turned to nature, Murillo is esteemed less highly, and Rembrandt has been restored to his place among the giants.

CHAPTER XVI

JACOB ISAACSZ VAN RUISDAEL
1628/9–1682
Dutch School

NICOLAS POUSSIN
1594–1665
Classical School of France

AT this point of our survey of the field of painting France swings into the line of vision. There had been other French painters before Poussin, but the latter was the greatest up to his time, and has had so important an influence upon subsequent French art, that in our selection of prominent names he comes first.

When we compare his *Et Ego in Arcadia* with Ruisdael's *Waterfall,* we are conscious at once of a vast difference of feeling, both in the attitude of each painter's mind toward nature and in the impression produced upon our own. We experience before Ruisdael's a sense of strenuousness and sadness, very different from the serenity and idyllic sweetness of Poussin's. We are face to face, in the one case with the realities of life, in the other with the pleasant dream of a world that only exists in the imagination. Yet Poussin composed the surroundings of his figures from real landscape—that of Italy; probably, however, not from one scene, but with a selection from many; while Ruisdael's landscape, which has such an air of stern reality, was actually bor-

rowed—in its general character, at any rate—from the
work of another painter, Allart van Everdingen.

It will occur to you, perhaps, as strange that a Dutch
painter of the seventeenth century should have borrowed
from any one instead of studying straight from nature;
just as it may have struck you that the scenery of the
Waterfall is not suggestive of Holland.

The fact is that Ruisdael, during his first and, as
many consider, his best period, painted pictures thoroughly Dutch in character, studies of the landscape
round his native city of Haarlem, showing a marked
fondness for massed clouds and warm sunshine. But
they met with little encouragement from his own countrymen, and he moved to Amsterdam. In the latter city
was established Allart van Everdingen, who had begun
as a painter of the sea, taking trips on the Baltic for the
better study of his subject. But on one occasion the
vessel had been driven by storm on to the coast of Norway; and, while he waited for a chance of getting home,
he made a number of sketches of the country, with its
rocky shore and pines and waterfalls. Returned to
Holland, he used this material for pictures, which, partly
because of their unusualness, were very popular. Ruisdael, then, finding his own work neglected, determined
to give the public what they seemed to want, and out of
his own head invented landscapes similar in character
to Everdingen's. Their very wildness and sternness
may have attracted him, fitting in with the sadness and
gloom that were gathering over his own spirit; for this
picture and all the productions of his later life are im-
printed with melancholy. And well they might be; for

he was evidently of so little account in his own day, that the date of his birth is doubtful, and scarcely more is recorded of his life than that, after working unsuccessfully in Haarlem, he moved to Amsterdam, and thence returned to his native city in poverty, to die in an almshouse.

In respect of sadness he is akin to Rembrandt, who also lived in the company of sorrow; and these two artists strike the only note of intense feeling in the Dutch art of the seventeenth century, which, as a whole, is distinguished by its equable and contented attitude toward life. Yet in the intensity of Rembrandt there is no bitterness; and even in this landscape of Ruisdael's we may discover a strain of tenderness. For, contrasted with the inhospitable wildness of the coast and the restless tumult of water are the quiet composure of the little spire nestling amid the trees, and the gentle evidences of quiet life in the string of cattle passing down to drink. But the noblest feature of the scene is the fine sky with its masses of cloud. The mountainous land and waterfall may have been invented or borrowed; but this at least has been studied by Ruisdael from the nature of his own land. And the skies of Holland are proverbially grand, partly because the prevailing course of clouds is from the west, so that huge volumes of vapor come continually rolling in from the North Sea, and partly because the land, being uniformly level, affords least obstruction to the vast appearance of the sky and to the gathering and passage of the clouds. None of the Dutchmen of the seventeenth century had been so impressed with the vastness and buoyant force and freedom of the sky as Ruisdael; in which respect he anticipated the achievements of modern Dutch artists, who have found in the skies of Holland an inexhaustible theme.

I think it is capable of demonstration that every landscape-painter of powerful imagination and serious poetic feeling has reveled in the representation of the sky. It is as if his spirit leaps from the definiteness and circumscribed limits of the earth into the limitless, unexplorable vastness of the air. The ground is local, tethering him by the foot to what man can examine and know; the sky, however, at some point ceases to be merely an envelope to the earth and mingles with that ether in which the whole universe swims. May we not believe that Ruisdael, compelled to fashion an unreal, or, at least, an alien land, to tempt his customers, satisfied both his love of country and the sincerity of his study of nature by the ardor with which he threw himself into the representations of the skies? Nor is there anything unduly sentimental in such a belief, for the artist is also human, and has his pride in himself and his preferences, and does best what best he loves.

And now let us turn again to the picture by Poussin. " I too have been in Arcadia "; in that sweet spot, undisturbed by nature's violence or the tumult and clang of human life. It exists nowhere, and yet everywhere is to be found. It was Poussin's fortune to discover it.

He was born of a noble but poor family in Normandy, that hardy country from which William went forth to conquer England, and, some eight hundred years later, Millet, to conquer, after a long-drawn-out conflict, the appreciation of his own countrymen. Poussin learned painting in the local town of Les Andelys, and then proceeded to Paris, where he spent much of his time in drawing from casts and in copying prints after Raphael and the latter's pupil, Giulio Romano. By the time that he was able to visit Rome, he was in his thirtieth year, a man of matured mind, nourished upon the antique and upon the suave, balanced style of Raphael; with a standard, therefore, fixed, and a mind capable of doing its own thinking.

It was well for him that it was so, since the Italy of his time was in its decadence. The last of the great masters had died with Tintoretto. They had been succeeded by many clever painters, but by none of commanding genius. On the one hand were Guido Reni and Carlo Dolci, saturated with sentimentality; on the other, Salvator Rosa, following Caravaggio in depicting what was impetuously powerful, and yet again Tiepolo, a brilliant and vivacious decorator. Poussin, amid this uncertain flux of energy, attached himself to Domenichino, a painter of much strength but poor as a colorist. Meanwhile he pursued his study of sculptured low-reliefs, practising modeling as well as drawing.

The effect of this is apparent in the grouping and drawing of the figures in this picture, for they are arranged as in a low-relief: the woman slightly in advance of the two stooping figures, while the fourth figure is only slightly behind these. The three planes in which the figures stand are flattened as far as possible into one; and the figures are relieved by the contrasts of light and shade, instead of being detached in their separate envelopes of atmosphere. The method, in fact, is a sculptor's rather than a painter's.

This is the first point to notice; and the second is the influence of Raphael. The latter can be traced in the serene composure of the whole composition, obtained by the perfect balance of the full and empty spaces, and by the harmonious grace of the lines that oppose and repeat one another with studied calculation, as well as by the grace of gesture and suave refinement of expression that characterize the figures. Both these influences combined to make the rendering of the subject an ideal one; and, except in the superior tact of taste displayed by Poussin, do not distinguish his pictures radically from those of the many other followers of Raphael and the antique. But here steps in a third influence, that of the Italian landscape; and, by combining the latter with the other two, Poussin originated something new, and became a model for other painters, establishing a principle of perfection that has served as a standard for French painting down to the present day.

Before his time the landscape was subordinated to the figures; even Titian, whose landscapes are so beautiful, felt them primarily as backgrounds. But in this picture of Poussin's it would be hard to decide whether the landscape accompanies the figures or the figures the landscape. In fact, both ingredients are of equal importance.

The love of landscape is particularly characteristic of northern nations, and it would seem that Poussin had it, but not in the way in which the Dutchmen felt it. They loved the landscape for its own sake; Poussin, for the

ET EGO IN ARCADIA   LOUVRE, PARIS   NICOLAS POUSSIN

way it could be made to contribute to the feeling of his figures. The latter were mostly classical in feeling; and thus he became the father of the so-called "classical" or "heroic" landscape. We can understand how it happened.

The visitor to Italy is apt to find that the Italian landscape makes a unique appeal. In every direction it seems to suggest pictures, presenting itself to the eye in ready-made compositions; moreover, it is continually a pictorial setting to the towns and villas, and, in the neighborhood of Rome especially, to the antique ruins. Many of us must have felt this; and, also, that there is a curious relation between the pictures in the Italian galleries and the landscape outside; that the latter, in fact, with its inexhaustible suggestion of stately compositions, must have had a great influence upon the imagination of Italian artists in the direction of helping to suggest the "grand style" of Italian painting.

To this Italy, then, of pictorial landscape came Poussin, already full of the spirit of Raphael and of classic sculpture, and with a fresh eye that recognized a kinship of feeling between the landscape and the style of figure-work which he had learned to admire. He had discovered a country in which the classical figures and those of Raphael could move and have their being. If we turn to the picture we shall feel, I think, how completely the persons belong to the scene in which we find them: they are naturally at home in it; they are part of it; it is Arcady, and they are Arcadians.

Strolling along in the pleasant sunshine, the woman and the three shepherds have chanced upon a tomb.

There are traces of an inscription on it; and the father, stooping to rub away the lichen and moss, reveals the words, "Et Ego in Arcadia." I too, a nameless one, crumbling forgotten within these stones, I too have lived and loved in this region of innocent delight, where man is in perfect accord with his surroundings; rising and lying down with the sun, and nourished upon the bosom of mother earth; mind and body healthy, since conduct and desire are in conformity with nature. It is the country of youth, eternally young in an old world, wherein the children sport and happy lovers stray, and even the aged may linger if they have kept some freshness in their souls. Correggio and Raphael had lived there; and it is the latter, maybe, who calls from the tomb to welcome Poussin to the charmed spot.

We have thus examined the character and feeling of Poussin's work, and found that it was not originally inspired by nature, but founded on a direct study of the antique and upon Raphael's interpretation of the same; and that, when it did receive an inspiration direct from nature, the latter was not used naturally, but to harmonize with the ideal conception of the figures. Let us now inquire how it was that his work became the source of what is called the "classic" and "academic" in French art.

We must remember that the French race has a strong infusion of Latin blood, and that it had been brought under the influence of the legal and social system of the Romans. At the break-up of the empire Italy was overrun with foreigners, and the character of its people became changed, the continuity of its institutions and traditions broken. These, however, survived in France; and the French, much more even than the Italians, are the inheritors of those qualities and ideals which made up the greatness of the Roman people.

Briefly, they comprised a fondness for system and a capacity for organization; a tendency to skilful adaptation rather than to originality; less regard for ideas than for fundamental principles, and especially for those of construction, for what is technically called the " architectonics." The Romans were great builders, and reduced the art of construction to a system, so that the major part of it could be carried out by unskilled labor. With this intention, they laid special stress upon form, logical relationship between the parts and the whole, and the dignity of the mass.

Let us see how the inheritance of these qualities by the French affected the history of their painting. In Poussin's time the throne of France was occupied by Louis XIV, whom the court painter Lebrun was flatteringly depicting in his paintings and tapestries as a Roman conqueror. Full of the Roman spirit, he played the *rôle* of an organizer. To perpetuate the purity of the French language, he established the Institute of France, composed of forty members. To this day the selection of these " Immortals " is determined less by their contribution to thought than by the perfection of their style,—by their mastery, in fact, of the architectonics of their craft. With the same zeal for system and organization, Louis founded an academy of painting and sculpture and an academy in Rome for the instruction of French artists. These, being official institutions, needed a system of principles. This was discovered in the art of Poussin.

In it was exemplified a diligent regard for the architectonics; a careful building up of parts so as to produce a balanced and harmonious whole; a preference for ideal or abstract perfection of line and form and spacing over the representation of character or sentiment; an avoidance of what is original in favor of a tactful reproduction of ancient models; and, in general, the preëminence of style over subject-matter. Poussin's color was a weak point; but that mattered little, for color—both the skill in it and the appreciation of it—is an affair of individual temperament, whereas line and form and composition are fundamental. It was on the side where painting touches sculpture and architecture, not in its special province of color, light, and atmosphere, that a standard of excellence could be established.

Granted the usefulness of establishing a standard, no better one could have been devised. For, although, as we shall discover, the existence of a fixed official standard will tend toward dry formalism, and almost every painter that achieves greatness will do so by breaking away from the rigidity of the academic style, yet the advantage of the system will continue. Its maintenance will be justified by the very high general average of skill that it insures.

It is Poussin's title to a place in history that he was the father of this classic or academic system, which made the École des Beaux Arts in Paris the greatest training-school of art in the modern world.

CHAPTER XVII

JAN VERMEER OF DELFT
1632–1675

Dutch School

JAN STEEN
1626–1679

Dutch School

W E have spoken of Dutch painting as having been an art of portraiture, owing to the intimate observation with which the artists represented the persons, scenes, and places of their daily life. This is particularly apparent in those pictures of outdoor and indoor life which are distinguished as a branch of painting by the general title, *genre*. This class of subject was not invented by the Hollanders of the seventeenth century, but was brought to such perfection by them that it has come to be particularly identified with the School.

Before the separation of the Dutch from the Flemish School, Pieter Brueghel, the Elder, and Pieter Aertz, who was born in Amsterdam, may be mentioned out of many genre painters of the sixteenth century. The Hollanders, however, of the succeeding century gave a new character to the art, affecting both the subject and its treatment.

While Brueghel's pictures are small, the early genre was usually on a larger scale than the Hollanders adopted, and the canvas was apt to be crowded with figures. If, for example, the subject was a winter

[261]

scene, the painter would represent as many aspects as possible of the human activity which enlivened the frozen canal and its snowy banks, thus giving a vivacious record of life which is very interesting and often very amusing. On the other hand, while some of the Hollanders continued to paint scenes animated with many figures, the general tendency was toward small canvases with one or two. Now are they actively employed; for the most part they are doing nothing in particular. In fact, by this time the artist had become less intent on depicting the incidents of daily life than on interpreting its spirit; and the life selected is less frequently that of the ale-house and the peasantry than of the well-to-do burghers. And with this change there developed a finer technique. In painting those little pictures to embellish some parlor wall, the artists were chiefly concerned to make their pictures as beautiful as possible, to be enjoyed not as representations of this or that, but for their expression of beauty. So they aimed to make the pictures fine in color and as exquisite as possible in craftsmanship; with the result that, as painters, the best of these genre artists of Holland have never been excelled. If you look at their pictures to see what they "mean" or what they "are about," you will often not be interested. They must be studied for qualities which have nothing to do with the subject; namely, for those of color, tone, light and shade, and skilful brushwork; in a word, for their revelation of the artist's love of beauty and love of his work, as the expression of it.

The great French sculptor, Rodin, once said of these men: "How they loved their work! and to love his work is the first condition of an artist." "Indeed," he added, "any one who loves his work is an artist"; a remark which on the face of it may appear astonishing, but is full of wisdom and beauty. For Rodin at that moment was not using "artist" in the narrow sense, but in the comprehensive one that we have suggested elsewhere; namely, that an artist is one who fits a form to the vision, thought, or purpose of his brain.

Now, of all the genre painters of Holland, Jan Vermeer is accepted as the finest technician, and, because the number of his known pictures is small compared with the general productiveness of the school, it is reasonable to assume that much of the skill and charm of the technique is due to the loving work he expended on it. As a counterpart to him I have set Jan Steen, because the latter frequently, as in the present example, painted subjects involving a great number of figures, and represented them actively participating in some domestic scene. He was an exception to the general rule that these genre artists did not in their pictures tell a story or illustrate an incident. But while Steen did this with inimitable zest, so that the subject, as subject, is brimful of interest and enjoyment, it is not upon this that his sole or chief merit rests. He was also a consummate technician; at least in his best pictures, for he was little appreciated as an artist by his contemporaries, and some of his pictures exhibit hasty or careless workmanship.

Before studying these two men and their work particularly, let us note the influences which produced this extraordinarily accomplished school of genre, and recall a few of the other artists who shared the honors with Vermeer and Steen.

Holland is a little country, so that the fame of an artist could travel quickly and readily attract students. Thus it came about that two men—Hals and Rembrandt—exercised an immense influence upon the younger painters, and were the direct cause of the Dutch School as a whole being so proficient.

While Hals himself never painted genre, his portraits, especially those wonderful portrait-groups, or "Corporation Pictures," now to be seen in Haarlem, inspired a revolution in the method of painting. In the first place, his example was felt in the direction of composition. He taught others how to combine a number of figures, so as to create an appearance of unity in the composition without impairing the effect of naturalness and spontaneousness in their poses and gestures. Secondly, he achieved this, not only by the arrangement of the lines and masses of the figures, but, still more, by harmonizing the colors. He introduced harmonies of *tone*—a point we will discuss presently. Thirdly, this method of tonal painting encouraged great refinements of color, which developed in Hals a very skilful manner of brushwork, directed toward making the actual painted surface as beautiful as possible. Lastly, this joy in surfaces led him to take delight in the forms, colors, and textures of all the accessories of his subject, so that through him the painters learned to study and render the beauties of furniture, fruit, flowers, articles of glass and metal ware, and the innumerable other objects of "still-life."

Hals's genius was of the objective kind, involving an eye of very extraordinary observation and refinement and a great gift of rendering external appearances. Thus his influence could be, and was, exerted upon others directly. On the other hand, Rembrandt's influence was indirect, for his genius was of the subjective kind, working from within himself. It was the state of his mind, the way he felt toward the world outside that determined his way of rendering it; so that even his method of painting could not be imitated by others. Yet, to some extent, his method of rendering, as well as his way of feeling, exerted an influence.

Rembrandt's tenderness for old age, which began with his early devotion to his mother, is reflected in some of the genre pictures of his pupil, Nicolaes Maes, such as *Old Woman Spinning* and *Asking a Blessing,* in the Rijks Museum, Amsterdam. In the same gallery hangs *Dreaming,* sometimes called *A Reverie,* in which Maes expressed with corresponding tenderness of expression the mood of a young girl, as she gazes out of an open window. Similar feeling appears in the work of another pupil of Rembrandt's, Gerard Dou, whose *Young Mother* is one of the treasures of the Hague Gallery. The pictures we have mentioned here, and some others by Maes, are almost the sole examples in Holland genre of the artist expressing human sentiment.

On the other hand, there were very few genre artists who were unaffected, however indirectly, by the principles of Rembrandt's chiaroscuro. The small rooms of Dutch interiors offered surprises of light and shade, dim recesses and random floods of light from window or open door. While Hals had shown the beauty of light, Rembrandt revealed the mystery and fascination of obscurity, of varying intensities of shadow. Maes followed his master in using light and shade for the purpose of expressing emotion; but the other genre painters were content to adopt the method because of the additional charm which is lent to the scene. We have seen how Rembrandt bathed his forms in shadow, and out of the latter drew various parts of his picture into greater or less degree of illumination. Out of the obscure hollow of his scene he built up a composition with light. This principle it was that the genre painters adopted.

Thus it came to be the usual characteristic of a Dutch genre picture that the scene represents a more or less obscure concavity, a hollow space filled with shrouded atmosphere, into which the light penetrates from a window at one side, falling variously on to the figures, missing certain parts of the same, flickering on others, and striking an occasional point with piquant intensity.

Now the important thing for the student to realize, in order fully to enjoy these pictures, is the fact of their concavity. You are not gazing *at* a flat pattern of light and shade, but looking *into* a hollow space, occupied by the figures and accessories; and the marvel, which grows in fascination as you come to know these pictures well, is the real appearance of the whole scene, the reality of everything in it, and the absolute precision with which every person and object occupies exactly its proper place in the perspective. In addition, there is the magic of endless diversities of colored light and shaded color, and, above all, the crowning beauty of a complete unity of effect. These Hollanders, in fact, built up their compositions by light-values, as we have seen that Velasquez did in his *Las Meñinas;* only, while the great Spaniard worked in a hollow, uniformly lighted, the Hollanders, inspired by Rembrandt, built up the lighted fabric of their compositions out of the shadow.

In the fascination which the artist himself felt in working in this way, and in the skill and loving labor which it involved, we can find sufficient reason for his abandoning the old kind of genre. He needed so few ingredients for his picture. It was the room in which he worked that now furnished the scene; and the few articles of furniture and objects of use or ornament were used again and again as accessories. He could get all the variety he wished by rearranging their positions; by regulating the quantity of light that came in at the window and by varying the poses and the costumes of the one or two persons whom he employed as models. Out of materials so meager Gerard Terborch, for example, composed little pictures in which the figures never number more than three. They are distinguished by the utmost refinement of color and by a skill of constructing forms in space that is unexcelled. Pieter de Hooch showed a preference for vistas: one room opening into another, beyond which is often a glimpse of street or garden, seen through an open door. He interprets the varying degrees of illumination with so much truth to actual appearance and such feeling for the beauty that the best of his pictures have been well called poems in light. Gabriel Metsu is most characteristically identified with the subject of the well-to-do burgher class: interiors furnished with solid comfort, in which perhaps a music lesson is being given or the lady is entertaining her guests, or receiving a present of game from a sportsman. For throughout all the genre pictures there crop out the evidences of the Hollanders' love of music, out-of-door sports, and gardening.

Jan Steen, as we have already noted, is distinguished by the number of the figures which upon occasion he introduced into his pictures. He, too, however, frequently composed with only a few; as in his many examples of the visit of a doctor to a lady patient, and in *The Music Master* of the National Gallery. It is in these less complicated subjects that he reaches his highest refinements of color-sense and brushwork.

By the way, in speaking of refinements or of fineness of brushwork, it is not to be understood that this involves minute and precise strokes, any more than when we speak of finely wrought surface we mean a highly polished finish. Dou's *The Young Mother* is an example of minuteness of brushwork and polished finish, and for this reason a great many people think it wonderful. It is, however, not on this precise manner of painting, but on the admirable skill with which the scene has been composed in space that the technical merit of the picture depends. And by the time you have studied the brushwork of the great genre painters, you will have less and less liking for Dou's, and fur-

ther will discover that as the art fell off in the hands
of lesser artists, it is just this petty style of brushwork
that is one of the features of the decadence.

For Dou worked largely with a tip of the small brush,
multiplying the points of paint with infinite patience.
Now patience is a virtue on general principles, but in
art it is better expended upon the study of a subject
than upon the rendering of it. When the latter stage
is reached, the greater artist replaces patient industry
by imagination and creativeness. We have seen that
Hals did not *imitate* appearances, but *interpreted* them.
It is not difficult to do the former; but to do the latter
well calls for an imagination that can create a new
vision of the thing seen, while to discover the stroke
which will suggest to others the impression received is
also an act of the creative imagination. Dou was in-
clined to imitate; but all the other genre painters whom
we have enumerated followed Hals in being interpreters.
We have seen that he, on his large canvases, used a big
brush, fully charged with pigment. These little pictures required a small brush, but it was proportionately
charged with pigment, which the artist applied not from
the point but from the side of the brush; allowing the
color to flow freely and in full quantity. And, since
they enriched their effects by broken color, that is to
say by laying over a mass of red, for example, strokes
of different tones of the same hue, their painted surfaces have what the artists call a rich *impasto;* meaning
a depth of pigment, composed of tones, as it were, firmly
kneaded together. Yet, notwithstanding its firmness,
there is no hardness or stiffness, as in the work of less

skilful painters. The pigment has been applied so fluently that its texture has the quality, which painters prize, of "looseness."

Tradition has pictured Jan Steen as a man of dissolute habits. It is founded on the fact that he owned a brewery and maintained what we should call a café in his own house. He was of jovial and companionable disposition, and no doubt, like most of the Hollanders of his day, loved a glass of good wine or beer; but it is now ascertained that the privilege of maintaining a brewery or café of this class was only granted to citizens whose reputation stood high in the community. But the best proof that Steen was not a victim to excesses is to be found in his pictures, which are the work of a singularly clear brain and a most sure hand. That some of them betray carelessness may reasonably be put down to the fact that his art was very poorly appreciated by his fellow-citizens, who had more regard for the man than the artist, and were more eager to buy his beer than his pictures.

There is always a relish to Steen's genre. By turns it is witty, ironic, gross, or genially humorous; our present picture being an example of the last. There sits the artist, rubicund and jolly, beside his buxom wife, diffusing an atmosphere of pleasantness throughout the whole family party. He is laughing as he watches the gravity with which a small son is playing a pipe in accompaniment to the song of the grandfather. Over the latter's head hangs upon the chimney a piece of paper, bearing the Dutch proverb, "While the youngsters pipe, the old folks sing." The whole scene

A LADY AT A SPINET   JAN VERMEER

BUCKINGHAM PALACE, LONDON

JAN STEEN'S FAMILY   JAN STEEN

MAURITSHUIS, THE HAGUE

is alive with naturalness; yet it is to be noted that there is no exaggeration of the part that is being played by each individual in it—a fault which too often characterizes the "humorous genre" of English and German painters of the nineteenth century. And a corresponding discretion and naturalness are apparent in the composition of the picture. There is a suggestion of actual roominess: hollow space occupied with atmosphere, while, notwithstanding the number of figures, there is no confusion. Each figure appears to have actual bulk and to occupy surely and simply its position in space. All these qualities result from the skilful rendering of the values of light; producing an illusion of actual forms, space, and atmosphere. If you were to compare this picture with some example of the "humorous genre" of even so good a painter as, say, David Wilkie, you would not discover in the latter so strong an illusion of atmospheric perspective. For his skill in painting was limited to suggesting the actual appearance of the separate forms, but did not extend to the power of placing them in a seeming environment of lighted atmosphere. This was the peculiar accomplishment of the Holland genre artists, of whom none was more proficient in this respect than Jan Vermeer of Delft.

It is usual to distinguish this artist by the name of the city in which his whole life was spent; for there was another of the same name who belonged to Utrecht, as well as two others, identified with Haarlem. He signed his name Vermeer, an abbreviation of the full Van der Meer, by which he was also known. The contemporary records of Delft testify, not only to a few facts of his life, but also to the high estimation in which he was held both as artist and citizen. Nevertheless Houbraken, publishing his *Great Theatre of the Netherlandish Painters,* thirty years after Jan Vermeer's death, made no mention of him. Perhaps this was the reason that during the eighteenth century the artist's very existence was forgotten and his pictures were ascribed to other painters. Indeed, it was not until 1860 that Vermeer began to come again into his own, through the researches made by a French critic, E. J. T. Thoré, who wrote under the pen-name of W. Bürger. Through him and others who followed his lead some thirty pictures, hitherto ascribed to one of the other Vermeers or to Pieter de Hooch or to other painters, have been restored to Jan Vermeer of Delft.

His pictures are few in number and for the most part small in size, but of great perfection. They include one or two views of towns, notably the *View of Delft* in the Hague Gallery; otherwise they are genre pictures, showing usually the small part of a room, lighted by a window at the left and occupied by one figure, or at most by three. Their special characteristic is that they reverse the arrangement of light and shade which the other genre painters learned from Rembrandt. Instead of placing his figures in light against a background of more or less obscurity, Vermeer places some shaded object, such as a chair or table, covered with a cloth, in the foreground, and shows the back of the room, where the figure or figures are, illuminated in a clear light. Nor usually is the latter a warm light, as in the case of pictures by de Hooch and others.

Vermeer displayed a preference for cool light and cool colors. His favorite scheme was an opposition of blue and lemon yellow, with which he often blended the contrasting warmth of red.

In our present picture the blue note appears in the bodice of the girl's dress and on the seat of the chair, while the yellow is struck in the gilt frame of the landscape on the wall. The frequent red is here replaced by the warm brown of the spinet. But the dominant note in this picture is black, seen in the marble flooring and in the ebony frame which surrounds the picture of Cupid. The girl's sleeves and skirt are of pearly white satin, and the plaster of the wall is pearly gray, luminous with the light that filters through the lower casement of the window.

Wherein consists the charm of this picture? It has not the interest of subject that one finds in Jan Steen's *Happy Family*. The figure also may seem unpleasantly stunted, an impression partly due to its being cut off above the feet by the front line of the picture. This was a frequent device of Vermeer's, adopted apparently to avoid a steep perspective in the floor. The reproduction, indeed, in black-and-white can not reveal the picture's essential charm, since the latter consists, firstly, in the color, secondly, in the luminosity.

We have indicated the color-scheme, but names of colors mean little or nothing unless you are familiar with the artist's work, in which case the memory of other color-schemes might help you to construct in imagination this one. Nor is the beauty of this color-scheme only a matter of hues of color, but much more the result of the tones of the hues and indeed of the tonal quality of the whole composition.

Let us briefly examine what artists mean by tone, tonal, tonality. When we describe a color as blue, we are speaking of its hue. But while a piece of blue silk, spread smooth upon the table, will show a uniform hue of blue, the effect will be different if the silk be bunched in a mass or suspended in folds, for then the light falls variously upon different parts of the fabric, and there will be a variety in the tones of the blue. Some parts will show the same tone that the blue exhibited as it lay upon the table. On the other hand, the raised surfaces, which catch more of the light, will show a whiter or higher tone of the blue; while in the hollows, into which less light penetrates, the tone of the blue will be of a lower, that is to say less white, tone. Tone, then, is the change which takes place in the hue of an object according to the quantity, quality, and direction of light reflected from its surface. The human eye, in most cases unconsciously, has acquired the habit of noting these "values," as they are called, of tone, and by this means observing the shapes of objects. Accordingly, the painter, when he wishes to make us see the shape of an object, models its forms in tones. But he may have another, and a finer, motive in using tone; and he will have if he is distinguished as a colorist; that is to say, if he use pigment, not merely to represent the appearance of objects, but as a means of composing color harmonies and rhythms corresponding to those of music. For in this case he will note more suitable

[278]

distinctions of tone and weave them more cunningly into a tonal harmony.

It will help us to grasp this idea if we take a specific example. Before, however, observing how the principle has been applied by Vermeer in our present example, I will ask you to form a mental picture of a simpler example, *Young Woman With a Water Jug,* which is in the Metropolitan Museum, New York. Imagine, then, the corner of a room, the walls of which are covered with gray plaster. At the left appears a casement, glazed with thick glass. It is opened inward a little way by the hand of a girl who stands facing toward us, with her back to the gray wall. Her other hand grasps the handle of a brass jug, which stands in a basin of the same color. It lies beside a yellow box on a table, covered with a Persian rug—dull red, blue, and yellow, which fills up the lower right corner of the picture. Over the back of a chair hangs a light blue cloak. Now mark the costume of the girl. The skirt and sleeves of her dress are blue, of very deep tone; her bodice is pale yellow trimmed with blue. Over her shoulders is a tippet of starched cambric, so thin that in parts the deep blue of the sleeve shows through. On her head rests a white cambric cap, shaped like a hood, through the flaps of which the light streams.

You may have already guessed that the dominant note of the color-scheme is the deep-toned blue of the girl's dress. Opposed to this is a smaller quantity of yellow in her bodice, in the objects on the table, and also in the pattern of the tablecloth. In the latter, also, is the opposition of dull red. At the same time it con-

tains some blue, and this hue also appears in the cloak
that is on the chair. Meanwhile—and this is very notable—the light which plays on the wall behind the girl
and filters through the flaps of her cap is slightly tinged
with blue. A suggestion of blue, in fact, prevails
throughout the picture. It presents a blue tonality; the
tonal scheme is constructed upon the dominant note of
color, with the subordinate hues and these tones introduced as contrasts. Now this is the usual manner of
composing the tonal harmony of a picture. Vermeer,
however, was a magician in the use of color, who treats
us to continual surprises.

For now turn to *A Lady at a Spinet*. The strongest
note of color in this picture is black. The tonality,
however, is based not upon it, but on the pearly white
of the girl's gown. The black, and the lesser oppositions of yellow, blue, and brown are introduced as crisp
and lively contrasts to the prevailing hue of the figure;
the spots which they make in the composition being so
artfully arranged that, while they give animation to the
scene, they continually bring the eye back to the quiet,
quaint little figure in the center. The tones of her
white satin gown appear as grays and blacks in the reproduction; but in the original—although the surface
has been somewhat injured by cleaning—it presents a
web of pearly tones, which the satin texture causes to
gleam. These tones are echoed in slightly grayer quality on the surface of the walls, the flatness and texture
of which cause them to be evenly and softly diffused,
thus subordinating them to the piquancy of the figure.
The artist then, in this case, may be said to have en-

meshed the lively notes of his composition in a web of pearly luminosity; for, face to face with the original, it is this circumambience of cool, fresh, lighted atmosphere that is the chief charm of this picture; beautiful in itself and in the way in which it draws all the oppositions of the color-scheme into a tenderly resonant harmony.

In this feeling for the beauty of natural light and in his skill in rendering it, Vermeer anticipated the open-air movement in painting, which we shall come to in the nineteenth century.

CHAPTER XVIII

WATTEAU has been called the first French painter; Hogarth was certainly the first English one. The previous painters in England had been foreigners, such as Holbein, Rubens, Van Dyck, Lely, Kneller, visiting the country for a longer or shorter stay. Those preceding Watteau, while French by birth, were altogether foreign in their art. We have seen how the greatest of them, Nicolas Poussin and Claude, lived in Italy and based their respective styles on the study of classic and Italian art and landscape. On the other hand, Lebrun, a pupil of Vouet who had studied in Italy, occupied the position of painter in ordinary at the court of Louis XIV, elaborating vast compositions and designs dictated by the monarch's vanity and intended to extol his fame, representing him as a classic hero and always in the act of conquest. Despite the size of his canvases, Lebrun was not a great painter, and there was nothing distinctively French or original about his work. On the contrary, both these qualities appeared in Watteau, hence the assertion that he is the first of French painters. And this notwithstanding the fact that he was really of Flemish birth, a native of Valenciennes, which had recently, however, become a part of the French dominions.

In his case, as in Hogarth's, a new kind of art sprang into existence, full-grown almost from its birth; both eminently characteristic of their times; the one distinctly French, the other as unmistakably English. Also, it is extremely interesting to note that each artist was, in a greater or less degree, influenced by the sister art of the drama.

Let us try to get an understanding of these two men by first examining the examples of their work. *The Embarkation for Cythera*—the island near which Venus was fabled to have risen from the sea, especially dedicated to her worship—was painted by Watteau upon his admission to full membership in the French Academy when he was thirty-three years old. It caused a great sensation, being entirely different from the official classic standard maintained by the Academy,—"a rainbow-hued vision of beauty and grace, such as had not been seen since the golden days of the Venetian Renaissance,"—yet strangely in touch with the French spirit of its own day. For the Grand Monarch had been dead two years, succeeded by his great-grandson Louis XV, a child now seven years old; and under the regency of Philip, Duke of Orleans, the dreary formality of the old court had been replaced by the gaiety of the new. True, the country was plunged in misery, and the shadow of the terrible Revolution which was to burst in the next reign was already drawing near. But at court the people frisked and frolicked, like lambs unmindful of the butcher; pleasure and love-making were their occupations, and Watteau's picture represents the graceful side of all this, detached from its wickedness and inhumanity.

Look at the picture—the trees, the water, and the sky all seem real; so, too, the ladies and gentlemen in their rainbow-tinted silks and satins. Yet the scene is also unreal; part of a world in which there is no ugliness, no hunger, no need of work or self-denial; a dream of the poets of old Greece reclothed in the semblance of the eighteenth century. Nor is it only the presence of the cupids that touches this strain of unreality; wreathed, as they are, in joyous circles in mid-air, clinging about the masts of the vessel, or winging their flight through the shrubbery as they summon the human votaries of pleasure. For the gilded vessel is ready to set sail to the isle of happiness, lying somewhere in that dreamy distance; lovers are already aboard, and the rest are being urged to follow. A statue of Venus adorns the woodland spot; yet it is but a symbol of the joy that awaits these pleasure-seekers in the island of dreams— when they reach it.

For it is the beauty of what is not yet attained, of the unattainable, expressed in this picture, that is one of the sources of its poetic unreality; and another is the exquisite pattern of its composition—the spacing of the foreground and the trees against the sky; the rhythmic curving line of moving figures; the delicate varieties of light and shade; and in the original the brilliant harmony of color. All is too absolutely attuned to what is only beautiful to be real; and yet, to repeat what has been said above, its poetry is based on realism. For "Watteau has this note of a great artist, that as a foundation for his poetry, his dream, his idealism, he lays a constant and minute study of nature."

When Watteau was a lad in Valenciennes he was continually filling his mind with the appearances of things and practising his hand in drawing; especially absorbed on the occasion of the fairs, when the market-place was gay with booths, and mountebanks and actors vied with one another in their antics and gestures. He reached an extraordinary facility in representing figures in action. To this he added from his studies in the Louvre a perfection of coloring derived from Rubens, Titian, and Veronese.

During those days of the Regency the light French comedies were again in favor, and the Italian comedies, which had been banished from the old monarch's court, had been invited back. Once more in the salons and gardens of the Luxembourg sported Gilles (the Italian equivalent of Pierrot), Columbine, Harlequin, Pantaloon, the doctor of Bologna on his donkey, and Polichinello,—characters evolved by Italian wit out of their prototypes as played by the Roman mimes. Sometimes the players acted in dumb-show, at other times from written plays, and often with words improvised by themselves, but always with their Italian skill of expression by gesture and facial play, in which they have been rivaled only by French actors and by the Chinese and Japanese. Watteau on some occasions derived his subjects directly from the Italian comedy, as in his famous picture of *Gilles* in the Louvre; but in all his work the indirect influence is plainly visible.

His figures move through the scene as if they were

enacting a comedy: in the case of our present picture, a very elaborate spectacle, but of lightest touch; no emotion, only the daintiest play of fancy; yet in its artistic aspect most serious and accomplished. For Watteau was no trifler; an earnest and indefatigable worker; serious even to sadness, a man of frail physique; nervous, irritable, not fond of company; a looker-on at life, not a sharer in its joys, except in the joy of his own art; and when he painted this vision of loveliness he was already dying of consumption. Note also with regard to his figures that, on the one hand, except in the case of the *Gilles*, they are small. Therefore we are not concerned with them individually and intimately, but only in relation to the whole scene, in which they play like puppets, creatures of exquisite grace, of easy movement, detached from us, inside the proscenium opening of the gilt frame. On the other hand, note the actual relation of those figures, in point of size, to the landscape. The latter is not subordinated to them, as in the Italian paintings, nor are they mere spots of accent in the surroundings, as in Claude's pictures and in the Dutch landscapes; but the two elements are so adjusted to each other, that, to use a theatrical expression, the *mise-en-scène* is perfectly balanced. It was this balance, coupled with the dramatic vivacity of the figures, which made Watteau's pictures a new thing in art.

Its newness is linked to that of Hogarth's by the influence that the drama exerted over both; otherwise there is no similarity between the two men in motive, though in their craftsmanship they were alike in being both accomplished painters. But while Watteau, as we have

said, was a sad, retired man, who found inspiration for
his landscape studies in the beautiful gardens of the
Luxembourg palace, which he peopled with the creatures of his own imagination, though having all a realist's feeling for, and knowledge of, nature and the
human figure; Hogarth, a jovial little man, fond of his
London and thoroughly acquainted with its aspects and
the life of its people, laid his scenes in the streets, the
drawing-rooms, churches, attics, madhouses—always in
some scene thronged with the rich, the poor, the actual
people living in his day. He neither extenuated, "nor
set down aught in malice." But, added to this painter's
joy of representing what he saw (and with what minuteness of detail you can see from this picture, remembering, as you study its extreme finish, that Hogarth began
life as apprentice to an engraver, and that in after life
he engraved a large proportion of his pictures)—added,
I say, to this purely pictorial motive is that of telling a
story, and one, too, which has a moral.

First of all let us read the story of this picture; or,
rather, this Act I of a very serious comedy of six tab-
leaux, entitled *Marriage à la Mode.* The scene is the
drawing-room of Viscount Squanderfield (note the allegorical significance of the name) ; on the right his lordship is seated, pointing with complacent pride to his
family tree, which has its roots in William the Conqueror. But his rent-roll has been squandered, the
gouty foot suggesting whither some of it has gone; and
to restore his fortunes he is about to marry his heir to
the daughter of a rich alderman. The latter is seated
awkwardly at the table, holding the marriage contract,

duly sealed, signed, and delivered; the price paid for it being shown by the pile of money on the table and the bunch of canceled mortgages which the lawyer is presenting to the nobleman, who, as you observe, refuses to soil his elegant fingers with them. Over on the left is his weakling son, helping himself at this critical turn of his affairs to a pinch of snuff, while he gazes admiringly at his own figure in a mirror. The lady is equally indifferent: she has strung the ring on to her handkerchief and is toying with it, while she listens to the compliments being paid to her by Counselor Silvertongue. Through the open window another lawyer is comparing his lordship's new house that is in course of building with the plan in his hand. A marriage so begun could only end in misery; and the successive stages of it are represented in the following five pictures of this famous series, which was issued in engraved form in 1745.

Of this masterpiece of Hogarth's, considered as the gradual unfolding, tableau by tableau, of a dramatic story, Austin Dobson writes: "There is no defect of invention, no superfluity of detail, no purposeless stroke in the whole tale. From first to last, it progresses steadily to its catastrophe by a forward march of skilfully linked and fully developed incidents, set in an atmosphere that makes it as vivid as nature itself, decorated with surprising fidelity, and enlivened by all the resources of the keenest humor." This is very high praise; but, observe, there is not a word in it which would be inapplicable if it were a play or a novel and not a series of pictures, that Mr. Dobson were criticizing. As Hogarth was not a dramatist or novelist, but a painter, we

THE EMBARKATION FOR CYTHERA

LOUVRE, PARIS

ANTOINE WATTEAU

THE MARRIAGE CONTRACT

WILLIAM HOGARTH

NATIONAL GALLERY, LONDON

need some further indorsement. Let Gautier, the French critic, speak: "Throughout the *Marriage à la Mode* series Hogarth perfectly merits the name of a great painter." Compare with this an extract from the writings of the American critic, Mr. John C. Van Dyke: "There can be no doubt that Hogarth's instincts were those of a painter. His feeling for color, air, values, his handling of the brush, his sense of delicacy and refinement in the placing of tones, all mark him as an artist whose medium of expression was necessarily pigment. The fact that his audience applauded him for his satires rather than for his painting does not invalidate the excellence of his art." And many other judgments to the same effect could be quoted.

So it is because Hogarth was distinguished by these qualities, which are among the hall-marks of painting, that he is reckoned a great painter; and because he was the first of Englishmen to be thus distinguished, and the subjects of his pictures are character studies of life in England, that he is considered the first of the English painters. For similar reasons, Watteau is called the first of the French painters.

The difference between the art of these two contemporaries, each representative of his race and period, is most interesting. The Gallic genius, influenced by intellectuality, seeks in each branch of art its separate special perfection; while the Anglo-Saxon, like the German, mixes sentiment with his abstract love of beauty: a sentiment either of emotions or imagination, of morality or religion. The Frenchman does not, as a rule, confuse his mediums of expression: that is to say, what can best be said in words, he leaves to literature; and, when through painting or sculpture he makes an appeal to the eye, it is to the eye, as far as possible, exclusively, that he is wont to appeal. There are many exceptions to this in French painting, the very popular Greuze being one; but, as a rule, the racial genius of the French is displayed in bringing to the highest point of perfection the special capabilities of the medium, whether in words, or paint, or what not. On the other hand, the Anglo-Saxon and the German, moved by sentiment, are apt to use their art to get at the sentiment of their fellow-men; quite as intent upon what they wish to say as upon their mode of saying it; sometimes more so. They will borrow, therefore, from other arts, as Hogarth did from those of the satirist and dramatist, and, we may add, of the preacher and the moralist.

To this ruling difference between the genius of these races there are numberless exceptions, yet the essential difference remains and must be grasped by all who would appreciate fairly the merits of both. Nor need we try to discover which is the better motive. To the French, their own undoubtedly, because it is fashioned out of their own characteristics. A heritage from Poussin, it has resulted in a very high average of accomplishment; so that no writers are more clever in writing than the French; no painters so generally skilled in painting; no sculptors, as a body, so expert in their particular craft.

On the contrary, while individual painters of the German and Anglo-Saxon races have regarded themselves primarily as painters and reached a high degree of accomplishment in their technic, there has been a tendency to think the subject of the picture of more importance than the way in which it is painted, and the latter has suffered in consequence. Hogarth, as we have seen, was not one of these; yet the admiration given to the story-telling and moral aspects of his work has done much to lead other painters to overlook the proper scope of painting, its true possibilities and limitations.

He himself was a perfectly typical product of his time, reflecting at least four very vital influences: Puritan morality; the power and independence of the middle classes; the love of the drama, and the rise of English prose.

The first two are closely interwoven. At the commencement of the eighteenth century there was this great difference between the conditions of England and France, that while in the latter the opposite extremes of the aristocracy and the proletariat stood wide apart, in England there was a powerful and independent middle class. It had its origin in the fifteenth century, when the mutual destruction of the nobles in the Wars of the Roses "gave honest men," as the saying was, "a chance to come by their own." It grew in numbers and in wealth, eagerly identifying itself with freedom of thought and speech, until by the seventeenth century it had developed that Puritan conscience which made a stand at once for morality and for religious and civil liberty. It was temporarily triumphant and then superseded in the matter of government by the Restoration, when lower moral standards and indifference to religion came to be in vogue. But the Puritan conscience survived, as it still does to-day; and in Hogarth's time made itself felt in a variety of ways. In a religious guise it reappeared in the preaching of John Wesley, and the rise of the Methodists; in literature, in the satirical writing of Swift, Addison, Steele, and Pope.

But the great event of literature during the latter part of the eighteenth century was the development and growth of English prose, particularly, in connection with our present study, of the modern novel. There sprang up a group of story-tellers: Defoe, Richardson, Goldsmith, Fielding, Sterne, and Smollett. Literature, seriously, humorously, or satirically, was interested in human life. The Puritan conscience, the sturdy middle-class common sense, the novelist's keen observation of life, tinged sometimes with bitterness, but always with humor—these are the influences to be detected in Hogarth's work.

Its affinity to the drama is no less evident. The figures are grouped in a scene rather than composed with the empty spaces of the background. They are strung across the scene, almost in the same plane, and are illuminated as if from footlights, the light of which does not explore the background. To appreciate this artificial form of grouping and lighting, the picture should be compared with Velasquez's *Las Meñinas*. In a moment we perceive that one is natural, and the other stagy.

In his portrait of himself, in the National Gallery in London, Hogarth has introduced a palette, on which is drawn a curved line. This is what he called the line of beauty and of grace. One may possibly trace his use of it in this picture: in the gesture of the right arm and hand of the heir; in the curve of the lady's pocket-hand-kerchief; more subtly through the line of her head and the hands of the Counselor Silvertongue; with a certain broken humility in the head and left arm of the lawyer who hands the mortgages, and with a pompous stiffness in the head and left arm of his lordship.

In his early efforts at painting, Hogarth produced miniature "Conversation Pieces"; that is to say, little subjects of figures grouped in the act of conversation: a style of picture which, as he said, had novelty. It was akin to the genre pictures, those subjects of real life which had occupied the Dutch of the seventeenth century. But there was this difference. The Dutch artists, depicting scenes of real life in the home, or streets, or taverns, were concerned almost entirely with the pictorial aspect of the subject; they did not include, as a rule, any study of character, much less any story-telling or dramatic motive. They looked at the outside, not the inside, of life. Hogarth was the first of the painters to do the latter. In his objective realism he is related to Dutch seventeenth-century art; but, under the influence of English literature of the eighteenth century, he went further and originated a new motive in painting. While Italian art in the eighteenth century was variously reproducing a faint recollection of its past, Holland itself aping the Italian, and Watteau shrinking from the present in a golden vision of dreams, Hogarth attacked the real. He is the father of modern realism in painting.

The great difference, then, between him and Watteau is that his pictures represent a study of character which analyzes the causes and results of human actions, while the French artist floats upon the beautiful surface of things. The one is terrible, seeing the world so clearly as it was; the other, altogether lovable in his disregard of what is gross and horrible, in his imagined perfection of beauty. But, in relation to the respective conditions of their countries at the time, Watteau's art was as a tangle of flowers, covering pleasantly a bottomless pit of destruction; Hogarth's, a rude awakening to a wholesomer condition; the one, a sad and sick man's craving after ideal beauty; the other, a healthy recognition of what was wrong.

CHAPTER XIX

SIR JOSHUA REYNOLDS
1723–1792
Early English School

THOMAS GAINSBOROUGH
1727–1788
Early English School

IN the same year, 1784, that Sir Joshua Reynolds's picture, *Mrs. Siddons as the Tragic Muse,* was exhibited at the Royal Academy, the famous actress sat for her portrait to his rival, Gainsborough. Sarah Siddons was then in her twenty-ninth year, in the prime of her beauty, and in the first flush of that popularity which was to make her the queen of the English stage for thirty years. She was the eldest daughter of a country actor, Roger Kemble, three of her brothers, John Philip, Stephen, and Charles, and one sister, Elizabeth, being also distinguished on the stage; while Charles's daughter, Fanny Kemble, carried on the theatrical traditions of the family until 1893. As a girl, Sarah acted in her father's companies; at eighteen married an actor named Siddons; and made her first appearance at Drury Lane Theatre in 1775, when she played Portia with Garrick. But on this occasion she failed to make a good impression, and retired in disappointment to the provinces, where she worked hard for seven years. Upon her reappearance in London in 1782, as Isabella in "The Fatal Marriage," her success was instantaneous. She became identified with parts of tragic pathos and queenly dignity, her favorite ones being Lady Macbeth, Queen Constance, Queen Katharine, Jane Shore, Isabella, Ophelia, Imogen, Portia, and Desdemona. Her power seems to have consisted not so much in the delivery of the words as in her "presence, mien, attitude, expression of voice and countenance, and in her intense concentration of feeling, which lifted and dilated her form, transporting her audience as well as herself." Her last appearance on the stage was in 1818. Thenceforth until her death, in 1831, she lived in retirement, as honored as a woman as she had been as an actress.

We can compare the two aspects of her personality in these pictures. Sir Joshua's exhibits her in an attitude of rapt contemplation, as if gazing into the world of the imagination and listening for the voice of inspiration; dressed in a costume which at the end of the eighteenth century passed for heroic. In Gainsborough's picture she appears as she may have done when Fanny Burney met her, in 1782, while paying an afternoon call at a friend's house. Mrs. Siddons had just become famous. She was on everybody's tongue, and Miss Burney makes this entry in her diary: "We found Mrs. Siddons, the actress, there. She is a woman of excellent character, and therefore I am very glad she is thus patronized. She behaved with great propriety; very calm, modest, quiet, and unaffected. She has a fine countenance, and her eyes look both intelligent and soft. She has, however, a steadiness in her manner and deportment by no means engaging. Mrs. Thrale, who was there, said: 'Why, this is a leaden goddess we are all worshipping! however, we shall soon gild it.'"

Her hair is frizzled and powdered after the fashion of the time, and surmounted by a large black, feathered hat; she wears a blue-and-gray-striped silk dress, with a buff shawl hanging from her arm, and holds a brown muff. The curtain at her back is red. On this arrangement of colors hangs a tale.

Sir Joshua, in the eighth of the discourses which, as president of the Royal Academy, he delivered to the students in 1778, laid down the principle that the chief masses of light in a picture should always be of warm, mellow color, and that the blue, gray, or green colors should be kept almost entirely out of these masses, and "be used only to support and set off these warm colors; and for this purpose a small proportion of cold colors will be sufficient. Let this conduct be reversed," he added; "let the light be cold and the surrounding colors warm, as we often see in the work of the Roman and Florentine painters, and it will be out of the power of art, even in the hands of Rubens or Titian, to make a picture splendid and harmonious."

It is said that Gainsborough took up the challenge and produced the *Mrs. Siddons* portrait; though others assert that it was in another famous portrait, *The Blue Boy,* that he did this. Whether or not it is true that he deliberately painted these pictures to refute his rival's theory, matters very little beside the fact that they do refute it. For one of the chief charms of Gainsborough's work is the delicacy of his color-harmonies, in which he was entirely original. But this story brings out very sharply the difference between these two artists: Reynolds regulating his art and life on safe and arbitrary principles; Gainsborough, an original student of nature, influenced by a dreamy, poetic temperament; the one, also, a man of the world; the other, simply an artist.

Sir Joshua was born at Plympton, four miles from Plymouth, in Devonshire, in 1723. His father, rector of the grammar-school, early trained him in classical studies, intending his son to be an apothecary; but he displayed such an inclination for drawing, diligently copying the prints which fell in his way, that the father yielded and sent him to London as a pupil of Hudson, then popular but now held in little esteem. After two years he returned to Devonshire and established himself as a portrait-painter in Plymouth, where he was taken up by Commodore Keppel, who, being appointed to the Mediterranean station, invited the young painter to accompany him on his ship, the *Centurion*. Thus he was able to visit Rome, spending two years there in very close study, especially of the works of Raphael and Michelangelo. It was while painting in the corridors of the Vatican that he contracted a cold, which brought on the deafness which afflicted him during the rest of his life. Leaving Rome, he visited Parma, where he fell under Correggio's influence; then Florence and Venice, in the latter city studying the works of the great colorists. On his way home he stopped in Paris, making acquaintance with the work of Rubens. Arrived in London, he settled in St. Martin's Lane, and painted a portrait of his patron, Commodore (by that time Lord) Keppel, which laid the foundation of his fortunes. Later he established himself in Leicester Square, where his house, No. 47, may still be seen opposite the site of Hogarth's.

MRS. SIDDONS AS THE   SIR JOSHUA REYNOLDS
TRAGIC MUSE

GROSVENOR HOUSE, LONDON

PORTRAIT OF MRS. SIDDONS   THOMAS GAINSBOROUGH

NATIONAL GALLERY, LONDON

Van Dyck had been dead a hundred years. Though his memory was a great tradition in England, no Englishman had succeeded to his fame, and yet portraiture was the trend of painting that chiefly interested the English. Reynolds, coming back from his travels with well-considered rules which he would follow if it were possible for him to paint historical or ideal subjects, immediately adapted himself to circumstances and applied these rules to portrait-painting. Every portrait should be a picture as well as a rendering of the features of the original. He had learned how Michelangelo made the attitude and gestures of his figures so full of expression; what triumphs of light and shade were produced by Correggio; the dignity and sumptuousness of Venetian coloring; the decorative splendor of Rubens's pictures; the exquisite sentiment of Raphael's women and children, and the dignity that this artist gave to his heads of men. He had learned all this and much more, and set himself to combine as much of these different qualities in his portraits as he could. "No one," said James Northcote, a pupil of Reynolds, who wrote his life, "ever appropriated the ideas of others to his own purpose with more skill than Sir Joshua. The opinion he has given of Raphael may with equal justice be applied to himself: 'His materials were generally borrowed, but the noble structure was his own.'"

For example, in the *Mrs. Siddons* the pose of the figure, especially in the carriage of the head and left arm and hand, recalls Michelangelo's painting of *Isaiah* on the ceiling of the Sistine Chapel; while in the latter's *Jeremiah* may be seen the suggestion for the attendant figures, *Crime* and *Remorse,* in the Reynolds picture. If you compare the *Siddons* and the *Isaiah,* you will be conscious at once of particular similarities and yet of general difference. Each figure is represented as being under the influence of inspiration, as if listening to a voice. The latter in the case of the *Isaiah* is near, in that of the *Siddons* afar off; the prophet is *taking it into* himself to write it in the book; the actress, with her right arm extended, looks as if she may spring from her seat and impetuously *give out* of herself what she feels. Then note the different treatment of the draperies: in the *Isaiah* it is sculptural, the drapery is felt as part of the figure; in the *Siddons* it is arranged so as to make you forget the figure in the amplitude and superbness of its garniture, just as the actual personality of a great actress is enlarged and made magnificent by the atmosphere of emotion which surrounds it. It was so that Reynolds, intimate friend of the great actor Garrick and of the brilliant orator Burke, tried to represent the mighty impressiveness, the emotional grandeur, and intellectual splendor of the nobly spoken word. Throughout all Reynolds's work there is a strong inclination toward the dramatic representation: even the children— and none ever painted sweeter ones than he—unconsciously play some little part. Moreover, Reynolds lived in the grand world, and painted all the great and the fashionable people of his time; and sought to apply to portraiture the principles of the " grand style " of painting.

Look back to Gainsborough's *Mrs. Siddons,* and see how free from anything dramatic or " grand " it is; how simple and straightforward; true and sure in the drawing, so that one can enjoy the suggestion of vigorous, alert body and soft, firm flesh. It gives enjoyment to our tactile sense, which is much less excited by the Reynolds picture. On the other hand, quite as noticeable is the delicacy of the picture: its delicate refinement of expression and the delicate rendering of the face and hair; while we have already alluded to the choice and original beauty of the scheme of color-harmony. Altogether there is a rare quality of distinction in this picture which we shall not find in the Reynolds, for all its grandeur. It is also a much finer kind of distinction than appears in Van Dyck's pictures; and I think we may discover why.

This quality of distinction in a picture is not so much a reproduction of something in the subject as of something in the artist; else we might expect to find it as evident in Reynolds's picture as in Gainsborough's. No, you may find this quality also in a painted landscape; it is an expression of the mind and imagination of the artist, even as the touch of a musician is an interpretation not only of the music, but of the way in which the music affects him—an expression of himself, in fact.

Now Van Dyck, as we have seen, was very fond of the grand world and fashionable life, and, having great personal refinement, gave an air of exceptional refinement to his portraits; but it is very largely a refinement of beautiful clothes and elegant manners. We can hardly imagine Van Dyck condescending to paint a picture of a *Girl and Pigs,* as Gainsborough did; and he certainly did not paint landscapes,—whereas Gainsborough, while painting portraits for a living, painted landscapes for his own pleasure, and lived at Hampstead during the summer, that he might be constantly in fellowship with nature.

It was this love of nature and of simple things, and the faculty of seeing beauty in them, that gave such a choice distinction to his work, because it was the expression of his own simple, lovable personality. He had beauty in himself, and all his life it fed on simple delights—the joy of nature, of domestic happiness, of music, and of his own art.

He was born in the little town of Sudbury, on the river Stour, in the beautiful county of Suffolk, not far from East Bergholt, the birthplace, some fifty years later, of the great landscape-painter Constable. As a boy, he loved to ramble in the country, sketching; and showed so much inclination for it, and so little for any other kind of study, that when he was fifteen he was sent to London and placed under the care of a silversmith, who procured him admission to the St. Martin's Lane Academy. Here he worked for three years under the painter Frank Hayman, who was distinguished by being addicted more to wine and pugilism than to art. Gainsborough's eighteenth year was an eventful one. First, he hired three rooms in Hatton Gardens and set up as a painter on his own account; then, meeting with little encouragement, returned to Sudbury; there fell a victim to the charms of a young lady of seventeen, Miss Margaret Burr, who had an annuity of one thousand dollars; married her, and established himself in the country town of Ipswich. After this eventful year, he worked on for fifteen years happily and quietly, continually studying in the open air and executing such small commissions for portraits as came to him, until he had succeeded in discovering for himself a manner of painting suited to his needs, and had developed an extraordinary facility.

In 1760, by the advice of a friend and patron named Thicknesse, he moved to Bath, at that time the most fashionable city outside of London. Its hot medicinal waters had been famous in Roman times, and still the gay world congregated there to drink them and to dance and talk scandal in the Pump-room, where Beau Nash reigned as an autocrat among the wits and macaronis.[1]

Gainsborough's success was immediate, but with increasing wealth there was no alteration in his simple method of living. He worked four or five hours a day, and devoted the rest of his time to the society of his wife and a few friends who were musical. For music now became a passion of his life, so that it was said he painted for business and played for pleasure, constantly mastering some fresh instrument.

So passed fourteen years, when, in 1774, Gainsborough moved to London, was commissioned by George III to paint a portrait of himself and the queen, and became the rival of Reynolds. He died in 1788, having contracted a chill while attending the trial of Warren Hastings, and was buried by his own request in Kew churchyard. On his death-bed he sent for Reynolds. There had been misunderstanding and estrangement between the two. It was now forgotten. Reynolds caught his last dying words, "We are all going to heaven, and

[1] Slang word for the fashionable dandies of the day.

Van Dyck is of the party"; acted as one of the pall-bearers at his funeral; and subsequently pronounced a eulogy. In it he said: "If ever this nation should produce genius enough to acquire to us the honorable distinction of an English school, the name of Gainsborough will be transmitted to posterity in the history of the art, among the very first of that rising name."

Reynolds himself only survived Gainsborough four years. He was buried with much pomp in St. Paul's Cathedral, near to the grave of its architect, Sir Christopher Wren.

The contrast between these two artists is almost the difference between art and artlessness. Reynolds was learned in what other painters had done, and had reduced his own art to a system; he was a man of the world, and represented his subjects with a well-bred consciousness of good manners. Gainsborough found out almost everything for himself; never lost the simple, natural way of looking at things and people, and painted, not according to rule, but at the dictates of what he felt. Reynolds planned out his effects; Gainsborough painted on the spur of the impression which the subject aroused. Reynolds's art was based on safe general principles; Gainsborough's was the fresh and spontaneous expression of his temperament,—depending, that is to say, on feeling rather than on calculation. His temperament, or habit of mind, was dreamy and poetic, gentle and retiring, including a small range of experience. Reynolds, on the other hand, was a man of large experience and of business capacity; intimate with Samuel Johnson, Oliver Goldsmith, and other celebrities of the day;

a man of knowledge and clever conversational power, whose pictures by their variety prove his versatility. Consequently, when the Royal Academy was established in 1768, he was elected president by acclamation, and was knighted by George III, an honor that has ever since been bestowed on the holder of this office.

These two men were at the head of the group of portrait-painters who, in the latter part of the eighteenth century and early years of the succeeding one, added luster to the new growth of art in England. Foremost among the other names in the group are Romney, at times quite as able as Reynolds or Gainsborough; Sir Henry Raeburn, a Scotchman; John Hoppner; and Sir Thomas Lawrence.

CHAPTER XX

JOHN CONSTABLE
1776–1837
English School

JOSEPH MALLORD WILLIAM TURNER
1775–1851
English School

WHAT a contrast these pictures present of splendid audacity and serene simplicity! The one an amazing vision of the imagination; the other, a loving record of something intimately familiar. Turner's was painted in 1829; one of the finest works of this master, who is a solitary figure in landscape art, unapproached by others, although, as we shall see, he combined several motives that others had been or would be seeking after. Constable's picture appeared six years later, an excellent example of the painter who may be regarded as the father of modern landscape.

The Valley Farm, known also as *Willy Lott's House,* is on the little river Stour in the county of Suffolk, England, near the mill at East Bergholt where Constable was born; for he, like Rembrandt, was a miller's son. It is a characteristic bit of English scenery, not grand or romantic; just a tiny bit of a little country, the conspicuous features of which are its verdure and rich cultivation; so homelike that those who love it, as Constable did, get to have a companionship with every detail, learning to know the line of its hills, the winding of its streams, and the position and character of every tree and object in the familiar scene. It was along the banks of this little river that he strayed in boyhood; and to it that he came back, after a stay in London where he studied at the schools of the Royal Academy, and copied the pictures in the galleries, especially those of Hobbema and Ruisdael. But he soon tired of looking at nature through the eyes of other men. "There is room enough," he wrote to a friend, "for a nature-painter. Painting is with me but another name for feeling; and I associate my careless boyhood with all that lies upon the banks of the Stour; those scenes made me a painter and I am thankful." This is the kind of spirit which, we have seen, actuated the Dutch landscape-painters of the seventeenth century; and, indeed, their love of nature was reincarnated in Constable. For in the lapse of time their contribution to art had been forgotten; the Dutchmen themselves had followed after strange gods, and, like the painters of France and England, had forsaken the direct study of nature for an attempt to reproduce the grandeur of the classic landscape.

He was not satisfied with a copying of nature. It was to him so real and personal a companion, that, in the first place, he tried to make it live in his pictures; that the clouds might move and overhang the spot, that its atmosphere might penetrate every part of the scene, and that trees and water, and the very plants by the roadside might move and have their being in it; and secondly, he put his own personal affection into his representation. Then, too, in the matter of color, which cannot be gathered from the reproduction, he dared to paint nature green, as he saw it, and the skies blue, with the sunshine either yellow or glaring white. This scandalized the people of his day. "Where are you going to place your brown tree?" said a patron of his, speaking of an unfinished picture. For the older men, even Gainsborough to some extent, transposed the hues of nature into browns and grays and gold, producing a very charming harmony of tone, but one that was arbitrary; not true to nature's facts, but adopted as a pictorial convention.

It is, then, because of this closer fidelity to the hues of nature, and to the effects of movement, of atmosphere and of light, which are the manifestations of its life and moods, and because he interpreted nature according to his own mood,—was, in fact, the first of the temperamental landscape-painters,—that Constable is called the father of modern landscape. For these are the qualities that particularly have occupied the artists of the nineteenth century, and have caused the most original and vital branch of painting at the present time to be that of landscape.

On the threshold of this new movement stood Turner, alone among his fellow landscape-painters, the most imaginative of them all, who was less concerned with the truth of nature than with her splendors and magic. No one has equaled him in suggesting the mystery of nature in its sublime forms. One turns to the *Ulysses Deriding Polyphemus,* not to be drawn toward it and made to feel at home, as in the case of the Constable, but to be lifted up and filled with wonder of its strangeness and mysterious grandeur.

The incident depicted in it is from Homer's Odyssey. The hero, Ulysses, in his voyage from Troy to his home in Ithaca, stopped at the isle of the Cyclops, and with his followers approached the cave of Polyphemus. The monster devoured six of the crew; but the hero plied him with wine, brought from his vessel, and, while he slept, put out his single eye by gouging it with a red-hot stake. The mariners then escaped to their ship, while Polyphemus in his pain and impotent rage flung rocks in the direction of their voices. We see his huge form writhing on the top of the cliff; the sailors scrambling up the masts to loosen the sails; the red oars flashing upon the water; a bevy of sea-nymphs around the prow drawing the ship to safety through the green water; the latter, gilded with the reflections of the rising sun, that paints with gold and crimson the little clouds, floating in the vaporous sky, wherein are rifts which reveal further depths of blue. But really the incident was of very little account to Turner, except as it furnished him with a peg upon which to hang the splendors of his own imagination; far enough away from our actual experience to permit him a perfect liberty of treatment.

A man may shut himself up in his house and lead a very solitary life, as Turner did, and yet unconsciously be a part of the influences of his time. And those early years of the nineteenth century were a period of reaction against the eighteenth century reign of prose, its cold calculation and small and elegant precision. The spirit of Romanticism was in the air. It is not usual, however, to regard Turner as a Romantic painter, yet his work combines qualities which reappear more distinctly in other men. We shall consider the Romantic movement in painting in another chapter; meanwhile here are two definitions of it, that will include Turner, as having, at least, romantic tendencies. Walter Pater says, "It is the addition of strangeness to beauty that constitutes the romantic character in art"; again, Dr. F. H. Hedge, "The romantic feeling has its origin in wonder and mystery. It is the sense of something hidden, of imperfect revelation."

The mystery of this picture, its spaces of light and darkness, that the eye explores but cannot fathom, we are conscious of at once. Moreover, when we think about it, we are sure that, if our eye could pierce the shadows and closely discern the formation of the rocks, definitely learn the structure of the ship and the appearance of its sailors, peer into the distance and discover exactly how each mass of cliff succeeds another—if, in a word, our eye could grasp everything and convey the facts distinctly to our understanding, we should not enjoy the picture as we do. It is the sense of something hidden, of imperfect revelation, that is one of the sources of its enjoyment.

And then the strangeness of the picture,—that arch of rock, an actual aspect of nature, though an unusual one; the huge, roughly hewn figure of Polyphemus; a sky, full of surprises to people who seldom see the daily pageantry of sunrise,—but it is less in detail than in general character that the picture is strange. The artist has taken a theme of old times, when the world was young and things loomed very big to its unformed imagination. For to the ancient child-mind the world seemed very big, and its empty, unexplored spaces, peopled with shapes and fancies that were vague and large. Whether it was the myths of old Greece, or those of the Norse mountains, or German forests—the earliest ones are concerned with personages vast in size, only half formed in shape, vague and elementary; and it is the suggestion of this vastness and shapelessness, of the early beginning of things, this great strangeness, in a word, that helps to make the present picture so impressive.

Once more compare it with Constable's. One is part of a vast new world; the other, a little spot that for ages the hand and heart of man have shaped.

Whether Turner felt toward nature the wonder which his pictures inspire in us, may be doubted. His life was a strange contradiction to the splendor and imagination of his work. Like many other great landscape-artists he was city-bred. The son of a barber in London, he early showed a talent for drawing, and the father hung the child's productions on the wall of his shop and sold them to his customers. By degrees the boy obtained employment in coloring architectural designs, and at fourteen was entered as a pupil in the schools of the Royal Academy. The following year he exhibited his first picture. He worked with indefatigable energy, and during vacations went on walking tours, sketching continually and painting in water-colors; so that, by the time he was twenty-four and admitted as an associate to the Academy, he had exhibited pictures which ranged over twenty-six counties of England and Wales. During this early period his most conspicuous success was made in water-color, in which medium he developed an extraordinary facility and skill. He would brook no rivalry. Girtin was at that time the most admired artist in water-color; he set to work to surpass him. Having done so, he practically abandoned this medium for oil-colors, and then threw down a gauntlet to the popular admiration for the French landscape-painter Claude. That artist had published a "Liber Veritatis." Turner would outrival him with a "Liber Studiorum" though the drawings, engraved under the artist's supervision, were not studies but finished water-color pictures. In fact, this collection of seventy-one out of the hundred plates originally planned, while a monument to Turner's genius, is also the assertion of a rivalry that, in itself unworthy, was conducted in a spirit scarcely fair. For Claude's "Liber Veritatis" is simply a sketch-book, and the sketches were engraved after their author's death, indeed, not until Turner's day. But the latter's finished productions were issued under his own eye.

Turner's rule of conduct, in fact, was "aut Cæsar aut nullus." Having established his supremacy over rivals, at least to his own satisfaction, he set himself to conquer a universe of his own. During a period of twelve years, beginning with this picture of Ulysses and ending with that of a tug-boat towing to a wrecker's yard a ship of the line, *The Fighting Téméraire,* and *The Burial of Wilkie at Sea,* he did his greatest work. For then his imagination was at its ripest and richest; displayed particularly in the majesty of moving depths of water, in skies of vast grandeur, and in the splendor of his color-schemes; moreover, the workmanship of his pictures was solid, and he still based his imagination on the facts of nature. But, as time went on, the need of continual experimenting—which every genius feels—

VALLEY FARM (WILLY LOTT'S HOUSE)   JOHN CONSTABLE

NATIONAL GALLERY, LONDON

ULYSSES DERIDING POLYPHEMUS   JOSEPH MALLORD WILLIAM TURNER

NATIONAL GALLERY, LONDON

seemed to take undue possession of him, so that the study of nature became constantly less and the independent invention more and more. It was no longer the forms of nature that interested him, but her impalpable qualities of light and atmosphere, and perhaps even more the intoxication of the actual skill in using paint, until one may suspect that he was more enamoured of the magic of his brush and paints than of the qualities of nature which he was supposed to be representing. So daring, almost to the point of recklessness, were his experiments, that his later pictures have deteriorated, until their original appearance can only be guessed. On the other hand, in his fondness for atmospheric effects, and particularly in his efforts to raise the key of light in his pictures, he was anticipating, as we shall see, some of the most interesting developments of nineteenth-century painting.

And during all these years, while as an artist he was absorbed in the pageants, the mystery, and the subtlety of light and atmosphere, his life as a man was morose and mean; his house in Queen Anne Street dirty and neglected; and, finally, it was in a still more squalid haunt in a wretched part of London, which he frequented by his own choice, that he was found dead. When his will was opened, the curious contradiction that he was fond of hoarding money and yet refused to sell the majority of his pictures, was explained. He had left his works to the National Gallery, his money as a fund for the relief of poor artists. A strange mingling of greatness and sordidness, of boorish manners and kindly humanness!

HOW TO STUDY PICTURES

Constable, on the other hand, led a happy, simple life in the village of which he wrote in one of his letters, published by his friend, the painter Leslie, " I love every stile and stump and lane." It was on out-of-door life, for he painted, as he expressed it, "under the sun"; observing the big clouds as they rolled inland from the North Sea, with their attendant effects of light and shadow. For it is these shadow effects of the northern countries that have made them the home of the natural landscape. In sunny Italy, where the air is for the most part bright and clear, the landscape makes an appeal of lines and masses; the artist finds in it suggestion for composition, hence the stately pictures by Nicolas Poussin and Claude, who lived in Italy, and of the English Wilson, who visited Italy and saw nature through the Italian influence.

But in a country where the sunshine is comparatively rare, Constable learned to appreciate the value of it; the ample comfort of its occasional breadth, the subtle charm of its brief gleams, piercing the rain-cloud and sparkling upon the grass and leafage. The sky, not spread with an undisturbed ceiling of light, but built high with clouds, that shift continually and change their aspects, taught him to observe the varying luminosity of the atmosphere; not to take light for granted, or to represent it by some uniform recipe for glow, but to study the infinite variety of its manifestations—with what degrees of strength or faintness it saturates the air, and how it colors the objects upon the ground.

Constable became, in fact, the first of the modern school of open-air painting. Some of his pictures were exhibited at the Paris Salon during the years 1822 to

1827, and the interest that his work aroused and the impression produced by it are to be reckoned, as Delacroix himself affirmed, a powerful influence in the creation of the French school of *paysage intime*. The Englishmen, however, of that date, paid Constable little honor. It is true he was made an associate of the Royal Academy in 1819, after which he moved from Suffolk and established himself in what was then the village of Hampstead on the northern outskirts of London; but it was not until he had been honored with a gold medal by the French that the Academy admitted him to full membership. Nor did this increase the public's appreciation; he died at Hampstead in very meager circumstances, but with the happy expectation that some day his pictures would be understood and valued. The expectation has been fully realized.

Such tardy recognition has been the lot of many painters great enough to create something new. Turner would not have been so highly esteemed in his own generation, but that Ruskin, the most admired writer upon art in his time, was his enthusiastic advocate, extolling him, indeed, with an extravagant enthusiasm that has been followed by a reaction. Ruskin claimed for him every virtue of a painter; and the later discovery, that he was not so great as his advocate claimed, has somewhat obscured how great he was.

Moreover, the world has now become so persuaded of the beauty of the natural style of landscape-painting, that it is distrustful of the imaginative. In its praise of Constable it pooh-poohs Turner.

This is a foolish and ignorant attitude of mind. The

proper one for the genuine student is to recognize that in art, as in any other department of life, a man should be judged, not by standards of measurement, but by what he himself is. Now to a man who loves nature Constable must appeal; but where is the man whose love of nature, being simple and real, has not, once or twice or oftener, felt taken out of himself, so that the facts of sky and earth seemed little to him beside the wonderful exaltation of spirit that the same suggest? It may be on some mountain, or in the presence of a sunset, or beside a little brook, anywhere, at any time, but some time or other to the lover of nature will come a moment in which the facts of the landscape are swept into forgetfulness, and all he is conscious of is a sense of his soul being strengthened, purified, exalted. It is so that Turner's best pictures may affect him.

As we approach the development of modern art, we become more and more involved in the question of nature-study. But let us realize that nature is practically the same to-day, yesterday, and forever; it is our own attitude toward it which is variable. Nature is a mirror in which the artist and ourselves are reflected. Therefore, it would be just as foolish to affirm that a mirror should reflect only such and such objects, as to limit our appreciation to particular kinds of artistic motive. The proper attitude of mind is one of being actively ready to receive impressions of all kinds.

CHAPTER XXI

JACQUES LOUIS DAVID

1748–1825

Classical School of France

FERDINAND VICTOR EUGÈNE DELACROIX

1799–1863

Romantic School of France

EACH of these pictures—David's *Oath of the Horatii* and Delacroix's *Dante and Virgil*—represents a breaking away from what had gone before. David's was a protest against the art of Watteau and his successors, Van Loo, Boucher, and Fragonard; Delacroix's, in turn, a protest against the art of David. The one was an attempt to revive the purity of Classic style by going even further back than Poussin, namely to the ancient Roman sculpture itself; the other, to express the fervor of modern life through the medium of romance. David's picture is cold, calculated, and self-conscious; Delacroix's impassioned, less formal in arrangement, the characters being absorbed in their various emotions.

Compare the two pictures, first of all, from the standpoint of their subjects, in each case a dramatic one: David's drawn from the early days of the Roman Republic, Delacroix's from Dante's " Inferno." And, first, the David. Jealous of the growing power of the young city, the neighboring tribe of Curiatii has invested it; Rome's very existence is imperiled. There are three brothers in the ranks of the enemy who, like Goliath in the Bible story, march up and down in front of their com‚ rades, challenging any three Romans to fight with them. Let a combat of three against three decide the issue. Now within the walls is one Horatius, who has three stout sons. He will give them up, sacrifice them if need be, as champions of the Republic. They are eager for the honor, notwithstanding that their own sister is betrothed to one of the three Curiatii. But between their loyalty to country and to sister they have no hesitation. They will fight for country; and to this highest of all purposes the father with prayer and blessings devotes them.

But observe the three brothers in the picture. Their attitudes are almost identical, like those of well-drilled supers on the stage. Let us admit that this device expresses the unanimity of their feeling; they are moved as one man, with a single patriotism, and, as we may judge from the hand of one encircling another's waist, by a single bond of brotherly affection. Yet still there is more than a suspicion of staginess in their pose. Perhaps David had seen Corneille's tragedy of the Horatii, written one hundred and forty-five years before; at any rate, its representation became very popular in Paris after the appearance of this picture, influenced by which the great actor, Talma, played the part, no longer in a periwig and court-clothes, but in the Roman costume. Again observe the secondary group of women. Do we feel convinced that the elder daughter betrays real grief, or her sister genuine sympathy, or that the mother's act of enfolding the little children in her arms is more than a bit of maternal conventionalism? In a word, are we really stirred by all this representation of pathos and heroism?

Now let us study, from the point of view of subject, the *Dante and Virgil*. The incident depicted may be read in Dante's "Inferno," Canto III, though the details are not closely followed in the picture. The poet of Florence, escorted by him of Mantua, has reached the shores of Acheron, that lake encircling the city of Dis (Pluto), against which leap up the fiery waves of Phlegethon. Upon the shore linger the souls of those who lived in life without praise or blame, moaning to be taken across the water, even if it be to hell. But Charon drives them back with cruel words and blows of his oar, as he takes the shade of Virgil and the living man into his crazy boat. To its gunwale cling the unhappy shades, one convulsively gripping it with his teeth; another has lost hold and sinks into the water, in which two more flounder, clutching each other as the living will when drowning. Above these writhing forms stands Dante, aghast with horror, leaning toward the Mantuan, who alone is calm, serenely fixed amid the tumult, eternally poised and youthful.

In this picture Delacroix has attempted to seize and convey by an immediate representation all the anguish and the tumult that the poet's song renders by separate stages. It was the work of a youth of twenty-three, already a master. David, a veteran of seventy-four years, when he saw it, exclaimed, "Where does it come from? I do not recognize the style."

For it does not depend upon line as David's picture,

but upon colored masses. It is true that the figures in
the water are arranged so as to produce a certain wild
rhythm of movement, like agitated waves; but none of
the figures are inclosed in hard lines, the contours having
neither the assertion nor the precision of David's. To
repeat, it is an arrangement of colored masses: of dark
greenish-blue sea, the pallid ivories of flesh tints, Virgil's
drabbish-green robe, and Dante's drab one; his crimson
becchetto, and the echo of its color in the fainter distant
glow of fire,—a turbid harmony of color, wherein the
nude bodies appear as a *motif* of pain and the crimson
is a crash of wrath. It is the work of a man who feels
in color, as a musician does in sounds, and who plays
upon the chromatics of color, somewhat as the musician
upon the chromatics of sound. It is the work, not of one
who uses color merely to increase the reality of appearances, as the majority of painters do, but of one of that
smaller band, headed by the Venetians and Rubens, who
make the color itself a source of emotional appeal.
Delacroix was a colorist; and David, drilled in the Academic school which says line and form are the chief es-
sentials, seeing the picture, asked, " Where does it come
from? "

It came, in the first place, out of the imagination of
a colorist, who conceives his pictures in color; sees them,
I mean, in his mind's eye, as a composition of color, before he begins to resolve the whole into its parts, and
work out the separate details of form. Indirectly it
came out of the heart of the Romantic movement which
had spread over Europe. Delacroix was inspired by the
influence of Goethe, Scott, Byron, Victor Hugo, and the

other poets and writers who had broken away from the coldly intellectual viewpoint of the eighteenth century, and its study of manners, to explore the passions of the human soul, and the variegated colorful life of the emotions.

David was a part, Delacroix a product, of the French Revolution, which opened a new chapter in the history of the world and also in that of painting. It had begun in protest against an extravagant and wanton court and an impotent monarch; had passed through a period of madness and horror, and culminated in an extraordinary outburst of national enthusiasm and individual energy. France, as a nation, was reborn, and—which had more influence upon the world at large—out of this Revolution, and the American one which preceded it, was born anew the idea of individualism. David represented the protest, and had no small share in promoting it; Delacroix, the fervor of personal feelings, let loose by individualism.

It was in 1784, in Rome, after he had completed his studies at the French Academy, that David produced the picture of *Brutus* and this *Oath of the Horatii.* In them he went back to the original Roman models upon which the Classic style of Poussin, then the model of the Academic school, had been founded. Here are the semi-circular arches and the vaulting, which were the most characteristic developments of Roman architecture, and columns such as the artist may have copied from the Baths of Marcellus. And against this background the figures are set as if carved in low relief, like those on the column of Trajan, of which David was so fond. By comparison with Italian painting and with that of France during the seventeenth and eighteenth centuries, this picture of the Horatii was severely simple. Then, too, what a simple severity of lofty patriotism it represented!

Its success in France was immediate. The people, tired of the voluptuous insipidities of Boucher and the others, welcomed its severity; while the principles of freedom and love of country that it inculcated gave at once a definite voice to the floating theories of the time. Republicanism, the old Roman brand of it, simple, unselfish, frugal, began to be considered the panacea for all the ills from which the French branch of the Latin race was suffering. David proved to be the strong man, fitted to the hour, and his influence, first asserted in this picture, played a big part in the subsequent Revolution. When the latter commenced he was forty years old. He was elected a deputy in the Convention, and appointed Minister of Fine Arts. In this capacity he was a despotic dictator; imposing his Roman taste even upon the costumes of the deputies and ministers, and from these upon the people, and organizing public fêtes in the manner of Republican Rome. "He applied art to the heroism of the day, gave it the martial attitude of patriotism, and inspired it with the spirit of Robespierre, Saint Just, Marat, and Danton. Robespierre is said to have spoken from the tribune slowly, rhythmically, artistically. Under the same starched methodical precision David concentrated the volcanic force of his appeal to patriotism." In the first consciousness of individualism, everybody was strutting and posturing self-consciously,

OATH OF THE HORATII   LOUVRE, PARIS   JACQUES LOUIS DAVID

DANTE AND VIRGIL   LOUVRE, PARIS   EUGÈNE DELACROIX

like actors upon a stage. The times were artificial and theatrical.

And how greatly this man was penetrated by the spirit of his age is illustrated in his manner of presenting to the Convention his portrait of Marat. The people asked for their murdered man back again, longing to look once more on the features of their truest friend. "They cried to me: 'David, take up your brush, avenge Marat, so that the enemy may blanch when they perceive the distorted countenance of the man who became the victim of his love for freedom.' I heard the voice of the people, and obeyed." [1]

His portraits, however, are free from this sort of rhodomontade, intensely direct and real. "In them, he is neither rhetorical nor cold, but full of fire and the freshness of youth. Before any face to be modeled, he forgot the Greeks and Romans, saw life alone, was rejuvenated in the youthgiving fount of nature, and painted—almost alone of the painters of his generation—the truth.

"David was one of the first of the men of the Revolution to come beneath the spell of the Little Corporal. One day while he was working at his studio at the Louvre, a pupil rushed in breathlessly: 'General Buonaparte is outside the door.' Napoleon entered in a dark-blue coat 'that made his lean yellow face look leaner and yellower than ever.' David dismissed his pupils, and drew in a sitting of barely two hours the stern head of the Corsican. Thus he passed into the service of Napoleon." [1]

He was appointed Imperial Court Painter, and

[1] Richard Muther: History of Modern Painting.

executed that colossal picture which has handed down to posterity a true presentation of the ceremonial pageant that took place in Notre Dame on December 2, 1804. The moment selected is that in which Napoleon, already crowned, is placing the crown upon the head of the empress. The *Coronation* was the great work of his imperial, as the *Marat* had been of his revolutionary period. He had been so intimately identified with both that, after Napoleon's final fall in 1815 and the succession of Louis XVIII, he was banished and sought refuge in Brussels, where he died in 1825. He left behind a legacy of so-called "classicalism," carrying on that of Poussin, which under various modifications has been preserved by the official Academy, as the basis of instruction in and the proper aim of painting. These academic principles, however, no longer confine the student to an imitation of Roman subjects and models. But, even as David permitted himself to be a naturalist in his portraits and in other subjects, such as the *Death of Marat* and the *Coronation,* so the Academy encourages still the study of nature, but within certain limitations.

It lays especial stress upon what it calls the ideal line, and ideal beauty of form and composition. Nature must be corrected to conform with the ideal representations handed down to us from Greek and Roman sculpture, and the paintings upon Greek vases. As Delacroix, mocking at these principles, said: "In order to present an ideal head of a negro, our teachers make him resemble as far as possible the profile of Antinous, and then say, 'We have done our utmost; if, nevertheless, we fail to make the negro beautiful, then we ought not to introduce into our pictures such a freak of nature, the squat nose and thick lips, which are so unendurable to the eyes.'"

This extreme view, which would exclude any subject that is not capable of being idealized, is no longer maintained by the Academy. Yet it still insists upon the prime importance of the line; and, as a result, the figures in academic pictures are usually in graceful poses and inclosed by sharp outlines. A comparison of the *Horatii* with Delacroix's *Dante and Virgil* will show the distinction very clearly. But, as a matter of fact, in nature the forms of objects are not sharply outlined. Even when a dark tree cuts against a light sky, the atmosphere that intervenes between it and our eyes tends to blur its edges. Now these effects of light and atmosphere depend not so much upon the way the picture is drawn as upon the way it is painted, and this again is connected with problems of color.

Accordingly, the Academician, precise about form, disregards problems of light and atmosphere and color; while the colorist, who cares most for these qualities, and sees nature as an arrangement of colored forms in harmonious relation, very often disregards the beauty of form, and, because of what he aims at, cannot make the lines of his objects so precise and ideally perfect. On the other hand, it is the little irregularities and indistinctness of line that give character to forms and suggest that they have the capacity of movement and are alive. The academic figure, notwithstanding its beauty, is by comparison inert and rigid. You may realize this point by a reference to these two pictures we are studying. The figures of the men in the *Horatii* have come to ges-

tures and positions of energy, and hold them as if cast in
bronze. The women have been placed in pretty attitudes
of amiable sentiment, and remain as if modeled in wax.
But in the *Dante and Virgil* there are life and movement: terrific action, put forth and sustained in the
figures of Charon and of the two men who grip the gunwale; action of another kind in the Dante, as he gazes
with horror and balances himself in the rolling boat; even
the latter moves, and the shades, although exhausted to
impotence, are moving.

This picture of Delacroix's has been called "in a pictorial sense the first characteristic picture of the century." That is to say, while the art of David and his followers was virtually a translation of sculpture into
painting, Delacroix's once more asserted the independence of painting, and its possession of certain qualities
and possibilities which no other art possesses in the same
degree. For, in the place of the tinted forms of the
Academicians, Delacroix had introduced the wonder of
color, used for purposes of expression by such masters
as the Venetians and Rubens.

Delacroix, in fact, was one of the greatest colorists of
the nineteenth century, using the word in the sense of
one who thinks and feels and expresses himself by means
of color. He nurtured himself upon the works of the
colorists in the Louvre, especially upon Rubens. Every
morning before his work began, it is said, he drew an
arm, a hand, or a piece of drapery after Rubens. It was
from Rubens also, and Titian, that Watteau, the great
poet-painter of the eighteenth century, had drawn inspiration. And Delacroix, like him, was proud, self-re-

liant, delicate from his youth up, and for many years sick in soul and body. But, whereas Watteau drew from the licentiousness of the Regent's court the food for his dreams of poetry, Delacroix into his closed studio admitted the mighty impulses which had been let loose by the Revolution.

Liberty had given larger bounds to individualism, and the first of the arts to reflect this was literature. The measured prose, conventionally correct verse, and somewhat pedantic rhetoric of the eighteenth century had been succeeded by an outburst of the imaginative faculty. The movement began in Germany with Goethe; in England with Wordsworth and Scott, Coleridge, Byron, Shelley, and Keats; and in France with Victor Hugo. During a visit to London, in 1825, Delacroix saw the opera of Goethe's "Faust" performed in English, while he had already discovered Shakspeare, Byron, and Scott to be his favorites. His own romantic nature flamed up by contact with theirs; he was possessed with their souls and became the first of the Romantic painters. He took many of his subjects from the poets of his preference, not to translate into literal illustrations, but to make them express in his own language of painting the most agitated emotions of the human heart.

But the representation of agitated emotions necessitated the introduction of a good deal that was horrible to those who swore by the ideal line and perfect balance of composition. "How can ugliness," they cried, "be beautiful?" Victor Hugo produced his play of "Hernani" in 1829; and around him and Delacroix was waged the battle between the Classicists and the Romanticists. Poussin's phrase was repeated by the Classicists—" Painting is nothing more than drawing." "Had God intended to place color at the same height as form," wrote Charles Blanc, "he would not have failed to clothe his masterpiece man with all the hues of the humming-bird." And this "critic" called Delacroix "the tattooed savage who paints with a drunken broom."

To these and similar denunciations, continued for many years, Delacroix himself in one of his writings has contributed a reply. It pleads for a wider conception of the idea of beauty. Winckelmann, the great German archæologist of the eighteenth century, had asserted, " The sole means for art to become, aye, if possible, inimitably great, is the imitation of the ancients." " The marble manner only requires a little animating." " The highest beauty is that which is proper neither to this nor to that person "—that is to say, *not individual.* This was practically the doctrine of the Classicists. To it Lessing, another German, replied that truth to nature was the first condition of beauty; and Goethe expanded it by saying that everything natural was true as far as it was beautiful. The English Keats chimed in, " Truth is beauty, beauty is truth." Delacroix's words are: " This famous thing, the Beautiful, must be—every one says so—the final aim of art. But if it be the only aim, what are we to make of men like Rubens, Rembrandt, and, in general, all the artistic natures of the North, who preferred other qualities belonging to their art? . . . There is no recipe by which one can attain to what is ideally beautiful. Style depends absolutely and solely upon the free and original expression of each master's peculiar qualities "—*upon individuality, in fact.*

There are, among others, some important considerations in these views of the Romanticists, which may be put in the following familiar way. It is quite possible for an exceedingly pretty girl to be very stupid; there is also such a thing as the beauty of character; we enjoy the beauty of the slimness of the silver birch, and the rugged stanchness of an oak; there is a charm about a Gloucester fisherman as well as an *Apollo Belvedere.* On the whole, we do well to be interested in people for what they are rather than for what they might be; individual character is always worth studying; when it is exhibited under the stress of powerful emotion, it is conspicuously so. The artist himself may be a man of marked individuality of character; it is better for the world that he should express himself freely, instead of within the tight groove of some conventional method.

The Classicists were intrenched in the official fortress of the Academy, and for long years resisted the attempts of Delacroix to obtain entrance. Indeed, it was not until twenty-two years after his death, when a great collection of his works was exhibited, that France realized how grand an artist it had lost. Before he died, other men with other motives, as we shall see, rose up to challenge the official standard of excellence; for the history of painting in the nineteenth century, centering in Paris, has been one of continually new assertions of individualism. Our sympathies, quite possibly, will be with the rebels, but that should not blind us to the value of the academic principles of painting.

If there is to be an official and permanent standard, the Classic is the best for the purpose. The standard to be serviceable must be one that can be reduced to a reasonable certainty. In painting, composition and line are the elements which can most readily be formulated; and, when founded upon the canons of antique art, are established upon a basis that the continuing judgment of the world has approved. Given this central body, there is the perpetual inducement for independent spirits to fly off at a tangent from it, which is productive of vitality. The classical ideal provides at once firm groundwork for the average student and a starting-point for independent genius. Permanence and progress are alike insured.

CHAPTER XXII

THÉODORE ROUSSEAU
1812–1867
Fontainebleau-Barbizon
School of France

JEAN BAPTISTE CAMILLE COROT
1796–1875
Fontainebleau-Barbizon
School of France

THREE miles from the landscape-forest which adjoins the Palace of Fontainebleau lies the little village of Barbizon. After 1832 it became the headquarters of a group of painters whose school and studio were the forest. They were the second protest of the nineteenth century against the formalism of academical teaching, and, though the artists varied individually, they were all united in their first-hand study of nature, so that they are distinguished as the Fontainebleau-Barbizon School.

Once before there had been a Fontainebleau School, the term being applied to that group of Italian artists —among them Leonardo da Vinci, Andrea del Sarto, and Cellini—whom Francis I invited to decorate his palace. With these men the subject had been the human figure, used with the artificial intention that decoration permits; whereas the group that appeared three hundred years later was concerned with nature, represented naturally. It comprised Rousseau, the acknowledged leader, Jules Dupré, Corot, Diaz, and Daubigny; the sheep and cattle painters, Troyon, Van Marcke, and Jacque; and

[347]

Millet, the painter of the peasant. This new group was related to the Dutch School of landscape-painters of the seventeenth century, through the English Constable.

The latter, learning of the Dutchmen, had revived the natural study of landscape and carried it further than they, introducing into his pictures the greens of nature, truer effects of air and light, and the suggestion of movement in the foliage. During the years from 1822 to 1827 Constable's pictures had been appearing at the Salon, and had been awarded a gold medal. Delacroix, the colorist, was attracted by them; and other painters, tired of the frigid unreality of the classic school, welcomed these nature-studies, and through them were induced to study also the works of the old Dutch landscapists in the Louvre. Among the many, thus influenced, was Rousseau, who had worked in the studio of the classicist Lethière, but, dissatisfied with the latter's grandiloquent canvases, had taken to wandering about the plain of Montmartre with his paint-box, and in 1826 had produced his first little picture.

But another influence played its part in shaping the future of the new school. Romanticism was in the air; Delacroix and others were making their pictures the medium of emotional expression. Accordingly, by the time that the Barbizon men had found themselves, their art was distinguished not only by truth to nature but also by poetic feeling. Of the two whom we are considering, we may say that Rousseau was the epic poet of the group; Corot, the lyric.

Of this lyric quality in Corot's work we may be conscious if we turn to *Dance of the Nymphs*. It yields a suggestion of music and of songfulness; exactly how, it may be hard to explain; but, perhaps, the reason is that there was constant music in the heart of the man who painted it. He sang as he worked, played the violin at intervals, and regularly attended the opera. Comparing himself with Rousseau, he once said, "Rousseau is an eagle. As for me, I am only a lark, putting forth some little songs in my gray clouds."

On the other hand, the epic quality in Rousseau's picture may not be so immediately recognizable; we shall better appreciate it when we have examined the motives of his work more closely. Comparing the example here reproduced with the one by Corot, we note this great difference, that Rousseau's shows a solidity of form and a power of clear decision in the lines inclosing the forms, whereas Corot's masses are by comparison dreamy and unsubstantial, the outlines blurred. Rousseau insists upon the form of objects and the character of their forms, while Corot escapes as far as possible from the actual things and renders the effect which they produce upon the senses. He sought to represent the essences of things; the fragrance, as it were, rather than the flower.

Both these men were city-bred. So, indeed, have been most of the great landscape-painters; a fact which may seem strange, until we remember how apt we all are to long for that which is farthest away from our actual life. Corot's parents were court dressmakers in the days of the first Napoleon, in comfortable circumstances, so that their son never wanted for money. Rousseau's father was a tailor, living up four flights of stairs; and

Rousseau himself was well on in manhood before he ceased to know the bite of poverty. Corot received the usual classic training and then went to Italy; but it was not until he had paid three visits to that country, and had reached the age of forty-six, that he came under the influence of Rousseau and the course of his art was changed. Even then some ten years elapsed before he perfected that style upon which his fame chiefly rests. Rousseau, on the other hand, found his true bent early.

The critic, Burger-Thoré, writing in 1844, asks a question of Rousseau. "Do you remember," he says, "the years when we sat on the window-ledges of our attics in the Rue de Taitbout and let our feet dangle at the edge of the roof, looking out over the chaos of houses and chimneys, which you, with a twinkle in your eye, would compare to mountains, trees, and outlines of the earth? You were not able to go to the Alps, into the cheerful country, and so you created picturesque landscapes for yourself out of those horrible skeletons of walls. Do you still recall the little tree in Rothschild's garden which we caught sight of between two roofs? It was the one green thing that we could see; every fresh shoot of the little poplar wakened our interest in spring, and in autumn we counted the falling leaves." "From this mood," as Muther says, "sprang modern landscape-painting, with its delicate reserve of subject, and its vigorously heightened love of nature."

Notwithstanding this nature-love in his heart, the young Rousseau at first devoted himself to mathematics, aiming to become a student at the Polytechnic Institution. The fact is interesting as showing that he combined the instincts of an artist and a scientist, a point we shall return to later. Meanwhile, as we have seen, he entered Lethière's studio, and watched him paint such subjects as *The Death of Brutus* and *The Death of Virginia*. But there was nothing in them to satisfy the youth's love of nature, and he began his wanderings with his paint-box in the country round Paris. The year 1833 found him for the first time in the forest of Fontainebleau, and the following year, at the age of twenty-two, he painted his first masterpiece, *Côtés de Grandville*. It was accepted at the Salon, and awarded a medal of the third class.

No further concession, however, could be allowed to a young man so dangerously independent from the academical standpoint, and for thirteen years, indeed until after the Revolution of 1848 and the fall of the " Bourgeois King," Louis Philippe, his pictures were excluded from the official exhibitions. Even then, officialdom, although it could not ignore this leader of a new movement, slighted him by singling out his followers, Dupré, Diaz, Troyon, for the Legion of Honor in preference to himself. It is true they were older men, but what Diaz thought of the slight to Rousseau may be gathered from the words in which he responded to the courtesies tendered him at the official banquet. Rising on his wooden leg, he gave the toast, " Here 's to our master who has been forgotten." In the following year, 1852, Rousseau himself was admitted to the Legion. At the Universal Exposition of 1855, the world discovered how great an artist he was; but by this time other shadows were beginning to creep over his life.

He had married a poor, unfortunate creature, a mere child of the forest, the only feminine being he had found time to love during his toilsome life. After a few years of marriage she was seized with madness; and, while he tended her, Rousseau himself became the victim of an affection of the brain, which darkened his last years. The end came in 1867, the year of another Universal Exposition. He had served as one of the heads of departments on the jury, and in the natural routine should have been awarded the higher rank of officer in the Legion of Honor; instead of which it was given to a man twelve years his junior, Gérôme. It was the climax to the tragedy of his life, and he survived it only a few weeks. In the churchyard of Chailly, near Barbizon, his body rests beneath a stone erected by Millet— a simple cross upon an unhewn block of sandstone, which bears a brass tablet with the inscription, "Théodore Rousseau, Peintre."

What a contrast the happy peace of Corot's life presents! His father had apprenticed him to a linen-draper, but after eight years consented to his becoming a painter. "You will have a yearly allowance of twelve hundred francs," he said, "and if you can live on that you may do as you please." Twenty-three years later, when the son was elected to the Legion of Honor, this allowance was doubled, "for," as the father remarked, "Camille seems to have some talent after all."

We have already alluded to his beginnings as a painter, how he went through the usual course of study of the figure and attempts at classical landscapes after the manner of Poussin. When he paid his first visit to Italy, he was so attracted by the moving life on the streets of Rome and Naples that he longed to transfer it to his sketch-book. But the figures would not remain still long enough to be treated methodically, as he had learned to draw; so he set himself to try and obtain with a few strokes the general effect of the moving picture, and with such success that after a time he could rapidly suggest the appearance of even so intricate a scene as a ballet. This skill was to stand him in good stead, when he should seek to represent the tremble of foliage in the morning or evening air. It taught him also, by degrees, the value of generalization; of not representing details so much as of discovering the salient qualities of objects, and of uniting them into a whole that will suggest rather than definitely describe.

But all this time the inspiration of his work was Italy and the Italian landscape; it was not until he had returned from his third visit thither, and was forty-six, that the landscape of France began to appeal to his imagination. He became acquainted at last with Rousseau, and with the aim of the Barbizon artists to represent nature as surrounded by air and light, and he set to work to learn the method of painting these qualities, reaching finally a style that is peculiar to himself.

It is so closely a result of his personal attitude toward nature, particularly toward the dawn and evening, which were his favorite moments, that a letter to Jules Dupré, in which he describes his sensations at these moments, gives one an understanding of his style:

One gets up early, at three in the morning, before the sun; one goes and sits at the foot of a tree; one watches and waits.

One sees nothing much at first. Nature resembles a whitish canvas on which are sketched scarcely the profiles of some masses; everything is perfumed, and shines in the fresh breath of dawn. Bing! The sun grows bright, but has not yet torn asunder the veil behind which lie concealed the meadows, the dale, and hills of the horizon. The vapors of night still creep, like silvery flakes, over the numbed-green vegetation. Bing! Bing! — a first ray of sunlight — a second ray of sunlight — the little flowers seem to wake up joyously. They all have their drop of dew which trembles—the chilly leaves are stirred with the breath of morning — in the foliage the birds sing unseen — all the flowers seem to be saying their prayers. Loves on butterfly wings frolic over the meadow and make the tall plants wave— one sees nothing—yet everything is there—the landscape is entirely behind the veil of mist, which mounts, mounts, sucked up by the sun; and, as it rises, reveals the river, plated with silver, the meadows, trees, cottages, the receding distance—one distinguishes at last everything that one had divined at first.

How spontaneous a commentary upon his pictures of early morning—nature in masses, fresh and fragrant, the "numbed-green" of the vegetation, the shiver of leaves, and the twinkling of flowers, the river plated with silver, and the sky suffused with misty light!

In the same letter he describes the evening:

Nature drowses — the fresh air, however, sighs among the leaves—the dew decks the velvety grass with pearls. The nymphs fly—hide themselves—and desire to be seen. Bing!—a star in the sky which pricks its image on the pool. Charming star, whose brilliance is increased by the quivering of the water, thou watchest me—thou smilest to me with half-closed eye! Bing!— a second star appears in the water, a second eye opens. Be the harbingers of welcome, fresh and charming stars. Bing! Bing!

EDGE OF THE FOREST OF FONTAINEBLEAU   LOUVRE, PARIS   ROUSSEAU

DANCE OF THE NYMPHS   LOUVRE, PARIS

COROT

Bing!—three, six, twenty stars. All the stars in the sky are keeping tryst in this happy pool. Everything darkens, the pool alone sparkles. There is a swarm of stars—all yields to illusion. The sun being gone to bed, the inner sun of the soul, the sun of art, awakes. Bon! there is my picture done!

This expresses the dreaming of a poet, and during the last twenty-five years of his life, when his best work was done, it was in this way that he worked. Years ago his father had given him a little house in Ville d'Avray, near Paris, and thither during the summer the old bachelor repaired with his sister. The time was spent in filling his soul with visions of nature, which, when he returned to Paris, were transferred to canvas. This picture that we are studying was painted in 1851, before Corot had reached his final style. It still shows some traces of classic feeling, particularly in the introduction of figures; but also a taste of what was to follow in the soft blur of foliage that tips the slender stems in the center. Later on he generalized even more freely; his trees become masses of softly blurred leafage, silhouetted tenderly against the delicate vibration of the sky, trembling indistinctly as in a dream-picture, while here and there, like the introduction of the word "Bing" in his letter, are little accents of leaves or bits of tree-trunk, vibrating sharply like the twang of a violin string.

Rousseau's advice, on the contrary, to his pupils was, "Form is the first thing to observe." The point to be noted is that, whereas Corot had begun by observing form and had then escaped as far as possible from it, Rousseau, first and always, based his art upon it. Indeed, at the middle period of his life the scientific instinct asserted itself, and for a while he sank the larger feeling for the whole in too exact a representation of detail. But, during his great periods, he exhibited a mastery in the delineation of the impressiveness of form that has never been surpassed. His favorite tree was the oak, with sturdy arms supporting its weight of leaves and branches, and strong roots, in between the rocks, grasping the firm earth. The strength of nature, her deep embedded force, putting itself forth in stout and lusty growth, continuously vigorous; the mighty force of clouds that replenish the earth; the vastness and grandeur of the sky in the full glory of midday, or the superb pageant of the sunset, as in this picture; in a word, the perennial strength of nature, as contrasted with the little lives of men—such was the theme upon which he spent his life. While Corot drank in nature, nature to Rousseau was entirely outside himself. He was in love with her for her own sake.

This was a grander attitude toward nature than that of Corot. The latter, in modern phraseology, was a temperamental artist; that is to say, he chose from nature what suited his moods and painted her with a certain invariableness of manner, as if there were nothing in nature except what he felt about her. All that he did was lovely, but it was limited in scope; whereas Rousseau, with his broad impersonal vision searching nature for what she had to tell him, painted in every picture a different subject. It was the phases of her inexhaustible story, a story as old as mankind and that will outlive the last of humanity, that he treated; and it is for this reason, because he suggested the continuity of her elemental forces, even while depicting a certain phase, that one may rightly describe him as the epic poet of the Barbizon School.

The truth of this would be more evident if we had the opportunity of seeing a number of Rousseau's pictures alongside of a number of Corot's; but even from the comparison of these two examples I think it may be gathered. The *Dance of the Nymphs* is a morning poem; breathing the freshness of a world that, despite of time, is forever innocent and young. The creatures that enliven it, nymphs and satyrs, are the effervescence of fancy, removed very far from the responsibilities and daily experiences of life. The figures which Corot introduces in his landscapes are always embodiments of the spirit of the scene, like the Dryads, Naiads, and Oreads of the old Greek imagining. But in Rousseau's Sunset Scene another day of labor is finished; rest is brooding down upon the tired earth; creatures nearer to nature than beings in the shape of humanity are taking their fill of water before they too settle down upon the earth, that mighty bosom from which all things draw nourishment and on which all rest. Those same cows—or others like them—will inhabit the same scene to-morrow; those sturdy trees and branches will survive another and another day, as they have weathered many; that boulder will defy the effort of time to remove it. The scene, as Rousseau painted it, is typical and elemental; not alone a spot on the edge of the forest of Fontainebleau, but a poem of universal import, whose theme is the ever-present one of earth's enduring strength, and of recurring toil and rest. Rousseau reached this power of elemental expression by continually concentrating his great faculty of observation upon the fundamental qualities of nature, which as compared with man's moods and changes are the same yesterday, to-day, and forever. Corot, on the contrary, nourishing his moods on nature, ended by interpreting these moods of his own rather than nature herself. He is not the great descriptive, epic poet, alive to the mighty forces that underlie the vastness of his subject, but the sweet, lyric singer of a few choice moments. As he said himself: he is the lark; Rousseau, the eagle.

For Corot recognized Rousseau's superiority not only in wider sweep of vision but in his mastery over form; and form is the foundation of all great painting, whether of the human figure or landscape. It is with the close study of forms of nature that all great landscape-painters have begun, even if, like Corot, they subsequently try to merge the form in the expression of the sentiments which the objects of the landscape arouse. For the painter cannot represent spirit to the mind, except by representing to the eye a real suggestion of the form in which it is embodied. This is the lesson of all the landscape-painting which has followed upon the new movement of the Fontainebleau-Barbizon artists.

Landscape to-day is the most living branch of painting; nowhere more so than in our own country. American painters have continued the nature-study and poetic feeling of the Barbizon men, and often have gone farther than they in the rendering of light and air and of the manifold variety of nature's coloring. But whenever we come upon men of commanding talent, such as

George Inness, Alexander Wyant, Homer Martin and Winslow Homer, and very many others among the living, we shall find that while often they prefer to subordinate form to poetical impression, it is with the precise and patient study of form that they first began. Upon this firm foundation they have subsequently erected the spiritualized fabrics of their poetic fancies. They have not builded castles in the air, but delicate structures planted firmly upon the facts of earth. Hence the hold they take upon the perceptive faculty; for they reach us first through our experience, and then delight our imagination.

CHAPTER XXIII

JEAN AUGUSTE DOMINIQUE INGRES   *AUGUSTE RENOIR*
1780–1867   *1841–1919*
Classical School of France   *Impressionist School of France*

INGRES, living to the great age of eighty-seven, had ceased painting before Renoir began. Why, then, do we couple them for comparative study?

The fact is that the lives of these two men form an arch, which, springing from the eighteenth century, spans the entire period of the nineteenth. The art of each is built upon a basis diametrically opposed to that of the other—Ingres's on line, Renoir's on color; but the curve of the one melts into the curve of the other, both uniting in an arc of beauty, which completes the expression of the French genius, as revealed so far in painting.

Ingres was David's most famous pupil, bred to his master's Classicalism; and he was the bitterest opponent of Delacroix and the Romanticism which the latter represented. Renoir belongs to the group of Impressionists, who were intent on rendering their subject in its actual environment of lighted atmosphere. Yet, unlike the rest of the Impressionists, Renoir was not only an innovator but also a continuer of the French tradition. His art carried forward the French art of the eighteenth century, which, as we have seen, was inspired by the example of Rubens. He represents the most characteristic element in French art, its northern inheritance from Flemish art; as contrasted with the southern influence, derived from Italy. It is the latter which Ingres represents. For he soon abandoned the classical formalism of his master and became an eager student of the Italian artists of the sixteenth century, particularly of Raphael.

It was not, however, in the way of imitation that Ingres approached the masters of the High Renaissance, but to study the principles of Italian idealism. The latter, he found, was based, not, as in the case of David's, upon formulas derived at second-hand from antique sculpture, but, as in the case of Greek idealism, from the first-hand study of nature. Ingres, in fact, by a different road reached the same end as Renoir: for both of them nature was the basis of their art. But, while Renoir resumed the tradition of Rubens, Ingres became a continuer of the still older one—the Greek. Each in his own way—Ingres by line and form, Renoir with the added means of color—once more emphasized the importance of design: the principle that a picture first and foremost should be decorative; and both, by reliance upon tradition, maintained the importance of style.

In the foregoing paragraph we have summarized the part played by these two artists in the story of modern French painting. Let us now enter more fully into each point and try to discover its bearing upon the general situation of modern art.

Ingres was the champion of the Classic, as opposed to Classicalism; Renoir, not in words but in deeds, represented a protest against modern Impressionism. It is around these two facts that their influence upon modern art revolves.

In the first place, let us clearly distinguish between the meanings of Classic and Classicalism. On the face of it, Classic implies the real thing; Classicalism is a more or less insincere and false kind of way of understanding and applying the lesson of the Classic. An artist adheres to the Classic tradition when he founds his own art on the principles involved in Greek art. A Classicalist, on the other hand, is one who ignores the principles and tries to reproduce the manner rather than the spirit of Greek art.

This distinction was very well stated, so long ago as 1711, by the third Earl of Shaftesbury in his forgotten work, *Man, Matters, Opinions, and Times.* In criticizing those who try to reproduce the manner instead of the spirit of the Classic, he says, "We should not *imitate* but *emulate* the Greeks, for we shall be most like the Greeks when most like ourselves." Compare with this the dictum of Winckelmann already quoted in the chapter on David: "The sole means for art to become, aye, if possible, inimitably great, is the imitation of the ancients." Winckelmann was the prophet of Classicalism. Classicalism, in fact, is *imitation* of the Greek, while the real thing, the Classic tradition, involves *emulation* of the Greek.

In what consists that Greek spirit and practice which the modern artist may emulate? In the first place the Greeks sought inspiration in and based their art on nature; but, in the second place, they were not crude naturalists, imitating nature. How then shall we explain their attitude toward and use of nature? They recognized the beauties of nature, but found nature operating against her own beauties at every turn. They noted that nature lessened the significance of her beauties by over-repetition and contradicted them by incongruous oppositions. Nature, in fact, is too prodigal and at the same time too haphazard. Art must correct this by employing the two great principles of selection and ordered arrangement.

Let us interrupt the argument for a moment with an illustration. I have seen a famous actor spend nearly fifteen minutes on the stage in the act of dying. It was explained, as if it were an artistic virtue, that he had visited hospitals to study the prolonged agony of death and reproduced or imitated the natural conditions on the stage. What was the result? The audience, at first riveted with interest, slackened into weariness and became restless. In plain English, it grew bored. Instead of enhancing the significance of the death-scene, the actor made it tiresome. The reason is that he was depending upon nature instead of upon art. Had he, after close observation of the incidents of dying, selected such as seemed most characteristic of this particular form of death and then arranged these in an orderly sequence of increasing poignancy, until it culminated in the final agony, the scene would have made no strain on our patience, but gripped us and held us spellbound and left us with a keen, realizing sense of the import of the tragedy. The actor, instead of exhibiting the tricks of imitation, would have proved himself an artist by his capacity to enhance the significance of nature.

It was this difference between nature and art—a

difference so often overlooked and at no time more than the present day—that was so clearly understood by the Greeks.

The next question is, how did the Greeks enhance the significance of nature, or, as we may put it, raise nature to her highest coefficiency? In a word, by selecting and organizing with a view to the expression of pure beauty. From the wide-flung beauty of nature, they learned the principles underlying all organic beauty; the beauty, that is to say, which is inherent in a thing created with organs that have special functions to perform in relation to the whole. Thus in a thing as small as a leaf they could discover all the principles of organic beauty. It has its central sap-duct about which all the structure of the leaf is built. Contrasted with the main line of growth are the auxiliary ducts, which, connected by tangential curves and radiating on either side in rhythmic repetition, form a sequence of variation in correspondence with the gradual swell and diminution of the leaf's form. In fact, the principle of beauty involved is that of all organic beauty, the combination of contrasts and repetition, rhythmically related in a harmony of growth, wherein all the parts perform with least waste and most efficiency their natural functions in the life of the whole. Needless to add that the beauty of the leaf is but a part of the larger organic beauty of the tree, differing in form, but similar in the principles of its growth to every part in the harmonious whole.

Now these principles of rhythmic contrasts and repetitions, harmoniously organized to secure the perfect function of the whole life of growth, the Greeks applied

MADAME RIVIÈRE   JEAN AUGUSTE DOMINIQUE INGRES

LOUVRE, PARIS

AT THE CONCERT   AUGUSTE RENOIR

PRIVATE COLLECTION, U.S.A.

to the rendering of the human form. Note, first, that it was living form and the life of form, the life of growth and the growth of life, which the Greek sculptor sought to express. The conditions of life in Greece gave him abundant opportunity of studying the nude form in movement. He could watch, for example, the young men, as they trained their bodies for feats of strength and speed in the *palaestra;* and note how unnecessary or wasteful movements were gradually abandoned and the necessary ones were still better and better adapted to the purpose in hand. Also by comparing the methods of experts he would note that one surpassed another in some certain way. It might be that one excelled in the development of his torso, another in his legs, a third in carriage of his torso or in the swing of legs and arms. So observing, always with an eye to which particular development or action was best suited for the end in view, he could at length obtain a synthesis of grace and efficiency. Thus he made, for example, his statue of *discobolos;* a figure so harmoniously developed, with action and gestures so rhythmically coördinated to the purpose of the game, that were such a man to be found in actual life he would be the ideal discus-thrower.

For the Greek ideal of beauty was essentially a practical one; it was no mere abstract perfection of proportion, harmonies, and rhythms, but the finest possible coordination of these qualities with a view to perfecting the functional relation of each and every part in the growth of an organic unity. If you examine a photograph or cast of the *discobolos* you will find that the figure presents a perfect equilibrium, owing to its being built up by a series of contrasts and repetitions in the disposition of the various parts. Meanwhile, it is not a stationary equilibrium, but a moving one; an instant of concentration between the accumulation of momentum and the letting of it loose. There is no suspense of action, still less rigidity of pose. One can feel in the pose the energy which has produced it, and also feel in anticipation the movement by which the energy will be released.

Perhaps we can now appreciate how Ingres' devotion to the Classic tradition caused him to revolt from the Classicalism of David. The latter imitated what Winckelmann advocated, the "marble manner," and his figures, imitated from antique sculpture, notwithstanding their excessive gesticulations, are lifeless blocks. Ingres, on the other hand, was led by the example of the Italians to the true source of art from which Italians and Greeks alike had drawn. He based his idealism on nature.

He was least good, because least himself, in some of his monumental decorations; as for example in his altarpiece, *The Vow of Louis XIII,* where he allowed himself to be influenced by the conventions of composition adopted by the Italians for works of this character. On the other hand, he was at his best and most himself when, in emulation of the Greek attitude toward nature, he composed such masterpieces as *Œdipus and the Sphinx, The Source,* and the *Odalisque.* For in all these the nude forms possess the suppleness of living movement, while at the same time their curves and planes flow into one another in a sequence of rhythms more perfect than that of nature. The natural beauty has received enhanced significance through being controlled and organized by the artist's design. It is, in a word, the design of these compositions which is the measure of their beauty.

Ingres' mastery of design is equally apparent in his portraits, such as the present one of *Madame Rivière,* in which the rhythms of the composition are secured by the pose of the figure and the lines and planes of the draperies. For it is upon the planes even more than the lines that the beauty of this composition depends. The linear design, it is true, is most distinguished for the languorous grace of its pattern of contrasted and repeated curves. They intersect so artfully, forming here a closely woven web, like the interlace of reflections on the ripples of a shallow brook, here sweeping boldly around smooth open spaces. But, after all, these lines are only the contours of a scheme of concave and convex planes. The pattern of the composition is not that of a *flat* map, but of a map in *relief;* and it is upon this rise and fall of surface, varied so cunningly, as plane melts into plane, now spherical, now cone-shaped, here broad and smooth in area and there drawn into reedlike flutings, that the artist's consummate skill and feeling have been expended. Ingres has felt his subject in its *plastic* bulk and has composed it with the rare feeling for what we have described elsewhere as the "tactile-values."

In brief, then, Ingres in this work, and in his other pictures, proved himself a great designer, whose composition is beautiful in its arrangement of lines, but is also distinguished by the rarer quality of being constructed out of form, presenting a relief-pattern of planes, which not only please the eye, but stimulate the imagined delight of touch. This, too, is the secret of Renoir's art.

Renoir owed much to Ingres. At first a follower of Manet, he adhered to that principle of composition, common to all the Impressionists, that the canvas must be first and foremost decorative. In this direction he was influenced by the purity of Ingres' designs. But the latter affected him further, for they inspired in him the feeling for plastic design. It is in this respect that Renoir differs from Manet and Monet, and, indeed, from all the Impressionists except Degas, who also was an admirer of Ingres. For the Impressionists, noting how the effect of light is to flatten the appearance of objects, were partial to flatness in their compositions. Renoir, however, like Degas, following Ingres, abandoned the flat decoration in favor of the plastic. But he differs from Ingres in the fact that his method of building up the roundness of his forms is the Impressionistic one of rendering the values of light in *plein-air*.

Instead of posing his figures, as Ingres did, in a studio, where a cool light falls upon them from one direction, Renoir placed them in open sunshine, where the warm light is diffused over the whole form. He paints them in their environment of lighted air, rendering the diversities of its effect upon the infinite facets of color-value, presented by the flesh and draperies. Note how this feeling for color differs from Ingres. The latter, although he taught that form was everything, color nothing, could yet display a refined sense of color. But it was in the choice of *local* colors. In our present example, the lady's dress is cream; the shawl of a similar color, embroidered in dull red and green; the cushions are a cold blue. The color scheme, in fact, is distinguished by a severe refinement; but it is almost as devoid of nuances as the bald statement of its hues.

Renoir, however, had he adopted the same scheme of local color, would have elaborated what is at most a melody of color into a complex orchestration. Each local color would have been broken up into a diversity of tones, according as the quantity, quality, and direction of the light variously affected the surfaces, and, more than that, he would have united all these contrasts and repetitions, these sequences and rhythms of color-value into a harmony of luminosity. The figures and their surroundings would have been built up into a plastic composition that would seem to be constructed out of light.

This result was not achieved by Renoir in his early period, when he was still pursuing schemes of black and gray and white, which he, in common with Manet, learned from the example of Velasquez. But when Manet himself stepped out into the open air and began to paint objects in the full warmth of sunshine, Renoir followed his lead and outdistanced him. For then it was that Renoir, consciously or unconsciously, began to resume the tradition of French painting, which had been violently interrupted by the Revolution. He joined hands with the decorative painters of the eighteenth century— from Fragonard back through Boucher and Lancret to Watteau—and so reëstablished the bond which unites modern French painting to Rubens. And it is a bond which includes even the Classic Ingres; for it is based on style.

Renoir, like Ingres, stands for the prime importance of decorative design, and not for a design of flat composition, but one that is plastic. Both these artists—one from the point of view of pure form, the other from that of form as the embodiment of luminous color—were a virtual protest against the flat decorative compositions alike of the Classicalists and the Impressionists; and accordingly played their part in bridging over the gap which had been separating modern painting from the old art of the Italians and Flemish. Both also in their modern attitude toward nature carried forward the old tradition. Ingres modernized the principles of art he had learned from Raphael, the Florentine master of form; Renoir brought "up to date" the art of the Flemish colorists by applying to it the principles of modern open-air painting.

The example of Renoir, *At the Concert,* was painted in 1880, and marks the date when his earlier use of black, gray, and white was yielding to the luscious splendor of his later palette. It is interesting to compare the composition with that of Ingres' *Madame Rivière.* Renoir's also is constructed on a system of intersecting arcs, full of languorous suggestion, and reveals a similar feeling for plastic volume of form and tactile values. That the surfaces seem broader and simpler than those in Ingres' composition is because in the case of the latter the photograph could reproduce the linear arrangement, whereas here it is powerless to suggest the even greater subtlety of the color-

values. The original alone can give an idea of the
nuances of color with which the flesh parts softly palpi-
tate and the draperies and hair vibrate. It is indeed in
his treatment of nude forms that Renoir is at his best.
He has nothing of the torrential force of Rubens; but
replaces it by a more subtle and exquisite sense of color
and a feeling at once more natural and refined.

CHAPTER XXIV

GUSTAVE COURBET	*ARNOLD BOECKLIN*
1819–1877	*1827–1901*
Realistic School of France	*Romantic German School*

GLANCE at these two pictures—Boecklin's *Isle of the Dead* and Courbet's *Funeral at Ornans*—reveals at once a great contrast.

In Boecklin's composition the horizontal line is subordinated to the vertical ones; these spire up or tower in bastion-like masses, lifting our imagination with them. In Courbet's, however, the almost level line of the landscape shuts down like a lid upon the parallel horizontal group of figures; the only vertical line that detaches itself is that of the crucifix; but this is too slight to overcome the impression that the composition holds our thoughts to the ground.

These differences of composition correspond to the differences of the artists' motives. Boecklin sought to produce an effect of solemn grandeur, of tranquil isolation, not unmixed with awe; of contrast between the monumental permanence of the island and the frailty and insignificance of the boat, which carries the mourner and the dead over the shifting water to the dead's long home. On the other hand, in Courbet's picture there is no grandeur either of sentiment or appearance; none of the awe that belongs to isolation nor much of the solemnity that attaches to a funeral, for even the ecclesiastical ceremoniousness is offset by the grave-digger in his shirt-sleeves and by the presence of a dog. As for the crowd, some few are mourners, but the rest, drawn thither only by curiosity, or in some cases, as we may judge from their costumes, in an official capacity; all very ordinary every-day people, going through with the business according to the usual routine. For, while Boecklin's picture is a vision of the imagination, Courbet's is a record of facts, the fact of committing a corpse to the ground, as the artist had seen it in his native town of Ornans; a record, so entirely prosaic, that very likely it repels us at first, though it may end by fascinating us for the very reason of its uncompromising truth to reality.

Courbet, in fact, was a realist; Boecklin, a painter-poet. The two ideas, although wide apart, are not absolutely separated, for we shall see presently that the German's poetry was based upon reality and that the Frenchman's realism could yield a measure of poetry. Yet, for a while, it will be better to study the two separately.

We have noted how the classic motive, under the influence of David, marked the beginning of the nineteenth century, and was carried on by his followers, particularly by Ingres. Also that it was attacked, on the one hand by the Romanticists, under the leadership of Delacroix, and on the other by the group of artists at Barbizon who made the study of nature their motive; and that amid this group of naturalists Millet was the great naturalist painter of the peasants, representing them exactly as they appeared in the pursuit of their daily employments.

But in 1850, when Courbet painted the *Funeral at Ornans,* Millet was known only to a few beyond the limits of Barbizon; none of those Barbizon men had as yet influenced the world; Paris itself, the center of the arts, was the citadel of Classicism. If it was to be stormed, it must be by a personality more robust and with more love of giving and taking hard blows. Such a one was Courbet.

Ornans, his birthplace, is near the beautiful valley of the Doubs, close to the western boundary of Switzerland, and it was here as a boy, and later as a man, that he absorbed the love of landscape, of streams and waterfalls, overhung with rocks and trees, and of quiet pools where the deer steal down to drink; subjects that often occupied his brush. That they did so, in itself marked his difference from classic painters of his time, who cared nothing for landscape; but his main difference was of a much more positive kind.

He was by nature a revolutionary, a man born to oppose existing order and to assert his independence. Of massive build, with a sprinkling of German blood in his veins, broad-shouldered, thick-necked, with a face framed in black hair, and features that might have been modeled from an Assyrian bas-relief, he had that amount of bluster and brutality which makes the revolutionary count in art as well as in politics. And in both directions his spirit of revolt manifested itself.

He started for Paris with the purpose of studying law; but, being arrived there, began to study art. Yet he did not attach himself to the studio of any of the prominent masters. Already in his country home he had had a little instruction in painting, and now turned for more to the masterpieces of the Louvre. Even in front of these, however, he did not play the part of a submissive student. He looked them over to see what he could gain from them, and gradually discovered a method of painting that would best serve his purpose to be independent of everybody, to see with his own eyes and to paint just what he saw. At first his pictures were not sufficiently distinctive to arouse any opposition, and were admitted to the Salon. So, too, was *The Stone-Breakers,* in which he first displayed his characteristic self. This picture, representing two laborers in uncouth costumes by the roadside, one kneeling as he breaks the stones, the other planting his figure firmly to sustain the weight of a basketful of stones which he is moving,—a picture in which there is no grace of composition, but the strongly painted rendering of an actual episode in the lives of the poor,—declared itself amid the classical surroundings in the Salon of 1851 as, " a rough, true, honest word, spoken amid elaborate society phrases."

Then followed the *Funeral at Ornans,* which the critics violently assailed: " These burlesque masks with their fuddled red noses, this village priest who seems to be a tippler, and the harlequin of a veteran who is putting on a hat which is too big for him "; " A masquerade funeral, six metres long, in which there is more to laugh at than to weep over "; " The most extravagant fancy could not descend to such a degree of triviality and hideousness "; " He means to sneer at the religious ceremony, since the picture has a defiant and directly brutal vulgarity. He has taken pains to expose the repulsive, ludicrous,

[383]

and grotesque elements in the members of the funeral party."

It will discount the force of these so-called criticisms, to remember that *The Stone-Breakers,* such a subject as Millet might have chosen, was slighted because it represented mere laborers in ragged and dirty clothes, "an excessively commonplace subject,"—and that Millet's pictures of peasants were being rejected by a public accustomed only to the peasants of the comic-opera stage.

Indeed the real offense of Courbet's pictures was that they represented live flesh and blood; men and women as they really are, and as really doing the business in which they are engaged,—not men and women deprived of personality and idealized into a type, posed in positions that will decorate the canvas; frigid, marbleized figures like those of Ingres, or tinted and china-like, such as those of Bouguereau. Among these classical and semi-classical painters, whose art was built on formulas, this huge peasant pushed his way, elbowing them roughly, treading intentionally on their toes. They winced at the realities of life—very well, he would give them the realities as strongly, and, if need be, as disagreeably as possible. He spent his evenings at a restaurant where younger artists and the young writers of the school of Balzac congregated. "I am a democrat," he would tell them; and this too, mind you, in the days of Napoleon III. "By doing away with the ideal we shall arrive at the emancipation of the individual. I admire Velasquez, because he saw things with his own eyes, but these imitators of Raphael and Pheidias—pah! It is the greatest impudence to wish to paint things one has never seen, of the appearance of which one cannot have the slightest conception. Better paint railway stations, the views of places through which one travels, the likenesses of great men, engine houses, mines and manufactories, for these are the saints and miracles of the nineteenth century." He advocated painting things as they are, and proclaimed that *la vérité vraie* must be the aim of the artist. So at the Universal Exposition of 1855 he withdrew his pictures from the exhibition grounds and set them in a wooden booth, just outside the entrance, with a big lettering over the door, " Courbet—Realist."

Like every revolutionary, he was an extremist. He ignored the fact that to every artist the truth of nature appears under a different guise according to his way of seeing and experience; and he chose to assert that art is only a copying of nature and not a matter also of selection and arrangement. But in periods of deadness and insincerity, the mute appeal of a Millet living afar off in the quiet woods is unheeded; it needs a big combative fellow, with self-advertisement and beat of drum and loud-voiced blustering exaggeration, to get a hearing and compel a following. It was this part to which nature had fitted Courbet, and which he played with gusto, to the dismay of the academical painters, but attracting the younger men to a fresh study of nature and compelling older men, like Bouguereau and Gérôme, to infuse some semblance of life into their pictures; giving a death-blow also to the idea that prettiness is beauty.

In his contempt for prettiness he often chose subjects which may fairly be called ugly; but that he had a sense of beauty may be seen in his landscapes; and that mingled with it was a capacity for deep emotion, appears in his marines, these last being his most impressive work. Moreover, in all his works, whether attractive or not to the student of mere subject, he proved himself a powerful painter, painting in broad, free manner, with a fine feeling for color, and with a firmness of pigment that made all his representations very real and stirring. Since his day, and in consequence of his pounding influence, painting has to a considerable extent broken loose from the shackles of conventional formulas, and the sickliness of mere prettiness and sentimentality. The painter, instead of being satisfied to tint his pictures, has learned the lesson of painting, and gone again to nature for his motives and instruction. Modern art thereby is more vigorous and wholesome.

While recognizing this, however, we must not forget that Courbet went too far in condemning the Classicists, just as the latter exceeded reason in their wholesale condemnation of him. We cannot agree with them that to represent life as it really appears, is vulgar and commonplace; nor with him that painting needs no formulas, that it can ignore, for example, rules of composition; that it is impudence to paint what one has never seen, and foolish to learn of the great masters of the past; that "imagination is rubbish and reality the one true muse."

For while art should draw continual nourishment from nature, we must remember that nature is not art. For art displays itself in selecting from nature and arranging what it has borrowed in such a way as to produce a balanced harmonious ensemble. Thus, the wide landscape spread out before us, as we sit on a hilltop, may seem, as

FUNERAL AT ORNANS

COURBET

LOUVRE, PARIS

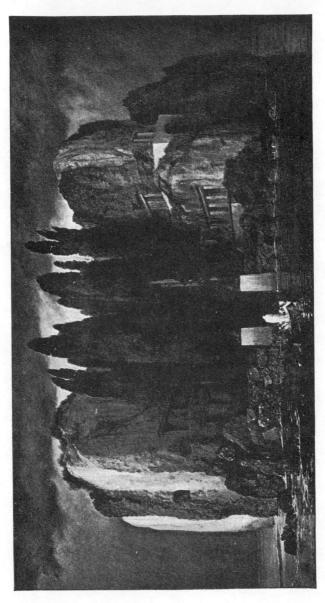

THE ISLE OF THE DEAD   METROPOLITAN MUSEUM, NEW YORK   BOECKLIN

is so often the case in nature, a perfectly balanced whole; yet, if the artist selects a portion of it suitable for the size of his canvas, he will have to adjust the parts of this part, add to them, or leave out some details, if he would make his picture balanced and harmonious. There is no doubt that Courbet himself did this in the case of his marines and landscapes, notwithstanding his assertions that he painted only just what he saw. In a word, he had the artist's instinct of selection, however much he may have kicked against the restrictions of rules.

And now that we realize something of the man and of his motives as a painter, let us turn again to his *Funeral at Ornans.* " A masquerade funeral," the critics called it; " a sneer at the religious ceremony,"—but surely the bearers are performing their task with a simple sense of responsibility; the coffin is not sensationally forced into prominence, but, on the contrary, introduced into the picture with much reserve; priest and crucifer may display no emotion, but they are showing ordinary attention to their duties; one of the little acolytes, as a boy will, is showing inattention, but throughout the rest of the group, the persons are exhibiting different varieties of feeling from deep affliction to almost complete indifference, just as one may observe to-day on any occasion of a largely attended funeral.

A sensationalist would have emphasized every point that could extract our sympathies—the coffin, the beauty of the service, the grief of the mourners, the yawning grave. Everything would have been keyed up to a dramatic intensity. But Courbet, with a wider vision, and perhaps a larger sympathy, has viewed the incident in its real relation to life. "Loss," as Tennyson says, "is common to the race"; death plunges a little circle of near and dear ones into grief, and causes a slight stir of respectful interest in a somewhat larger circle of social or business acquaintances; but the world, outside of them, goes on its way of work and pleasure, and nature, as typified in that level line of landscape, is absolutely indifferent. When you come to think of it, this picture, by merging the poignancy of grief in surroundings of mere respect, and by framing the little incident in the vast indifference of the world outside of it, has struck a deeper note of human tragedy than any highly-wrought-up spectacle of mere sorrow could have done. It also proves how much greater than his theories was Courbet himself. The reason is, that he had the faculty of great portrait-painters of seizing the character of his subject; not so much on the few occasions that he really painted portraits, but in a more general way in all his work. Whether it was landscape, marine, or men, women, or animals, that he painted, he represented the physical aspect of the subject with such force and actuality, that every one of his subjects suggests an actual individuality. You may note this in the faces and figures of the people round the grave. They are all real people, who for a few minutes have left their real concerns in a real world to pay their respects to the reality of death.

And now let us turn to Boecklin's *Isle of the Dead*. While Courbet stands firm and steady on the earth, the German painter-poet lifts our imagination into the upper region of the spirit. The little boat with the upright figure, robed in white (not in black, observe), is the focus-point to which the composition is adjusted, and to which our eyes are drawn in preparation for the start of our imagination. Compare this ferry-boat with that of Charon's in Delacroix's picture of *Dante and Virgil,* the agony of writhing forms, Charon's terrific energy, and in the distance the flames of Phlegethon. Here the boat with its quick and dead is isolated; an inexpressible calm broods over it; its littleness approaches noiselessly a greater calm, a vaster isolation. Its frailty upon the shifting water bears the chances and changes of mortality to a resting-place that has the suggestion of immemorial permanence. I find myself thinking of that solitary peak above Vailima, where what is mortal of Robert Louis Stevenson reposes. Far down below upon the island shore is the lapping of ocean that to human eye stretches shoreless; around and above the bed of rest, the sky's infinity; not " earth to earth, dust to dust, ' but the atom of spirit united to the Universal Spirit. So Boecklin has pictured the entrance of the Dead into the infinite seclusion from all we call the world, into communion with the immensity of the Elements.

It is characteristic of him that he has not attempted to lift our imagination to such heights by representing the island in a purely imaginary way, as a spot that the elements unaided have fashioned out of nature. Men have been here before; living, vigorous men, who have walled off the encroachments of the ocean, set up piers of hewn stone; possibly planted the cypresses, certainly honeycombed the rocks and builded up tombs. An island such as this may exist somewhere; it is not geologically impossible, and might have been wrought to its purpose of a burial-place, as this has been. Thus, always, Boecklin's imagination is based upon facts; and from these facts of knowledge we can proceed, step by step, to the point where knowledge ceases and imagination makes a leap into the beyond.

To appreciate this, let us glance at the process of Boecklin's own development as a painter. The son of a Swiss merchant, he was born in Basel, "one of the most prosaic towns in Europe." At nineteen he entered the art school at Düsseldorf, then the center of the school of sentimental and anecdotal pictures, but was advised by his master to proceed to Brussels, where he copied the old Dutch masters. In this way he learned the actual art of painting, which in Germany had been neglected, the subject being held of more importance than the method of representing it. From Brussels he passed to Paris, and studied in the Louvre, whence he made his way to Rome. Though he returned for a time to Germany and after 1886 lived until his death in Zurich, the country which affected his life, where he lived during that period in which his particular genius unfolded itself, was Italy. It was from the Roman Campagna, sad and grand, with its vast stretches, broken by ruins; from the fantastic rocks of Tivoli, where the Anio plunges down in cataracts, overhung with luxuriant growth of trees and shrubs and vines; from the smoothly sloping hills near Florence, dotted with villas and olive orchards, overlooking the valley and the winding of the Arno, that he drew the inspiration for his landscapes.

Like the Frenchmen, Poussin and Claude Lorrain, in the seventeenth century, and many other German artists of his own time, he introduced into his pictures "a harmonious blending of figures with the landscape." But, unlike these other painters, he does not depict some historical, mythical, or Biblical subject and then make his landscape conform to the action and sentiment of the figures. With him the love of landscape was first and foremost; whereupon, having conceived the mood and character which his landscape should express, he put in figures to correspond with them. This, as we have seen, is what Corot did, whose figures are embodiments of the spirit of the scene. But Boecklin went much further than he in this direction.

In the first place, in the range and variety of the moods of nature which he interpreted, so that his figures, the offspring of his landscapes, touch deeper and more varied notes. Here in the narrow solitude of rocks and trees, a hermit is scourging his bare back, before a rude cross, while a raven hovers overhead; elsewhere on a rocky hillside the silence is broken by the cry of Pan, who grins to see how he has startled the goatherd and his goats; or again, robed figures move in a stately single line through a sacred grove, while others bow before a smoking altar. Further, as the Greeks peopled their streams and woods and waves with creatures of their imagination, so Boecklin makes the waterfall take shape as a nymph, or the mists which rise above the water-source wreathe into forms of merry children; or in some wild spot hurls centaurs together in fierce combat, or makes the slippery, moving wave give birth to Nereids and Tritons. Yet even here his imagination works with originality. These sea-creatures, lolling on the rocks or floating lazily on the water, are full of sensuous enjoyment; there is cruelty in their faces as there is beneath the surface of the smiling sea. Nor are his centaurs shapely, with grand heads, like the Greek ones; they are shaggy and shambling with primitive savagery, creatures of a fierce time while the world was still in the making.

Boecklin's imagination went even further; he invented new forms, as in *A Rocky Chasm,* where there issues from a crevice a kind of dragon, web-footed, with long craning neck and a pointed feeble head, a creature as eerie as the dim abyss in which it harbors.

He was, in fact, a Greek in his healthy love of nature and his instinct for giving visible expression to her voices; a modern in his feeling for the moods of nature; and in his union of the two, unique. Moreover, he was a great colorist. "At the very time," writes Muther, "when Richard Wagner lured the colors of sound from music, with a glow of light such as no master had kindled before, Boecklin's symphonies of color streamed forth like a crashing orchestra. Many of his pictures have such an ensnaring brilliancy that the eye is never weary of feasting upon their floating splendor. Indeed, later generations will probably honor him as the greatest color-poet of the century."

Boecklin as well as Courbet was a man of fine physique and wholesome robustness; but, whereas the German's mind was as sane as his body, the Frenchman's lacked this admirable poise. He had always been a revolutionary in art, and lost no opportunity of being one in politics. From the consequences of his share in the Revolution of 1848 he was shielded by some influential friends; but, when the French army had been defeated by the Germans at Sedan in 1871 and the terror of the Commune had been established in Paris, he threw himself into the turmoil, and received from the self-constituted government the position of Minister of Fine Arts. He managed to save the Louvre and the Luxembourg from the fury of the mob, but in order to do so had to let it wreak its madness on the Vendôme column. Nevertheless, when order was restored, he was held accountable for the destruction of the latter, and was fined a large sum which more than swallowed up his fortune, and in addition he was banished. Broken in spirit, he retired to Vevey on the Lake of Geneva, to die.

CHAPTER XXV

DANTE GABRIEL ROSSETTI	WILLIAM HOLMAN HUNT
1828–1882	*1827–1910*
Pre-Raphaelite Brotherhood,	Pre-Raphaelite Brotherhood,
England	England

IN 1850, the year in which Courbet's *Funeral at Ornans* aroused the anger of the French critics, London was amused by the appearance of Rossetti's *Ecce Ancilla Domini* ("Behold the Handmaid of the Lord") and Holman Hunt's *A Converted British Family Sheltering a Christian Missionary*. It was not only the pictures, but even more the pretensions of their authors that excited ribaldry. A year before, these two young men, Rossetti being then twenty-one and Hunt twenty-two, had joined with another young painter, John Millais, and with three young sculptors, James Collinson, Frederick George Stephens, and Thomas Woolner, and with Rossetti's younger brother, William M. Rossetti, in forming a society. They had taken to themselves the title of the Pre-Raphaelite Brotherhood, and were in the habit of affixing to their signatures the letters, P. R. B.

The object of the Brotherhood was revolt against existing views and conditions of art; in its original intention not unlike the revolt of Courbet, a plea for realism. He was ridiculing the dry formalism of the Classicists, and scoffing at the way in which painters allowed themselves to be bound by the "worn-out" traditions of Raphael; advocating instead a representation of nature as it actually appears to the eye of the painter. In like manner the Brotherhood protested against the cult of Raphael, which, since its introduction into England by Sir Joshua Reynolds, had reduced the teaching of art to arbitrary rules about lines of grace and stately compositions, flowing draperies, and artificial poses, substituting a cast-iron system for the free and truthful rendering of nature. But while the sturdy Courbet flung all traditions aside and found his motives in the present, the Brotherhood, under the dominating influence of Rossetti, who, as we shall see, was already a deep student of Dante and filled with the spirit of the thirteenth and fourteenth centuries, sought the impulse of a new tradition in the painters who preceded Raphael: Fra Angelico, for example, and Botticelli.

These "Primitives" belonged to the springtime of the Renaissance, looking out upon the world with fresh young eyes; even their lack of skill in drawing and their *naïve* sentiment were refreshing in comparison with the stilted, pompous insincerity and soullessness of the modern followers of Raphael. Even the latter himself was attacked by Ruskin, who had stepped forward as the expounder and champion of the Brotherhood's ideals. After citing with what truth to the facts of nature the great masters, and especially Titian, rendered every detail of the foregrounds of their landscapes with most laborious fidelity, he proceeded to contrast the unreality of Raphael's conceptions, taking, as a text, his cartoon of *Christ Walking upon the Water.*

HOW TO STUDY PICTURES

Note [he says] the handsomely curled hair and neatly tied sandals of the men who have been out all night in the sea mists and on slimy decks. Note their convenient dresses for going a-fishing, with trains that lie a yard along the ground, and goodly fringes—all made to match, an apostolic fishing costume. Note how Peter especially (whose chief glory was in his wet coat girt about him, and naked limbs) is enveloped in folds and fringes, so as to kneel and hold his keys with grace. No fire of coals at all, nor lonely mountain shore, but a pleasant Italian landscape, full of villas and churches, and a flock of sheep to be pointed at; and the whole group of apostles, not around Christ, as they would have been naturally, but straggling away in a line, that they may all be seen. The simple truth is, that the moment we look at the picture we feel our belief in the whole thing taken away. There is visibly no possibility of that group ever having existed, in any place or on any occasion. It is all a mere mythic absurdity, and faded concoction of fringes and muscular arms, and curly heads of Greek philosophers. Now the evil consequences of the acceptance of this kind of religious idealism for true, were instant and manifold. So far as it was received and trusted in by thoughtful people it only served to chill all the conceptions of sacred history which they might otherwise have obtained. Whatever they could have fancied for themselves about the wild, strange, infinitely stern, infinitely tender, infinitely varied veracities of the life of Christ, was blotted out by the vapid fineries of Raphael. The rough Galilean pilot, the orderly custom-receiver, and all the questioning wonder and fire of uneducated apostleship, were obscured under an antique mask of philosophic faces and long robes.

And having made a stand for truth to nature and the probabilities of fact, Ruskin concludes with the statement of his belief that in modern times, and especially in northern climes where people are so much dressed up in clothes, the representation of physical strength and beauty can no longer be the highest aim of art; and in an age which is before all things intellectual, painting should make spiritual expression, instead of form, the object of its most serious study. The art of the new age must be religious, mystic, and thoughtful, and at the same time true to nature. And it was because the Pre-Raphaelite Brotherhood seemed to recognize this, that he asserted it was going to be epoch-making.

Probably no critic of art ever had such a knowledge and love of nature as Ruskin, and few have equaled him in the intuitive appreciation of what is fine in art. But he was so much bigger a man than a mere art critic,— a moralist, a scientist, instinctively religious, versed in literature, and possessed of rare literary gifts,—that he could not help looking at painting, as it were, through these different-colored glasses and wishing to have it conform to the color of each. He could not, at any rate he did not, recognize the independent status of painting: that it is not primarily a means of inculcating morals, of teaching religion or science, or of playing second fiddle to the more elaborately explanatory possibilities of literature; but that it is first and foremost a visible expression of material things, just as music is of immaterial ideas. The latter is independent of morals, religion, and of descriptive or dramatic story, although it may contribute very forcibly to all of them. So painting may; yet this is not its primary function. It is an independent art, whose chief concern is with external appearances.

Moreover, though Ruskin was as earnest an advocate of truth to nature as Courbet, he did not understand

the meaning of artistic truth. While Courbet sought
a powerful generalization of the whole subject, expressed by means of a broad and large technic, Ruskin
taught that the artist should render every characteristic
detail with minute exactness. If he painted rocks, for
example, he must show unmistakably to what particular
geological species they belonged; and in his foregrounds
must render the blades of grass and the flowers with
" the most laborious botanical fidelity." The artist,
whose proper function is to reveal to eyes less sensitive
and trained than his own " a new heaven and a new
earth," he would have had pother over nature with a
microscope, emulating the patient investigations of the
botanist and geologist. In fact, he preached—for he
was even more a preacher than an art critic—a sort of
religion of truth, that tended to enslave the artist's freedom of vision and imagination still more than the re-
quirements of the church had done in the days of the
Early Renaissance. The result was for a long time dis-
astrous to English painting and to English public taste;
for it established as a standard of excellence a petty rendering in smooth, precise manner of the little insignifi-
cances, at the expense of the larger truth of the whole.
Ruskin was fond of quoting from the Bible, but missed
the application of one text—"Woe unto you, scribes
and Pharisees, hypocrites! for ye pay tithe of mint and
anise and cummin, and have omitted the weightier matters of the law. Ye blind guides, which strain at a gnat
and swallow a camel."

The Brotherhood, as a compact group, bound together by a common regard for sincerity and high pur-

pose, lasted only a short time. Its members drifted
into separate lines of work, yet its influence upon art
both in England and on the Continent was far-reaching. However, the direction which it took may better
be considered after we have studied the two men,
Rossetti and Holman Hunt, who proved to be the
most distinctively original members of the disbanded
Brotherhood.

Ruskin's contention that modern art must be concerned with spiritual expression was realized in Rossetti;
that it must be religious in motive and truthful to the
minutest detail, in Holman Hunt. This will be apparent in a study of the two pictures here reproduced. In
The Blessed Damozel our interest is drawn toward the
face of the woman looking down; everything else is con-
tributory to the impression that it arouses; even the title
excites our wonder. Who is she, and why that expression of her face? In *The Light of the World,* however,
it is the matter-of-factness of the picture that first attracts us. Its title, even if we have not immediately
noticed the crown of thorns, makes us aware that the
figure is Christ. But there is here no grandeur of drapery, or noble pose, or elevated type of countenance.
The last is that of a man of the people; only the splendor of the gold-embroidered cloak and its jeweled clasp
suggest that the man is more than ordinary. He knocks
at a door, overgrown with vines and weeds, a door,
therefore, that has remained long shut. Every spray
and leaf and flower is lighted sharply by the lantern.
Behind the figure, forming a halo round the head, appears the full moon. We remember the text, " The

foxes have holes, and the birds of the air have nests; but the Son of man hath not where to lay his head."

The appearance of this picture in 1854 had a peculiar timeliness. For many years a great awakening had been going on in the Church of England, corresponding to the political, social, and industrial awakening that was spreading over the country as a result of the extension of the franchise by the first Reform Act, and of the introduction of steam and railroads. As a set-off to what seemed to many minds only a material revival, began a religious one, the nursery and stronghold of which was the University of Oxford, so that it became known as the Oxford Movement. Its aims were threefold: to uphold the direct descent of the Church of England from the days of the Apostles, to promote religious piety, and to bring back to public worship the beauty of ritual that it had had prior to the Reformation. Everywhere throughout the land the clergy and people had been asleep, the cathedrals and churches had fallen into decay, but the new spirit of devotion aroused a longing to revive the outward beauty of the past, and one of the most important phases of the movement became the Gothic Revival. The consequence was that, while the most energetic movement in French art at that time was toward a true representation of the world of to-day, the English one devoted itself to a renewal of the past; and not of the classic traditions, but of those of the Middle Ages.

One can now understand how this picture, *The Light of the World,* appealed to the religious feeling of its day. People saw in the doorway overrun with vines

THE BLESSED DAMOZEL   DANTE GABRIEL
                                      ROSSETTI

OWNED BY THE HON. MRS. O'BRIEN

LIGHT OF THE WORLD   WILLIAM HOLMAN
                            HUNT

KEBLE COLLEGE, OXFORD

and blocked with weeds, an allegory of what had been the condition of the churches and their congregations before the awakening; until Christ, with the lantern of truth, had stolen in upon the night of spiritual sleep, and aroused the sleepers with his knock. After its exhibition in London it went on a pilgrimage throughout the country, and hundreds of thousands of copies were sold in engravings.

In the first place it represented Christ, not in the conventional classic draperies, but in his capacity of priest, in the revived vestments of the church—the alb and cope; moreover, not with a head like a Greek philosopher's, but with the features of a man of the people and the expression of a visionary. In the second place, the picture was full of highly wrought detail; beautiful plant-forms that recalled the delicate traceries of Gothic decoration: metal-work and jewelry and embroidered needlework, the crafts which were being revived in the service of religion. Furthermore, the very exactness with which all these were rendered gave pleasure to a public, that under Ruskin's instruction had learned to look for two qualities in a picture—a beautiful story, preferably a religious one, and a patiently accurate representation of detail.

The success of the picture determined the future course of Hunt's work; which remained religious in subject and minutely realistic. He visited the Holy Land, that he might study the type and characteristics of the descendants of the Bible personages, the appearance of the sacred landscape, the customs of the people, their mode of life, and the implements and utensils of daily use. Accumulating the results of his researches, he sought by means of exact rendering of modern conditions to get as near as possible to the probable conditions of the past.

The most remarkable example is *The Shadow of the Cross,* in which he represents Christ in the carpenter's shop in Nazareth. He not only gave him the homely appearance of an ordinary artisan, but carried the truth to facts so far as to paint him naked except for a leather apron; a strong brown-skinned man, with the muscles shown and even the hair upon the breast and legs. In front of him is the bench at which he has been planing, and shavings of wood cover the floor. He has paused for a moment's rest and is stretching his arms, and the evening sun streaming through the window throws the shadow of his body upon the wall in the form of a cross. This suggestion is so solemn, and the intensely religious conviction of the artist so apparent in the picture, that, what might have been merely a dry archæological inventory, is lifted up to unmistakable nobility. And this, notwithstanding the harshness of coloring, the abrupt lines of the composition, the lack of atmosphere, and the baldness and metallic glitter of the textures. In fact, despite the absence of those qualities which one looks for in good painting, Hunt's pictures are strangely impressive.

Indirectly they gave rise to a new motive in religious painting. Touched by the human as well as the spiritual beauty of the Saviour's life, artists, such as Fritz von Uhde in Germany, and Lhermitte in France, have represented him as once more visibly moving among men. The former, for example, has interpreted the subject of *Let the Little Children come unto Me,* by a scene in a village school in the Bavarian Alps. From the sunshine outside the Saviour has stepped in, and the peasant children are gathered round with looks of wonder, drawn to him by the sweetness of his invitation. Lhermitte, on his part, among other kindred subjects, pictured a family of peasants at their lunch, bowing their heads, while Christ himself, seated at the humble board, pronounces a blessing on the food. Religion to these people is the chief solace of their lives of toil, and so unquestioning is their simple faith, that the miraculous appearance of the Christ, treated with utmost reverence, as it is, seems to have a touching and beautiful naturalness.

And now let us turn to Rossetti. His father, an Italian patriot, who had sought refuge in London, where he became professor of Italian at King's College, was a distinguished Dante scholar. His children were all gifted. Maria Francesca, the elder daughter, wrote a critical work, entitled, " The Shadow of Dante "; Christina, the younger, became celebrated as a poet; and their younger brother, William Michael, is a well-known writer and critic. Dante Gabriel, the subject of our present study, was poet as well as painter.

He was extraordinarily precocious, very early acquainted with Scott and Shakspeare, and the author at six years old of a drama in blank verse. But the chief influence of his childhood was the worship of Dante. He knew the poems by heart. " The mystical poet became his guide through life and led him to Fra Angelico, the mystic of painting." He attended Cary's drawing-school and the schools of the Royal Academy; but could not find in their systematic methods the help he wanted; therefore he sought the advice of Ford Madox Brown, and eventually of Holman Hunt. He was impatient to paint the pictures that thronged his brain, and impatient of the dry routine of steady instruction, and in consequence never acquired a complete command of drawing. Perhaps he was encouraged not to try for it, in consequence of his fondness for subjects from Dante and his instinctive feeling that they must be represented with the almost childlike simplicity of feeling, the mystic dreaminess and sweetly embarrassed manner of Fra Angelico and the other "Primitives" who adorned the early garden of the Renaissance. For in his heart he belonged to that time; it was as if the spirit of those children of painting had, after many transmigrations, become reincarnated on the banks of the Thames.

And while he persevered in painting, he was continually experimenting in poetry. The exquisitely beautiful poem, afterward pictured in *The Blessed Damozel,* was written in his nineteenth year. The picture was not painted till 1879, when he was fifty-one. In the interval he had known the woman who became to his life and art what Saskia had been to Rembrandt's. In 1850 he met Miss Elizabeth Siddal, a milliner's assistant, who was introduced to him as a model. According to William M. Rossetti she was " tall, finely formed, with a lofty neck, and regular, yet somewhat uncommon features, greenish blue, unsparkling eyes, large perfect eyelids, brilliant complexion, and a lavish wealth of coppery golden hair." She satisfied at once his conception of a perfectly balanced soul and body, of soul-beauty shining through the beauty of form, which was his ideal of woman. She became also his ideal of Beatrice, and as such he painted her many times. He loved her, but for some reason marriage was postponed for ten years, and then after scarcely two years of married life she died. But the memory of her abided with him, and almost all his subsequent painting was a representation, in one character or another, of his Beloved. And, with the years, her type of beauty expanded, losing its girlishness in richer ampleness, becoming more glorified in his imagination.

By the time that he painted *The Blessed Damozel,* he was broken in health, old before his time, and not far from death. In 1870 the volume of his poems had been published, and attacked violently by Robert Buchanan under the title of, "The Fleshly School of Poetry." Suffering from the loss of his wife, and being the victim of insomnia, he was wounded out of all proportion to the circumstances, fancied that a conspiracy had been formed against him, and became a prey to the most morbid sensibility. In his misery he grew more addicted to the use of chloral, which he had taken to alleviate insomnia. Only at intervals, encouraged by his friends, who clung to him, could he work.

There is, therefore, a great tragedy embodied in this picture. Read the poem, written in the springtime of his life, when yet he was only dreaming of what love might be. Is it not strangely prophetic, that even then, it was not the possession, but the loss of the Beloved, that filled his thoughts?

> The blessed damozel leaned out
>   From the gold bar of heaven;
> Her eyes were deeper than the depth
>   Of waters stilled at even.
>
>   .   .   .   .   .
>
> Herseemed she scarce had been a day
>   One of God's choristers;
> The wonder was not yet quite gone
>   From that still look of hers;
> Albeit, to them she left, her day
>   Had counted as ten years.
>
>   .   .   .   .   .
>
> It was the rampart of God's house
>   That she was standing on;
>
>   .   .   .   .   .
>
> So high, that looking downward thence
>   She scarce could see the sun.
>
>   .   .   .   .   .
>
> " I wish that he were come to me,
>   For he will come," she said.

Since those lines were written, she had come to him, possessed him, been taken from him, and become his forever.

Devotion to this one woman was the source at once of strength and of weakness to his art. Of strength, because, in the first place, it attracted him to outward appearances and gave form and substance to his dreams, and taught him to express the invisible through the visible, while enabling him to realize the conceptions with which his mind was stored and suggesting others to his imagination. On the other hand, it was a source of weakness, because it narrowed him to one type on which he perpetually harped with variations, so that masses of coppery golden hair, heavy-lidded dreamy eyes, a mouth with curling lips, and a long full throat appear and reappear with various degrees of exaggerated emphasis; while his imagination, absorbed in the contemplation of one idea, gives birth continually to one slightly varying form of highly wrought sentiment. He retreats from the manifold sensations of the open, sun-cleansed world, into a hothouse, whose air is laden with the fragrance of the orchid.

Yet we should remember that this single devotion to one type, while it limited his art, may have been necessary to it, the only thing that could have ripened the fruit of which it was capable. We have seen how Dante, and especially the poet's mystic love for Beatrice, filled his early thoughts. When he met Elizabeth Siddal, he met his own Beatrice; henceforth she was to be to him the incarnation of his own spiritual life, the inspiration of his art as the Florentine damozel had been to Dante's. Nor, while she was the companion and nourishment of his spiritual solitude, is it to be assumed that but for her he would have gone outside himself and nourished his art with the rains and sunshine of the actual world. As we have said, he did not belong to our own age, but to Dante's.

By the latter, and the poets of his time, who followed the " sweet new style " that had been derived from Bologna, love was regarded as the mark of the gentle heart and the service of love as the means of realizing the ideals of the spirit, so that the particular woman was rather a visible embodiment of these ideals than a being to be loved and possessed in a human way. If, as seems well-nigh certain, this was also Rossetti's conception of art and life, it is clear he could have found the best within him only by this exclusive devotion to one type.

He lived in a dream-world, thronged with emotions. These soul-thoughts, too deep, too wide, too vague and infinite to be captured by brush or pen, being inexpressible, he yet tried, as far as possible, to express, sometimes in poems, sometimes in pictures. The latter are brilliant in color, glowing with brightly hued fabrics, precious stones, and flowers; a world of glorious fancy, in which the figures live as in a trance. Never since Perugino had there been figures so wrapped in spiritual solitude as these. But Rossetti's are fuller of expression, suggesting not only mystic ecstasy but a wide range of spiritual expressiveness. Yet, like the Umbrian artist's, they are calm in attitude and slow in gesture, and through this very immobility express the most vivid intensity of inner life.

Though courting seclusion in his London home, at Cheyne Walk, Chelsea,[1] Rossetti nevertheless became the center of a group of men whose influence on art has been wide-spread. Among them were William Morris, Burne-Jones, Walter Crane, George Frederick Watts, Swinburne, the poet, and the novelist and poet, George Meredith. Through Morris and Walter Crane a new impulse was given to decorative art. Sick of the tedious,

---

[1] The home of artists, also, so wide apart as Holbein and Whistler.

soulless repetition of Renaissance ornament, these men went farther back to a study of Gothic and Celtic ornament, which led them to a study of nature's plant- and flower-forms as motives for decoration. Out of this arose a new spirit of invention, which spread over Europe and to some extent has appeared in America, resulting in the revival of a desire for beauty in objects of art-craftsmanship, and in an increase of original creative skill on the part of the designers, until decorative art has once more become a live one.

That phase of Pre-Raphaelism which is represented by Rossetti, "the painter of the soul," was continued by Burne-Jones and was welcomed in France by some artists who were tired of the long series of pictures dealing with the external life of peasants and social functions. They too began to try and express the subtle emotions of the spirit; and from France the new movement extended to Germany, Switzerland, Belgium, and Austria. The Brotherhood, in its beginning, had started a magazine, called the "Germ." Only four numbers appeared; but the seed, scattered, after long years brought forth flowers, the blue flowers of idealism.

CHAPTER XXVI

ÉDOUARD MANET
1833–1883
Impressionist School of
France

EDGAR HILAIRE GERMAIN DEGAS
1834–1917
Impressionist School of
France

IN comparing these two pictures we are drawing a finer line than has been required in most of our pairs. Here are pictures by two Frenchmen, exact contemporaries, both living and working in Paris before and after the war of 1870, friends and fellow rebels against all that the Academy stood for, and yet very different. The comparison may be profitable for this very reason, that in similar situations, similar even to the point that each man had private means and therefore was not forced to sell his pictures to live, two men could differ so profoundly in their artistic or creative impulses.

Manet's great work was to carry further and complete the teaching of realism begun by Courbet. The latter's realism consisted mainly in his point of view, in his habit of selecting subjects from nature and treating them as naturally as he could, with the sole purpose of representing the person or thing as it appeared to his eye. But while his subjects were realistic, his rendering of them in many respects was not. He painted realistic subjects with a recipe that he had invented for himself by studying the old masters. For example, he enveloped his pictures in what has been irreverently called "brown sauce"; moreover, his figures, rocks, waves, and trees, were real enough in form, but apt to be of a uniform rigidity of texture. Manet's further contribution was to add to realism of subject a realism of representation; to render the particular texture of each object and to surround all with nature's light and air. He restored to painting a knowledge of the truths which had been discovered by Velasquez.

This great artist had been forgotten during nearly two centuries. At length in 1857, on the occasion of the Manchester Exhibition, he was revealed to the English. The biography of him by Sir William Stirling was translated into French; Paris began to be aware of his pictures in the Louvre, and from them to be directed toward the Prado at Madrid, where the bulk of his work exists. Manet was the first to become a pupil of the Spanish master.

Now we may remember that Velasquez proved himself original, both in the way of looking at a subject and in his way of representing it; each distinguished by extraordinary realism, his motto being, "Truth, not Painting." He represented only what could be embraced by one comprehensive glance, subordinating everything to a vivid impression; and then represented what he saw as he really saw it. And the secret of that reality was that he saw everything through and in the light which surrounded it. Velasquez, like Rembrandt, painted light. But the latter, under his gray Northern sun, painted with light for the purpose of expressing the *inward* meaning of things, whereas the Spaniard re-

tired from the glowing Southern sunshine out of doors
into the gray light of his studio, for the purpose of representing realistically the *externals* of his subjects. He
discovered that the subject, viewed under these conditions, appeared much flatter than it was usually represented; that form, so viewed, does not stand out with
sharp contrasts of light and shade, but that it is really
composed of a series of planes, reflecting more or less
of light; and that the appearance of color also is the
result of various degrees of light reflected. Moreover,
he discovered that distance from the eye affects the
prevailing or "local" color of objects, the atmosphere
which intervenes introducing successive veils of gray;
so that the accurate rendering of those variations resulted in a new manner of representing distance,—
namely, not by lineal, but by atmospheric perspective.

Manet for some years had been studying the old masters, learning from them their different tricks of painting and producing pictures somewhat after their likeness. But all that he had learned was a knowledge of
mannerisms. Until he became acquainted with the work
of Velasquez, he had discovered no guiding principle or
firm basis. He was modern to the finger-tips; and the
Paris of his day, under the influence of Balzac, was vibrating with the realistic spirit. Courbet had demanded
that painting also should be realistic in subject and point
of view. But what about the method and technic of
painting? Was it satisfactory to serve up a modern subject in the old brown sauce of the Bolognese? If not,
how could a technic be found that would express in
painting the modern spirit of analysis and subtlety that

had been developed in modern literature? The answer was found in the art of Velasquez.

He had been dead just two hundred years; yet, strange fact, in his point of view he had anticipated the modern artistic tendencies toward realism, and, what was still more wonderful, had discovered for himself truths in nature that could be applied to painting so as to produce truth of artistic representation. The key-note of his discovery had been light; the study, the analysis, and the painting of light in all its different manifestations upon the surfaces of objects. To Manet, rediscovering the truth through Velasquez, and to the men who were drawn with Manet to this new-old source of inspiration, the watchword became "Fiat Lux," "Let there be Light." The rendering of values became the chief technical aim of the painter; nature was studied afresh, in order to search out and record the infinite manifestations of light; in place of a pompous grandiloquent style of meaningless painting, there grew up one distinguished by keen observation, subtle discriminations, and delicate truth of rendering.

At Nadar's gallery, in 1871, Parisians flocked to see the work of Manet and the other men of this new group. The catalogue contained a great deal about "impressions"—for instance, *Impressions of My Pot on the Fire; Impressions of a Cat Walking*. In his criticism Claretie summed up the impressions and spoke of the exhibition as the "Salon des Impressionistes." Thus was started the name "Impressionists," which unfortunately has stuck. For it is misleading, the distinguishing aim of the so-called Impressionist School having been to study light, so that they might fitly be called "Luminarists."

The object of the new group was to teach, that the first requisite of a painter is to be able to paint. This, of course, was an attack once more on the academical and classical school, which says the first requisite is to be able to draw. It tried to enforce its point by saying it did not matter what was painted so long as it was painted well: subject was of little account; the first consideration was the painter's ability to paint. This new creed was summed up in the phrase "Art for Art's sake." The conflict over these catchwords stirred up a great deal of dust, which, however, by this time has cleared away, so that we can better understand the matter at issue.

Remember, in the first place, it was a battle-cry, the rally of this new school of realism, against the insufficiency of Courbet's realism on the one hand, and the dry formalism, on the other, of the Academy. Now, as we have had occasion to remark before, men, when they get to the fighting mood, are not troubled overmuch about logic and reasonableness. It is not the well-weighed statement, recognizing both sides of the question, that will stir their blood; but a catchword, exaggerating their own side of it, to be flung at the adversary with a certainty that, when it reaches him, it will make him dance with fury. Such was this "Art for Art's sake," shouted and reshouted, partly because it involved a great truth, perhaps even more, however, *pour enrager les bourgeois,* or, as we say in English, to make the Philistine squirm; the Philistine being that person, either artist or layman, who is perfectly satisfied with mediocrity, and above all things does not want to have his pet notions disturbed.

Now, over in England, at the period we are considering, Ruskin was contending that the highest aim of art is to teach, to uplift, especially to teach religion; which, stated in an exaggerated way, implied that the subject is the main thing. Across the water from Paris came the retort, *À bas le sujet, l'art pour l'art.* Neither was altogether right, neither altogether wrong.

Will an art, that is based only on a keen eye and nimble fingers, satisfy men and women who have minds and souls?

On the other hand, will painting, based on beautiful ideas, satisfy us if it does not make its chief appeal to us through the eyes? if it does not reach our brain through the medium of enjoyment of the sense of sight?

Has not every art its medium of expression; the poet reaching our capacity for the highest through the medium of words; the musician, through that of sound?

But the painter, who cannot help approaching us through our sense of sight—will he, on the one hand, be wise in paying less attention to what he sees and the rendering of it than the poet does to his words, the musician to his sounds and harmonies? On the other hand, should he be satisfied to appeal *only* to our eyesight and leave our brains and souls untouched?

From the point of view of the layman he should not be; and those artists, who limit their appeal to the eyesight and the enjoyment derived from the sense of seeing, will have a limited following. But let us try to understand that the point of view of the layman and of the artist, however much they may draw together, must always be separate.

For what is the layman? He is the man who does not happen to be a specialist on the subject that is under discussion. If the subject is the buying and selling of silks, then the artist is among the laymen; but if painting, then, the buyer and seller of silks. Now, since the latter, if he is to be a good buyer and seller of silk, must find his occupation very absorbing,—so much so, perhaps, as to make other things seem of secondary importance,—can we not understand how the painter may become absorbed, even exclusively, in the rendering of light and atmosphere, and in the power of discriminating with most delicate assurance between different values? It is the thing he can do better than a great many others; it therefore exercises the keenest activity of his brain, and fills him with that stimulating joy which a man gets in doing what he knows he can do well. He may even not trouble himself about the effect his work will have upon other people; but if so, he differs from the buyer and seller of silk, who has to be concerned with the effect that his commodity will produce, when it is made up into a dress and worn by a lady at some social function. The able merchant is skilled in the values of silk and gives value to his public. It may be the better for the artist and for *his* public, if he can do the same.

Once more, then, I ask you to look at a picture through the eyes of the artist who painted it. In no other way can you be interested in this *Girl with a Parrot* by Manet. I might have selected for illustration that other picture by him in the Metropolitan Museum, *The Boy with a Sword,* one of his best works, in which he came nearest to the power of his master, Velasquez. But, besides being beautifully painted, it has a winsome charm of subject, which is not usual with Manet, so that the selection would have given a wrong impression of his work. The latter, as a rule, is quite uninteresting in subject, not infrequently downright unpleasant; what we must expect to find in it ordinarily is only the technical charm, the refined taste displayed in the color-scheme, and the subtle skill with which light and values, atmosphere and textures, are depicted.

The light in this picture is dull, uniform, and pervasive. The photograph has falsified the effect by making the background appear dark. In the original it is a drabbish gray, a slightly yellower gray than the dove-gray on the wings of the parrot, whose head, on the contrary, is a whitish gray. Again, the glass of water at the top of the stand is gray, but a much lower tone in the darker parts, and a much more sharply whitish tone in the high lights; while, still again, the pan on the floor is of dull pewter, a lighter gray than that of the wall and less light than the parrot's head. So far, you observe, the artist has played upon grays. As a musician might explain it, he has given several modulations of the chord of gray, including the major and minor, the augmented and diminished. In other words, he has made a color-harmony of slightly differing tones of gray; taking pleasure in observing and rendering those slight distinctions, and also in noting how differently the light is reflected from the different surfaces,—in a sort of dull and smothered way from the plaster on the wall; deep and lustrous from the bird's wing; more softly broken up from the feathers on the head; sharp and pellucid from the glass, and with duller luster from the pan. The result is, that by careful discrimination between the various actions of light, he has given us a real appreciation of the textures of the different objects—a refinement of realism in the way of painting that is far beyond the realism of Courbet.

The color of the gown is that of faded rose-petals; that is to say, very pale rose in the shadows, a pale straw-color where it catches the light. The modeling has been obtained by varying these two tones, according to the amount of light contained in the various parts of the silk; the only approach to shadows being some dove-gray tones, where you see the dark spots round the edge of the right arm, and under the hand and cuff of the left. Notwithstanding that the artist limited himself to these few tones, and chose a gown which hangs from the shoulders with very few folds, he has made us realize the balloon-like roundness of the garment, and, moreover, the existence of a figure underneath it. Again the expression, faded rose-petals, describes the prevailing hue of the face and hands; the latter are practically of the same color as the gown; yet we shall have no doubt, especially in the original, that the texture of the one is silk, of the others flesh, because of the method of the brushwork. Upon the dress it was laid on in sweeps; upon the flesh-parts, in circular strokes and dabs.

So far, then, as we have examined the color-scheme of the picture, it is a harmony of faded rose-petals and gray; but to prevent it from being tame, to make it resonant and vibrant, certain notes of positive color were introduced; for example, the black velvet band round the neck, a crimson tail to the bird, and the yellow rind of the orange. I may add that this clear note of yellow receives a dull echo in the drabbish-yellow sand, mingles with the rich brown of the wooden pedestal, and reappears more noticeably in the lighter brown of the girl's hair.

By this time I hope we have entered sufficiently into the point of view of Manet, when he painted this picture, to discover that the problem, as it presented itself to him, was not one of a girl or a parrot, but purely a painter-problem—to render by means of paint the real appearance of objects as revealed by light. By limiting the range of his palette, he increased the difficulty of the problem and thereby his own joy in solving it; and, moreover, produced a very delicate harmony of color, which to a sensitive eye gives somewhat the kind of pleasure that the ear receives from a delicate harmony of sound.

We are now in a position to understand the value of Manet's contribution to modern painting. Guided by the example of Velasquez, he once more introduced real light into pictures; sometimes bright light, sometimes, as in this example, subdued light, but light as it illumines space and is contained on the different surfaces of objects. To reënumerate: he rediscovered the natural truth, that objects in light appear flatter than they do when placed in a dark studio, with light shot down on them from only one direction; that in the light there are scarcely any shadows, and that modeling, therefore, is not to be obtained by lights and shadows, but by careful rendering of the planes of more and less light; and that by means of this careful study of values, the textures also of objects could be best expressed. Lastly, he rediscovered the subtleties of nature's color-harmonies as revealed by light.

Manet was sensitive primarily to the elements in his environment that appeal to the senses, to color, to texture, to light—to the delights of the eyes. Degas, on the other hand, was primarily moved by the relations between things, by the order and organization which various human activities brought into the environment. With a much more intellectual approach to the painter's problem, he analyzed the appearance of his ballet dancers to get at the underlying principles of movement and of form which were responsible for the perfection of their performance.

It was the way of these painters to frequent those places of public amusement where people gathered, and to paint Parisians at the races, at the ballet, in cafés and in the public gardens, off their guard and almost unaware that they were the stuff of which art is made. When Manet painted the *Bar of the Folies Bergères* he caught an instant of time with all the peculiarities of that particular moment—qualities of light and color, the degree of smokiness of the atmosphere—which would never re-occur in exactly like proportion; and moreover the barmaid was a specific person with her own personal life suggested though not probed.

Not so with Degas. His ballet dancers are types, one might almost say machines, for they lack all human

GIRL WITH A PARROT   ÉDOUARD MANET

METROPOLITAN MUSEUM, NEW YORK

THE REHEARSAL ON THE STAGE   EDGAR DEGAS

METROPOLITAN MUSEUM, NEW YORK

personality. He studied endless numbers of girls, practicing at the bar, performing, as in our picture, before the footlights, lazily waiting in the wings. When Degas painted a dancer it was a composite of all dancers, and was given the impersonal, objective quality that the painter had automatically acquired in his extensive study. It is this preoccupation with the type rather than with the individual, with the shapes and muscular movements produced by countless repetitions rather than the sudden, personal gesture of a single girl that is partly responsible for the classical quality in Degas' painting. It links him sympathetically with Ingres and sets a gulf between him and Manet.

Where Manet looked back to Velasquez, Degas acknowledged Ingres as his artistic master. Like Ingres, Degas is first and foremost a draughtsman, but where the older man makes his line define the edges, the limits of his form, and weaves patterns of a calligraphic richness over the surface of his canvas, Degas models his form in the impressionist manner with color, but defines the movements, the paths of muscular action, with a strong, vital line. In his earlier works you find that lineal definition of the edges which has already been remarked in Ingres. But as Degas matured, and particularly in his late works, the line became a hidden but never lost tension, and the arabesques of his patterns are like those of the ballet, never actually visible because they are always in process of change.

Edgar Hilaire Germain Degas was born in Paris in 1834, the son of a French father and a Creole mother. His family were well to do and, like Manet, Degas never had to worry about pot boiling. He was free to experiment and free to paint for painting's sake. He studied at the École des Beaux-Arts and in Rome and his earliest works, which are largely historical, won him some degree of recognition from the Salon which later he was to scorn and flaunt. In the late '50s and early '60s he turned more and more to genre subjects and to portraits. It was over a portrait he did of Manet and his wife that Degas quarreled with his friend. When he had got the painting home, Manet decided that his wife's portrait did not improve the picture so he summarily painted it out. Needless to say, Degas resented this bitterly as possibly did Mme. Manet, though history says nothing of her feelings in the matter.

As his individual style developed, Degas' interest narrowed to a few themes which he worked over and over—scenes at the race track—his only popular successes—ballet dancers rehearsing and performing, laundresses, and, in his latest period, the nude. The final preoccupation with the nude parallels that of Renoir to whom it presented, as to the Greeks, the final summation of the artist's problem, an endlessly puzzling, endlessly rewarding theme on which to exert his best powers.

The picture which we reproduce here is in many ways more characteristic of Degas' work than either the early genre scenes or the late nudes. The pastel *Rehearsal on the Stage* which hangs in the Metropolitan Museum of Art opposite an oil of the same theme and of similar composition was painted in the artist's middle period, when he was still exploring the aesthetic possibilities of space as well as of figures in movement. It is characteristic of the artist as of his time that the picture space is not shown as a box reaching back from the picture plane. Another artist in another time would have shown the footlights or their glow across the front of the picture, and the depth of the stage going back at right angles to the forward plane. But Degas turns his stage at an acute angle to the left so that the glow from the footlights comes from the right hand corner of the picture. One sees two men in the wings to the right, the performing group of dancers in front of the footlights, then the conductor off to the left, and finally the other girls whose turn is yet to come grouped in apparently haphazard fashion at the left. The depth of the stage recedes sharply back to the left and the various flies are marked as they project into the stage. By insisting that we view his scene from this acute angle the artist not only gives us a sense of being literally backstage and therefore "in the know", but he upsets our memory image of what a stage should look like and thereby forces us to look more closely. It is common experience that disturbance of the usual or habitual claims our attention as nothing else will. By this device Degas emphasizes our sense of actuality, and at the same time brings us sharply down to the present, to the immediate moment. The picture space clearly would go on indefinitely were it not for the frame which cuts it off. Thus the artist gives us a fragment of space as well as a single moment in continuing time.

The sense of immediacy, of a moment arrested on the canvas, is even stronger when you look at the tense, controlling gesture of the conductor, at the performing dancers caught in a patterned pose which as soon as the conductor's hands drop, will dissolve and form again. Contrast the taut precision of arms and legs and bodies, of the lines of tension that run from the conductor to the girls and back enclosing a geometric solid of space between them—with the relaxed, and somewhat skeptical figures of the two men watching from the right, and the luxurious stretch and yawn of the dancer who is behind the conductor's shoulder. These contrasting elements of relaxation, like violin bows unscrewed, serve to enhance the movement and the quality of the performing dancers.

Degas was once asked why he painted ballet dancers so much and he replied quite simply that he liked their pretty clothes. But it is surely permissible to assume that he answered the question only in part. He was fascinated by the pattern of legs and arms and bell-shaped skirts, put together as though on springs; by that precision of form which he found alike in the dancers and in the race horses, and even in women ironing. One feels the lines of the composition of our picture as the paths of movement and of tension. Note for instance the plumb line that seems to run down the center of the performing group, a controlling axis about which the design is shaped.

But there is infinitely more in this picture than the organization and arrangement of figures. The whole picture space is filled with light; light which brightens to an artificial brilliance near the footlights to the right and becomes dim and shadowed upstage to the left and back. Degas rarely painted sunlight except in his race track pictures of his earlier period. Artificial lights, and man-made patterns always interested him more than sunlight and natural forms. His ballet dancers are not human beings as nature formed them but are molded by a gruelling physical discipline to a form that could best fulfill the demands made upon it by the art of the dance. Renoir delighted in skin that "takes the light", warm radiant flesh tones. Degas' dancers are sallow, their skin has no appeal of texture or color.

In their techniques Degas and Manet show their peculiarly different sensitivities. In the *Woman with a Parrot,* if you examine the actual painting, you find that the texture of the paint itself counts for something. Manet painted, even more in his later pictures, with a full rich brush that allowed to the paint a quality of almost separate existence. Degas, before he gave up the use of oils entirely, mixed a great deal of turpentine with the oil, thinning it out so that it lost all body. He had none of Manet's feeling for the texture of paint itself, and his medium becomes exclusively a means to an end.

As we said at the beginning of the chapter these two painters differed in the kind of sensitiveness with which they responded to the demands of the artist's rôle; Manet is a descriptive or lyric painter, Degas an analytical. Manet selects from his visual experience those elements and details which give him the greatest satisfaction and rearranges them as one might flowers in a vase. Degas selects from a consciously narrowed and intensified experience the materials which he will weave into an entirely new form, something with an intoxicating sense of reality, but to an extraordinary degree transcending any reality of the here and now. In this sense he is as surely a classic as was his master Ingres.

CHAPTER XXVII

JAMES ABBOTT McNEILL WHISTLER   *JOHN SINGER SARGENT*
1834–1903   *1856–1925*
American   *American*

THESE pictures, like their respective authors, present a strange contrast. The Sargent, so brilliantly assertive, is the work of a reticent personality; while the Whistler, so tenderly reticent, is the creation of an artist who was brilliant and assertive.

There is an antithesis in these two cases between the man and his work that is by no means uncommon in the history of art. Without attempting an explanation of this, we may note, as helping toward it, that an artist puts into his work what there is of best and strongest in himself; also that some artists, holding their art very sacred, erect around it a barricade, and adopt a personal manner that, as it were, shall throw the world off the scent; somewhat as the plover wheels around in the air with noisy cry, in order to distract attention from her nest, which is tucked away remote from disturbance in a different direction.

The work of both these men has an original force, that has influenced countless other painters, and yet its inspiration was borrowed. Both owe much to the lesson of Velasquez; Sargent also to that of Frans Hals and

Raeburn, while Whistler gleaned from Manet and the Japanese. The originality of each consists in adapting what he has derived to the spirit of his own age and surroundings, and in giving his own work an independent vitality, that became, as I have said, an example to others.

This statement may serve as a useful definition of originality. The latter is rarely, if ever, doing something new, but giving to a thing that has been done before some new force and meaning. Now that we are reaching the end of our survey of painting, we may look back and see that the progress has been for the most part a series of renewals, of men carrying forward and farther what they had received from others. The most notable example of this in the whole story is that of Raphael, who has been called " the Prince of Plagiarists," and yet his work is unique. It is not the search after or discovery of new ideas that makes an original man, so much as his ability to reclothe the old with some newness of appearance or meaning out of his own stock of individuality.

When Sargent entered the school of Carolus-Duran he was much above the average of pupils in attainment. He had been born in Florence, in 1856, the son of cultivated parents; his father, a Massachusetts gentleman, having practised medicine in Philadelphia and retired. The home life was penetrated with refinement, and outside of it were the beautiful influences of Florence, combining the charms of sky and hills with the wonders of art in the galleries and the opportunities of intellectual and artistic society. Accordingly, when Sargent arrived in Paris, he was not only a skilful draftsman and painter, the result of his study of the Italian masters, but also,—which has had perhaps an even greater influence upon his career,—young as he was, he already had a refined and cultivated taste. This at once stood him in good stead, for his new master, though a very skilful painter and excellent teacher, was otherwise a man of rather showy and superficial qualities. He too had studied in Italy, but later in Spain, and it was chiefly upon the lessons learned from Velasquez that he had founded his own brilliant method. This method Sargent, being a youth of remarkable diligence with an unusual faculty for receiving impressions, soon absorbed. He painted a portrait of his master, which proved he had already acquired all that the latter could give him. Then he went to Madrid and saw the work of Velasquez with his own eyes; subsequently visiting Holland, where he was greatly impressed with the portraits by Frans Hals. Let us see how these various influences are reflected in his work.

In the accompanying picture we may trace the influence of Velasquez in the noble simplicity of the lines, in the ample dignity of the masses, in the single impression which the whole composition makes and the quiet sumptuousness obtained by the treatment of the black and white costumes, a treatment at once grand and subtle. Moreover, the whole picture has the highbred feeling and stateliness of manner, the powerful directness and at the same time self-restraint, that Sargent had found in the old Italian portraits. Yet the suggestion of the picture is thoroughly modern; not only do the ladies belong to to-day and vibrate with life, but in the actual technic of the painting there is vitality of brushwork: now a long sweep of a full brush, now a spot of accent, a touch-and-go method, brilliantly suggestive, terse, quick, vivacious, and to the point, qualities that are best summed up in the French word *esprit*. They are peculiarly French; and in his possession of them Sargent shows the influence of his training and life in Paris, and proves himself a modern of the moderns.

Yet in his case this *esprit* is rarely carried to excess; and when it may seem to be, as in some of his portraits of ladies, one may guess that he took refuge in this pyrotechnic display of brushwork because he could find nothing else in the picture to interest him. Usually, he seems to have received an almost instantaneous impression of his subject, vivid and distinct, to the setting down of which are directed all his subsequent efforts; and they are often long and patiently repeated. It is not a deep impression; as a rule, takes little account of the inward man or woman, but represents with amazing reality the visible exterior, illumined by such hints of character as a keen observer may discover in manner or speech and general appearance. Sometimes, however, it would appear that he had been unable to establish a sympathetic accord with his subject; and these are the few occasions when he seems mainly preoccupied with the technic, or the still fewer ones in which there are evidences of tiredness or fumbling in the brushwork.

In the acquirement of the latter a strong influence was

THE ARTIST'S MOTHER   JAMES A. McNEILL WHISTLER

LOUVRE, PARIS

THE MISSES HUNTER   JOHN S. SARGENT

NATIONAL GALLERY, MILLBANK

Frans Hals. From him Sargent caught the skill of modeling the faces in quiet, even light, of building them up by placing side by side firm, strong patches of color, each of which contains the exact amount of light the part of the face reflected, and of giving to flat masses of color the suggestion of roundness and modeling. While French *esprit* is noticeable in his portraits of ladies, his male ones recall rather the manly gusto of the old Dutch painter. Moreover, in his placing of the figures in the composition, and in the pure, luminous tones of his flesh-tints, he often reminds one of the Scotch artist, Raeburn.

In addition to portraits, he has executed some mural decorations for the Boston Public Library, the theme of which is the *Triumph of Religion*—illustrating certain stages of Jewish and Christian history. One portion presents in an intentionally complicated composition the confusion of gods and goddesses of Egypt; another, also with deliberate intricacy of arrangement, the persecution of the Jews under Egyptian and Assyrian tyrants. Then in the frieze below stand the *Prophets* of the Old Testament, those of *Hope* and those of *Lamentation;* large and simple forms, following one another in beautiful, simple lines of rhythmic gravity.

Upon the wall at the opposite end of the room appears a symbolic representation of the *Redemption of Man,* treated in the spirit of Byzantine decoration, but without the Byzantine formalism and unnaturalness in the representation of the figures. This panel, the latest executed, is the best, being a remarkable example of grafting the skill of modern painting upon the old stock of Byzantine mural decoration, which still remains, by reason of its flatness of treatment, its general simplicity of design and occasional elaboration of parts, the most distinctly mural form of color decoration that has ever been applied to a wall. The *Prophets* share this simplicity of design, but the other two panels, partly because of the confusion of their design,—although there is no reason why a pattern should not be elaborate and intricate,—still more because of the immense amount of literary allusion that they contain, and without a knowledge of which they are unintelligible, may be reckoned the least successful.

These decorations exhibit a very beautiful side of Sargent's mind that was only partially developed; a deeper insight into the significance of the subject than his portraits suggest. The latter are distinguished rather by an audacious vivacity of method, and an extraordinary appreciation of the value of the things which lie upon, or only a little below, the surface. In this respect he offers a great contrast to his compatriot, Whistler.

If you turn to the latter's *Portrait of the Artist's Mother,* you will recognize at once that "audacious" and "vivacity" are terms that cannot be applied to it; also, that the interest it arouses is a much deeper one than you feel in Sargent's picture. For Whistler, not a brilliant brushman, was interested most in what could not be presented to actual sight, but suggested only. Here it is the tenderness and dignity of motherhood and the reverence that one feels for it; not the first blossoming of motherhood, as in Raphael's Madonnas, but the ripened form of it. What the man himself is conscious of owing to it and feeling for it, what the mother herself may feel, as she looks back with traveling gaze along the path of hopes and fears, of joy and pain, that she has trodden. This miracle of Motherhood, most holy and pure and lovely of all the many miracles of life, continually repeated in millions of experiences, Whistler has represented once for all in such a way that this picture will remain forever a type of it.

By what means did he produce this universal, typal significance? Ultimately, of course, by the way in which he has composed and painted the picture; but, before that, through the attitude of mind with which he approached the task. If we succeed in understanding this attitude, we shall have learned a clue to all this artist's work.

You remember that Leonardo cared less for the appearance of things than for the spirit or essential meaning that was concealed behind the veil of the outward appearance. He was in this respect the opposite of Dürer, just as Whistler was of Sargent. He shunned the obvious, however brilliantly portrayed. Now the least obvious of the arts is music. Music steals into the soul of a man and fills it with impressions; into the soul of another man with impressions, varying according to his experience and feeling; and so on into the souls of countless others, with always varying impressions. Moreover, the impression received by each individual is not a definite one, or limited except by the individual's capacity. The impression grows and grows until it loses itself in a distance that we can seek toward but never reach; it passes into the universal.

Why has not painting the power to affect us so indefinitely? Because it must begin by representing concrete things: figures and objects that we can see and touch, and to which we have given names. Therefore much of our attention is distracted by voluntarily or involuntarily identifying these things which have names, so that the general impression, the essence of the artist's conception, of which these names are unavoidable accidents, is clogged and circumscribed by them. Accordingly, if the painter desires, as Whistler did, to raise his own art toward the abstract and universal appeal of music, it must be by diverting attention as far as possible from the means that he is obliged to employ.

At one period of his career Whistler almost completely discarded form and objects, relying, as far as possible, entirely upon the effects of color to produce the impression; calling these canvases, in which different tones of one or more colors would be blended, "nocturnes," "symphonies," "harmonies": terms borrowed from the art of music, the abstract significance of which he was striving to emulate. The public, being addicted to names and to being interested in concrete things, asked, "What are they all about?" and, receiving no answer, scoffed.

But even to Whistler these canvases were only in the nature of experiments. The pictorial artist cannot get away from the concrete; visible and tangible objects must engage his attention; he must found upon them his abstract appeal. Let us see how Whistler did it, interrupting for a moment our study of his paintings by a glance at his work in etching, for all through his career he was etcher as well as painter. Among his early works with the needle is a series of views of the Thames: the row of picturesque old houses that lined the water at Chelsea, where he lived for many years, the wharves, the shipping, boat-houses, and bridges. In the suggestion they give of constructive reality, of detail, and of the actual character of the objects represented, they are marvelous. Not even a man exclusively in love with the appearances of things could render them more convincingly. Then, having mastered the character of form, he set to work to make the objects in his etchings subordinate to the general impression he wished to convey; giving more and more attention to the evanescent qualities of light and atmosphere. Having learned to put in, he became learned in leaving out; and in his later series of Venetian etchings confined himself to a few lines contrasted with large spaces of white paper. But the lines are used with such comprehension and discretion, that they are sufficient to suggest the character of the objects, while the chief meaning is given to the empty spaces. These cease to be mere paper; they convey the impression of water or sky under the diverse effects of atmosphere and luminousness, and by their vague suggestiveness stimulate the imagination.

Remembering Whistler's preference for suggestion rather than actual statement, one can understand his fondness for etching, since the latter demands an effort of imagination, first of all upon the artist's part to translate the various hues of nature into black and white, and then upon the spectator's to retranslate these into hues of nature. And while this is so in the case of *color,* it is much more so when it comes to the point of creating an illusion of *atmosphere* simply by means of a few lines on a sheet of white paper. And a correspondingly keener imagination is demanded of the spectator, which may be a reason why many people prefer the master's earliest *Thames Series.*

In the *Portrait of the Artist's Mother* black and white again form important ingredients, combined with the gray of the wall and the very dark green of the curtain; the grave harmony being solely relieved by the soft warmth of the face. Is it necessary to say that this prevailing gravity, so choicely reserved, and this accent of tenderness, contribute very largely to the emotion aroused in our imagination? Reserve, if it is deliberate, is a quality of force and may be one of dignity. That it shall be so here is assured by the contrast between the upright line of the curtain and the diagonal curving line of the lady's figure, and by the quiet assertion of these two masses. Observe how the latter are painted so that they shall count as masses, with only enough suggestion of modeling to make us feel in one case the folds of the curtain and in the other the figure beneath the dress. The severity of these masses is assuaged by the two gathering-points of intimate expression, the hands and the head. The former are laid one above the other with a gesture of exquisite composure, their color rendered more delicate and tender by being shown against the white handkerchief.[1] The gray wall behind

---

[1] Compare Rubens' placing of the dead body on a white cloth in his *Descent from the Cross.* See page 206.

the head assists in creating an illusion of atmosphere, enveloping the head in tenderness, while the little accents of dainty suggestiveness that appear in the white cap soften the immobility of the face. In this is concentrated the calm and tender dignity to which every other part of the canvas has contributed. I speak of "calm and tender dignity," but who shall capture into exact words the qualities of mind and feeling which lie behind that searching gaze? That face speaks to each and every mother's son with different appeal; it speaks in a universal language, that each can understand but no man can fully comprehend. Yet, once again, let us note that the expression of the face is not an isolated incident, but the center and climax of a corresponding expression that in a more general way pervades the whole canvas; the result of the exquisite balance of the full and empty spaces and of the tender dignity of the color-scheme of black and gray.

Whistler's fondness for gray, which even caused him to keep his studio dimly lighted, may be traced to his study of Velasquez, as also his subtle use of black and white, and the preference he shows for sweeping lines and ample imposing masses. Often in the apparently haphazard arrangement of the masses and spaces there is a suggestion of the Japanese influence, as well as in the introduction of a hint of something outside the picture. Note, for example, the apparently accidental spotting of the picture on the wall, and the portion of another frame, peeping in, as it were, from outside. From both Velasquez and the Japanese he learned the power of simplicity and subtlety; the value of leaving out rather than of putting in; the charm of delicate harmonies, the fascination of surprise, and the abiding joy of suggestiveness. They helped him to give expression to the preference, which he shared with Leonardo, for the elusive rather than the obvious.

Whistler and Sargent belong to America, but are claimed by foreigners as, at least, citizens of the world, cosmopolitans. Sargent, with the exception of a few months at distant intervals, spent his life abroad; Whistler, after about his twentieth year, was a resident of Paris and London, occasionally visiting Holland. The artistic influences which affected both were those of Europe. Yet their Americanism may be detected in their extraordinary facility of absorbing impressions, in the individuality evolved by both, and in the subtlety and reserve of their methods, qualities that are characteristic of the best American art.

CHAPTER XXVIII

CLAUDE MONET
1840–1927
Impressionist School of France

HASHIMOTO GAHO
1834–1910
School of Japan

WE touched upon Oriental art at the very beginning of our story. Then it was the Byzantine offshoot of it that we were considering, and the efforts of Giotto to liberate painting from the shackles of its traditions. Now, however, it is the art of Japan that claims our attention, and it does so because, as we saw in the previous chapter, it was a source of some fresh inspiration to Western painting. A recent phase of the latter is represented in Monet, while Gaho was his contemporary in Japan. They were both landscape-painters.

We have seen that Manet was the founder of modern impressionism, yet in the minds of the public Monet stands forth as the most conspicuous impressionist; and, as his later pictures were painted not in masses of color but with an infinity of little dabs of paint, the public is apt to suppose that this method of painting is what is meant by impressionism. Now Monet, like Manet, was an impressionist, in that what he strove to render was the effect vividly produced upon the eye by a scene; and, working always out of doors, he went further than this,

[455]

in trying to represent the exact effect of a scene at a certain hour of the day. It is the fleeting, transitory mood of nature that he represents. For this reason he was one of the first to be attracted by the Japanese paintings and colored prints which began about the sixties to be brought over in considerable numbers to Paris. For one of the characteristics of Japanese work is, that it catches the fugitive gesture or movement in the elasticity of its momentary appearance.

But the method which Monet used to render his effects is a totally different matter from his way of seeing nature, and of itself has nothing to do with impressionism. Nor was he the originator of the method of painting in dots or dabs. The first to practise it was a French painter but little known, named Seurat, who had studied very closely the experiments in light and color made by certain scientists, among others by Professor Rood of Columbia University, and then applied the theory to the practice of painting. Seurat was followed by Pissarro, and then by Monet, and later by many others, among them our own American painter, Childe Hassam. But, since Monet stands out from all of them as the big original man, this innovation in the handling of pigments will be identified with him.

Let us trace the train of causes which led to this result. Though a Parisian by birth, Monet's early years were spent at Havre, where Boudin, the painter of harbors and shipping, frequently resided. It was he who, attracted by the young Monet's taste for drawing, advised him to go out of doors and study nature. The young man did so, but was interrupted in his studies by

being drawn as a conscript and drafted to Algeria.
Here he came under the spell of the brilliant Southern
sunshine. To his study of nature was added a special
enthusiasm for the effects of sunlight. This was increased when he visited England during the disturbed
period of the Franco-Prussian War, and became acquainted with the experiments in the painting of light
that had been made by Turner. Thus, a second time, an
English influence affected the course of French painting. Forty years earlier the appearance at the Salon of
pictures by Constable had stimulated "the men of 1830"
to go out to Barbizon and study nature; and now Turner
gave the stimulus to Monet to supplement and advance
the study which they had achieved. The rendering of
light became the problem of his artistic endeavors. Then
it was that on his return to France he became acquainted
with the principles of Seurat and Pissarro, and found in
them a practical means of fulfilling what was to be his
particular *rôle* in art as the leader of the "luminarists."

His aim was to render the appearance of nature as
seen in out-of-door light,—*plein air*, as the French
call it,—and especially the various effects of sunlight.
Aided by the experiments of the scientists and by his
own keen observation, he discovered certain facts which
had escaped the notice of less keen eyes unaided by
science; for example, that green, seen under strong sunshine, is not green, but yellow; that the shadows cast by
sunlight upon snow or upon brightly lighted surfaces
are not black, but blue; and that a white dress, seen under
the shade of trees on a bright day, has violet or lilac tones.
Science had proved that these are facts, and the keen,

cultivated eye of the artist corroborated them. Here was a new insight into realism.

Thus far, however, science had only opened up a new faculty of seeing; could it also suggest a method of reproducing in paint the effects thus seen? Professor Rood had made experiments by covering disks with various colors, and then revolving them and noting the color produced while the disk was in motion. This suggested a new way of applying the pigments to the canvas. Instead of blending them upon the palette, the artist placed them separately side by side upon the canvas, so that the blending might be done by the eye of the spectator, standing at the required distance from the picture. As Pissarro himself said, the idea was " to substitute the optical mingling for the mingling of pigments, the decomposition of all the colors into their constituent elements; because the optical mingling excites much more intense luminosity than the mingling of pigments."

If you stand close to a picture by Monet, you see only a confusion of dabs of different-colored pigments laid on the canvas with separate strokes of the brush-point, in consequence of which this method of painting has been called the *pointilliste* method. But, if you step further back, these dabs begin to mingle, until they no longer appear separate but merged into a single harmonious effect.

Let us refer to the illustration of the *Old Church at Vernon*. It reproduces pretty well the effect of the separate dabs—the points, or stippling, as they are also called; but, unless you are familiar with some of the originals of Monet's pictures, it will hardly suggest to you the blending of these dabs. The searching eye of the camera has reduced the effect of distance and mechanically registered the multiplicity of paint spots, so that the picture looks somewhat as it would if we were standing where we ought not to stand to view it properly—namely, close by. Accordingly we receive an impression of a gritty, confused surface, and of a very wabbly, unsolid-looking church, rising up into a sky that seems veiled in crape. For here again, and in the water of the foreground, the camera has played us false. It did so, you may remember, in the drab-gray background of Manet's *Girl with a Parrot,* making it appear too dark; and here the darkness of sky and water is even more exaggerated, since in the original they are a very delicate dove-gray.

For the hour represented is early on a summer's morning, when the vapors that have been sleeping over meadows and river are touched by the "rosy-fingered dawn" and, palpitating in the growing warmth, begin to float skyward and disperse. All the air is a-tremble with silky opalescent mist, through which trees and buildings glimmer scarcely more substantial than their reflections. You can now appreciate why the outlines of the church are rendered so uncertainly, why its mass presents so little of the solidity of architecture. The church, like everything else in the scene, appears to be trembling in the soft, quivering atmosphere. If you have witnessed such an early sunrise, and could see the original of this picture, you would not need my word to recognize the truth with which the phenomenon is represented.

HOW TO STUDY PICTURES

We may discover here a clue to the kind of motive which interested Monet, as well as to the method he adopted to realize it. It was not the church as a specimen of architecture that for the time being interested him, but its aspect under the influence of a certain evanescent mood of nature. With the same end in view, he painted his famous series of the *West Front of Rouen Cathedral:* under varying light-effects of early morning, of full sunlight, of fog, of the last rays of the sun, of afternoon, and so on. The venerable pile is represented with sufficient hint of shape and construction to make us realize its presence, yet it is not its material reality that affects us, but something quite as real, possibly even more so: namely, the influence upon our spirit of its presence when bathed in the tenderness, or glory, or mystery of light. The pictures will not give you the actual appearance in its whole or detail of the architecture as a photographic print would do. But imagine yourself dispensing with a lens and wooden box and a sensitized plate inside it, and receiving the impression of the lighted cathedral through your eyes on to the sensitized plate of your imagination, and so securing a spiritual impression, a spirit picture. It would be somewhat like what Monet produced in these cathedral pictures, and in a host of others, including the one we are studying.

It was indeed a higher kind of impressionism that Monet originated, one that reveals a vivid rendering, not of the natural and the concrete facts, but of their influence upon the spirit when they are wrapped in the infinite diversities of that impalpable, immaterial, universal medium which we call light, when the concrete loses itself in the abstract, and what is of time and matter impinges on the eternal and the universal.

This is the secret also of the spiritual impression produced by Corot's pictures of the dawn and evening; everything trembles on the edge of those gray skies of his through which the eye travels forward, until imagination takes its place and the spirit dips into the illimitable. For Corot could make us feel that the bit of sky which he reveals to us is a part of the infinite ocean of light. But Monet's range of expression is much wider than Corot's; partly because his sensitiveness to color was keener and more embracing, partly because he had found a new way of rendering the color impressions by means of paint. For this reason he has gone farther in the representation of light than Rembrandt, Velasquez, or Turner. He did not have to stimulate the appearance of light by surrounding it with shadows as Rembrandt did; nor was he bound to the tangible, visible objects of his subject, as was Velasquez, in representing their values or the amount of light which each contained; nor, again, tempted to escape from the tangible appearances, as Turner grew to be. The secret of his freer, fuller power is that he used a method of painting which, while it was clumsy and gross compared with the tenuous medium of light that he was representing, yet enabled him to suggest a higher key of light and more nearly to suggest the essential characteristic of light, namely, its vibrative quality.

For let us remember that light is a form of energy that travels in waves through space, until it reaches us, when it floods the sky and pours over all the earth, swimming through transparent objects, turned from its direction, as it is refracted in its course through objects of varying transparency, tossed in a shimmer of luminous reflections from the surfaces of opaque objects; an energy that streams, or throbs, and darts in and out, pulsating continually with vibrations.

It is an approximation toward this suggestion of movement that the *pointilliste* method of painting permits. When we try to read from a book whose print is too small for our eyesight, the little dots of black are apt to irritate our brain, until the whole page presents an unsteady, quavering blur, very painfully fatiguing because it oppresses us with a sense of feebleness. But suppose that, instead of dots of black, we are looking at dabs of color, which, when they blend, suggest a mass of foliage quivering with light; then the sensation is pleasant. Instead of the eye being distressed by the sense of feebleness, it has been gladdened by a surprise of new perception; and as our eye has had a share in creating the surprise, our imagination receives so much the pleasanter stimulation. We are not gazing helplessly at a blur, but likely to enjoy a sensation of vibrating color; color, that is to say, with all the stir of light about it.

The artist in another way also has made it possible for us to see more sensitively. For example, to our unaided sight a stretch of sea may appear to have a prevailing hue of blue, or, more definitely, perhaps, a greenish blue. Monet, on the other hand, with an eye that was by nature keener and trained to an exquisite sensitiveness, saw the blue and painted in blue dabs, noted the greenish blue and added dabs of green. But he saw much more; the presence of yellow it may be, or white in the strong sunshine,

OLD CHURCH AT VERNON   CLAUDE MONET

SUNRISE ON THE HORAI

HASHIMOTO GAHO

and of pink and rose and violet. All these constituent
colors he places side by side in minute patches, and immediately the latter begin to act and react on one another,
as a number of bright people will do upon one another,
when assembled together in a room. I will mention only
one recognized fact: red, yellow, and blue, being regarded as the primary colors, and the combinations of
any two of these—namely, red + yellow = orange, yellow + blue = green, blue + red = purple—being regarded as secondary colors, it has been demonstrated that
the juxtaposition of any secondary with the remainder
primary will heighten the brilliancy of each. Thus,
orange and blue are mutually enforcing; so green and
red, and yellow and purple. While this law applies
everywhere in painting, it applies with more subtlety and
vivacity when the color spaces, instead of being big, are
split up into an infinite number of tiny fragments; for
the result may be likened to an intricate web, scintillating
with numberless dewdrops. And there is yet another
source of vivacity in this method of painting; namely,
that the light is not reflected in broad masses from the
canvas, but from each one of these separate patches
dart reflections, which melt and mingle like the play of
light upon minute threads of gossamer.

In this way Monet and his followers have based their
method of painting upon the facts discovered by scientists in their study of light, and have thus made great
advances in the rendering of light by means of pigments.
It must be remembered, however, that the latter are poor
substitutes for the colored light which they try to reproduce. White paint, for example, which represents the

lightest or highest note of color in pigments, is infinitely inferior in luminosity to white *light*. So, while it is often said that these artists have raised the key of color, it would be more correct to say that they have raised the key of the shadows. By substituting for black and brown or red shadows delicate blue and violet ones, they have increased the general appearance of lightness, and by the increased vivacity and subtlety due to the *pointilliste* method of laying on the paint, have more nearly approximated to the effect produced upon the eye by the vibrations and the brilliancy of sunlight.

In this necessarily brief account of Monet's work I can add only one more particular—that it is absolutely objective. Corot was a poet at heart, seeking through nature to express his own subjectivity—himself; and this is the attitude of the majority of landscape-painters. Monet, on the contrary, was an eye, analyzing what it saw; the brain behind it was filled with passion, but with a passion aroused and satisfied entirely from without. The result is that, while most painters interpret through nature a mood of their own, Monet interpreted those of nature purely; and through the frame of his picture we gaze, as through an open window, at nature herself appealing to us, if we have eyes to see, *directly*.

Yet many people are honestly unable to admire his pictures. The eyes of some are physically incapable of blending into one the separate patches. Others, again, by their temperament have so marked a preference for the solidity and facts of nature, that this spiritualized suggestion of it troubles them. I think one is to be congratulated if one can appreciate both the tremendous reality of Rousseau, the spirituality of Corot, and also the marvelous suggestion to one's spirit and imagination that may be found in Monet.

Now it is the suggestiveness to spirit and imagination that is the key-note of the Japanese motive. Buddhism teaches the impermanency and unreality of matter; that matter is but a limited symbol of the universal soul. The Japanese laugh at our Western art, that tries to represent the human form and the forms of nature exactly. Our artists, they think, in the first place are feeding themselves upon what is not real, but an illusion; and, in the second place, are trying to make the spectator believe that what he sees on the canvas is a real man, or fish, or mountain. He is trying to prop up an illusion with a lie.

Now this is an idea not very dissimilar to the teaching of our own philosophers, from Plato to Herbert Spencer, but so far removed from our ordinary way of regarding this world and our relation to it, that I mention it only to get a starting-point for trying to understand how the Japanese feel toward art. We may state it briefly in the following way.

Matter is impermanent, the forms in which it appears to the eye are temporary. We ourselves were taught at school that the extent and shape of our earth are continually changing ; and in Japan these changes are very frequent and remarkable, owing to the volcanic nature of the islands and to the almost daily occurrence of earthquakes. "Rivers shift their courses," writes Lafcadio Hearn, "coasts their outline, plains their level; volcanic peaks heighten or crumble ; valleys are blocked

[469]

by lava floods or landslides ; lakes appear or disappear.
Even the matchless shape of Fuji, that snowy miracle
which has been the inspiration of artists for centuries, is
said to have been slightly changed since my advent to the
country ; and not a few other mountains have in the
same short time taken totally new forms.   Only the general lines of the land, the general aspects of its nature,
the general character of the seasons, remain fixed.   Even
the very beauty of the landscape is largely illusion,—a
beauty of shifting colors and moving mists."   This was
written in 1895, after the author had been living in
Japan for about ten years.

*This impermanent matter is the temporary manifesta-
tion of the Universal Spirit, which alone is eternal.*   In
every form of nature, great or small, resides for the
time being an atom of the Universal Spirit.   It is this
atom of spirit that is the life of the form in which it resides, determining its character.   The Japanese speak
of this inward spirit as " kokoro."

The highest aim in art, said Hashimoto Gaho, *is to
express this kokoro.*   A picture that gives merely the
temporary appearance of the objects of nature is not
a work of art; it becomes such only if it manifests an
expression of the "kokoro," or, in his own word, if it
manifests "kokoromochi."   At first sight this might
seem like Corot's expression of the spirit of dawn and
evening; but Corot put into his pictures what was in
himself, whereas with Gaho the " kokoro " was entirely
outside himself, residing in the object before him, actually there, whether Gaho himself were asleep or awake,
alive or dead, having nothing to do with himself.   Rous-

seau, therefore, to whom nature was an objective study, who tried to represent the strength that lies in the rocks themselves, and the sinewy vigor that directs the growth of the oak, comes nearer to Gaho's idea of it; and Monet also, who has been described as only an "eye." On the other hand, we remember that the old Greeks also believed that there was a spirit in the waterfalls, the mountains, the trees; but in their art they represented it in human shape, as nymphs, naiads, oreads, dryads. This aim, however, is the very opposite to that of the Japanese artist, who strives to get away as far as possible from the accidents of impermanent form. In his attempt to do so he simplifies, generalizes, and conventionalizes.

So do Western artists, but not for the same purpose or to the same extent. They want to represent the human form or the landscape as its material form really appears to the eyes ; but, not being able to imitate every hair on the head or every leaf and blade of grass, they are forced to give a general appearance of hair, of foliage, or of grass,—they simplify and generalize. Then they make marks on the canvas which are not like leaves, but which we have all agreed to accept as suggesting the appearance of leaves; in fact, they conventionalize: but, observe, mostly with the intention of forcing upon us the material fact of these things being leaves. Some of our artists, however, say : "We do not care about representing leaves, but only the impression produced on our minds by them"; and these men whom we call impressionists, because of their going farther in generalization and conventionalizing, approach nearer to Japanese art, by the example of which, we must remember, however, they have been largely inspired.

Now the Japanese artist, taught by his religion to value spirit more than matter, portrays material form only because he is obliged to make a material habitation for its " kokoro "; but he does not dwell on form. On the contrary, he tries to draw your attention away from the fact of his subject being a woman or a tree ; he eliminates as far as possible the aggressiveness of form, and accordingly simplifies, conventionalizes, and generalizes more than the Western artists do.

In the first place, he does not use oil paints, by means of which his Western brother gives solidity and elaboration to his objects. The Japanese artist paints with water-colors upon silk or paper, using thin transparent washes of color, manipulating his brush with a delicacy and decision that are superior to anything in Western painting. With one stroke of his brush, moving freely from the shoulder,—for he kneels on the floor and works above his silk or paper,—he can render, for example, a branch of a plum-tree, using the flat side and bearing more heavily on one end so as to render the shadow at the same time as the light part, and twisting the brush on to its edge to indicate knots or joints or such like. This in itself represents a wonderful skill in generalizing and simplification. It has led also to a wonderful skill and expressiveness in the use of line.

This is the second point to be noted: Gaho himself says that Japanese painting is founded upon line, that by varieties of modulation of its breadth and of dark and light the line itself may be made to manifest " kokoromochi."

Thirdly, the colors are laid on flat ; forming a pattern of very subtle harmony.

Fourthly, the composition is not based on set forms of balanced arrangement, but is distinguished rather by irregularity, by its unexpectedness and surprises. Nor is it designed to hold our attention entirely within the frame. Often the spray of a flower, or a branch, belonging to some plant or tree that we cannot see, peeps into the picture, as if to remind us that there are other things beyond this tiny view, and that the latter is only an atom of the universe. We have noted, in the previous chapter, Whistler's borrowing of this device in the *Portrait of the Artist's Mother.*

Fifthly, conventionalization is carried to a point where to Western eyes it seems strange. For example, we may look through a number of prints by different artists, and the women's mouths will all be represented by a similar arrangement of lines, which to us does not convey the idea of a natural mouth. To the Japanese, however, it does ; and they would retort that many of our conventions in painting seem to them equally unintelligible and unreasonable. For, remember, that conventions are a sort of shorthand appeal to memory and experience ; wherefore, since there is so much in the Japanese memory and experience that must remain unknown to us, we can never fully appreciate the conventions of their painting.

Every one of these characteristics of Japanese art that I have enumerated has influenced modern Western art. Space will not permit me to particularize, but if you will bear them in mind when you examine pictures by Degas and Whistler, the latter's Venetian etchings especially and the work of many American and foreign illustrators, you will be able to discover the traces of the influence unmistakably.

There is one other point among so many that might be alluded to. A Buddhist text declares that *he alone is wise who can see things without their individuality.* And it is this Buddhist way of seeing, as Lafcadio Hearn says, which makes the greatness of true Japanese art. One might explain this by saying that the Japanese artist discards the accident of individuality in favor of the type, but it is even more than this—that in the Particular he tries to express a portion of the Universal, regarding even his composition, for example, not as a complete finite arrangement but as a fragment of what he imagines as a universal geometry.

And now let us turn to Hashimoto Gaho's *Sunrise on the Horai.* The Horaizan is the Japanese Earthly Paradise ; the dream-place of peaceful and exalted contemplation. Gaho, contrary to custom, has represented it upon the mountain-tops and pictured it in the purest hour of all, in the freshness of early sunrise. The sun itself is veiled in the vapor that rises up from the steep valley, at the bottom of which are the rice-fields, whither the laborers are already wending for their day's toil. Down there are the lives of men, their joys and sorrows, the multiple units of the human hive. All below is clouded in uncertain mists, but up here it is clear and serene; the foreground, a miniature panorama of mountain scenery, with pines, the symbol of eternity, and pagoda pleasure-houses of the soul ; further back, a cone-like peak of spiritual desire and mountain ramparts, barring the approach as yet to the ultimate Beyond.

Study, first, the linear arrangement: the broken level lines of the foreground, the soaring lines of the peak, the lines as of longing piled upon longing of the mountain mass, and then that diagonal line that fades into invisibility. Then from its gradual lifting up into height, and from its flight into the immensity of distance, the imagination settles back to the assured certainty of the foreground and the intimacy of the pine-trees, those familar objects of the Japanese landscape.

Study, secondly, the exquisite gradations of tone, and the way the darks and lights are distributed in the composition, the occasional accents of dark, and the value of the empty spaces. There is perhaps nothing in painting which may give so pure and rarefied a joy as the way in which the Japanese artists give you the effect of definition melting into indefiniteness, and this picture of Gaho's is a fine example of the effect. It states just enough to render the imagination active, and then leaves it to its own wandering.

It is this suggestiveness to the imagination, moreover the decorative beauty and expressiveness of the lines and masses of the composition, and the choiceness and originality of the color-harmonies, rich or delicate, as the case may be, but always subtle, that are among the conspicuous charms of Japanese painting. These may be enjoyed, even when the subject refers to experiences that we do not share or is represented by means of conventions unfamiliar to us. In the accompanying example these limitations are scarcely to be felt.

CHAPTER XXIX

<table>
<tr><td>PAUL CÉZANNE
1839–1905</td><td>PAUL SIGNAC
1863–1935</td></tr>
<tr><td>Post Impressionist
School of France</td><td>Neo-Impressionist
School of France</td></tr>
</table>

IN preceding chapters we noted the beginning of a reaction against the impressionistic method of painting, as practised by Manet, Monet, and their followers. Renoir, resuming the tradition of Rubens, abandoned the flat decorative pattern of impressionistic composition for roundness of form and depth of planes; we have now to see how this principle was also advocated by Paul Cézanne.

Meanwhile, the older form of impressionistic painting has been criticized from another standpoint. It professed to rely upon pure pigments and to aim at luminosity of color; but, in the opinion of certain painters, did not place absolute reliance upon the purity of the pigment, and in its color harmonies stopped short of the highest possible luminosity. This group of artists have called themselves Neo-Impressionists, because they wished it to be understood that they were not opposing impressionism, but trying to enlarge its possibilities. At the head of this new departure in impressionism was Georges Seurat, who led the way in utilizing for the purposes of painting the principles discovered by scientists concerning the laws of light and color. It was, however, Paul Signac who developed the method most conspicuously.

Thus, at this point of our story of modern painting, we are brought face to face with two new movements, both of which are founded on the present-day study of nature. But, while one looks forward and calls in the aid of science to help it to further victories in the rendering of nature, the other looks back to the great days of Flemish and Italian painting, and experiments how the gap may be bridged over which separates modern impressionism from the monumental art of the past. Of the latter Cézanne has been the prophet, or, as he described himself, the pathfinder or primitive of the way; while the leader in utilizing the lessons of modern science was, as we have said, Georges Seurat.

It must be realized that painting, like every other department of life, is to-day emerging from a century of revolution. The upheaval began at the end of the eighteenth century, and the resulting confusion showed little sign of abating until the last quarter of the nineteenth. It was a revolution, not only political, but also religious, industrial, and social; affecting mankind's attitude toward life and toward the universal. Its new faith was science; its weapon, mechanical power; the goal of its striving, intellectual liberty and material progress. It is only by an effort of the imagination that the younger generation can realize how stupendous a change this revolution has wrought in life. Within the lifetime of a man of three score years and ten the old landmarks of society were submerged in the torrent of new ideas, and, it must be admitted, the old sanctities of life were well-nigh overwhelmed in the flood of material progress. For mankind became intoxicated with material progress and mistook it for civilization. To amass wealth and more wealth, to multiply the volume of mechanical production and to command new markets, to add to the conveniences of life by railroads, steamships, telegraphy, telephones, and so forth, to accelerate the pace of life and the wear and tear upon body and brain—these and a thousand other devices for securing material progress men treated for a time, not as a means to happier and better living, which is true civilization, but as in themselves the end-all and the be-all of life. In consequence of this materialism the ideals of life became vulgarized; ugliness spread like a blight over men's lives and their surroundings, interrupted by gross and stupid ostentation in the display of mushroom wealth.

These tendencies were reflected in the painting of the time. Not a little of the naturalistic painting represented the mere facts of sight; not a little of the impressionistic exulted in ugliness, while much of the classical Academic painting was occupied with meaningless display of flaunting nudity or the representation of far-fetched horrors and sensationalism. Brains and taste were too little in evidence in the exhibitions, the walls of which became advertising spaces for catching the eye of a giddy and ignorant public by vulgar and meretricious means. The reaction was inevitable, and it has grown around the art of Cézanne.

Cézanne was born at Aix, in Provence, and it was in this city of southern sunshine and glowing color that he spent the latter part of his life, aloof from exhibitions and the picture market. As a young man he visited Paris with the notion of adopting the profession of literature; but, having been introduced by his college friend Zola to Courbet and Manet, he turned his thoughts to painting. He passed by turns under the influence of Delacroix, Daumier, Courbet, and Manet, and was reckoned among the Impressionists, when he decided to leave Paris and devote himself to working out the ideas of painting which were fermenting in his mind.

He had already shown his independence of impressionism in certain still-life pictures: a green jar, for example, or brilliantly red and yellow apples, relieved with inky shadows, against a gray wall. He needed the blackness of the shadows as a dominant note in his colorscheme, and dared to paint them in defiance of the appearance of the actual shadows to his eye. He cut himself loose, in fact, from the Impressionists' slavery to the visual impression and asserted his right to suggest the *sensations* with which the visual had impressed him. All his life he continued to paint still-life, and while the later examples omit the violence of the black shadows, their color harmonies arrest one by their force. In the apparently haphazard way in which the objects are arranged there is no dignity of line, but their compositions present a magnificent mosaic of color-patches, which have been well described as having the grandeur of something primitive. One enjoys them without any thought of what they represent, and then to one's amazement begins to realize their essential fidelity to nature. They transcend the naturalistic by enhancing the significance of the merely visual impression and raising the latter to the higher plane of sensation.

In opposing the Impressionists' reliance upon visual impressions, Cézanne condemned the flatness of their compositions. It is true that the effect of light is to flatten the appearance of objects and to reduce the planes; meanwhile, what affects the imagination is depth of distance and bulk and volume of form. So, for the sake of suggesting the finer sensations of the mind, he would reject the evidence of the eye. Like the Impressionists, he adhered to the principle of the composition being a decoration; but instead of making the latter a flat pattern, he would construct it solidly in space. Thus he did not base the plan of his composition on the geometric forms of the circle, triangle, and rectangle, but upon their equivalents in bulk—the sphere, cone, and cube.

You may say that this is what the Hollanders of the seventeenth century did in their genre pictures; and it is true that their compositions represent the construction and placing of solid forms in a hollow space. But there is a difference in the motive with which they employed this common method. The motive of the Hollanders, while it aimed at making the picture a thing of beauty in itself, based the beauty on the representation of a scene. On the other hand, Cézanne cared as little as possible about representation; his motive not being, as we have said, to record the visual impression, but the mental or emotional sensation which the sight of the object had aroused in him. Hence he employed this method of solid construction in space in order to make his subject not more lifelike to the eye, but more impressive to the imagination.

This difference of motive is quite simple, when it has once been grasped; and grasped it must be, if we are to understand the latest trend of painting. The only difficulty in grasping it is the fact that we have become so accustomed to judging a picture chiefly and almost solely by the evidence of the eye. We have been brought to this by impressionism and the naturalistic motive, which dominated painting for half a century. It has been the painter's practice to represent his subject as much like nature as possible, and to base his claim to notice on the nature-like character of his representation. So we have gained the habit of admiring his work because it seems to us to be so lifelike.

But, when you come to think of it, this is as much as to say that it is only the things of the eye which are important, and that only visual impressions are to be valued. This, indeed, has been the actual, if unconscious, attitude of a great many painters, and of a large part of the public, toward pictures; and it corresponds to the materialistic standard which has prevailed generally in the affairs of life. We have been prone to judge a man by his capacity to get on, which in the final analysis means to make money. That he might possess intellectual and moral qualities of a high order went for little in popular estimation, unless he could coin them into money or the equivalent of money—power.

Now Cézanne's life and art were an artist's protest against this materialistic standard. It was not his part to preach the significance in life of the higher qualities of mind and feeling; but, as an artist, to illustrate it in his life and work; and this he did. He lived alone, with no thought of making money or gaining fame, and in his work sought to express the high thought and feeling with which the beauty of the visible world impressed him. So, like the Hollanders, he took for subjects, usually, the quite ordinary aspects of life: the landscape around Aix, some fruit or simple objects of still-life, some humble neighbor, man or woman. But, once more, it was not to make a concrete representation of them, such as the ordinary eye might recognize, but to render the abstract expression of some high sensation.

Before attempting to explain how Cézanne did this, let me try to suggest the impression produced upon thoughtful people by his pictures. Since his work depends almost entirely upon its color-qualities, no photograph can begin to reproduce its character. I must, therefore, ask you to take my word for the effect which it produces on painters and others who have come under the spell of it. They find themselves in the presence of something extraordinarily impressive. It seems to be a part of what is permanent; to be aloof from stress and change; to be an echo of the great silences, of immemorial time and infinite space; to hold in itself the enigma of man's brief life amid the eternity of the universe. We are moved by it, not to words, but to deep and strong emotion. We come out from the sight of a number of Cézanne's pictures as if we had been listening to a symphony of Beethoven's, played upon a grand organ.

What is the source of this profound impression? It is certainly not the subject itself. No; it is the high qual-

LANDSCAPE

METROPOLITAN MUSEUM, NEW YORK

PAUL CÉZANNE

THE PORT OF MARSEILLES

PAUL SIGNAC

LUXEMBOURG, PARIS

ity of Cézanne's imagination and his great gift of technical expression. Both represent emotion controlled by intellect; the sensations he experiences and renders have been lifted above mere feeling; the feeling has been *intellectualized*. Let the student who is sufficiently interested think this out for himself; recall what he has experienced of sentiment and emotion in pictures, poetry, plays, music, novels, yes, in life itself; then let him question himself as to whether he can not detect a change in the attitude of thoughtful people toward sentiment and emotion; as, for example, in the relation of the sexes. By this time he will have discovered that the growing tendency of the present is to intellectualize all manner of sensations; that is to say, not only to subject them to the control of reason, but to view them in relation to the large issues of life and living; in a word, to view the local, the particular, and the temporary in relation to the universal.

Now briefly to suggest characteristics of Cézanne's technique. We have noted that his compositions do not depend upon line; they are constructed of color-harmonies. These are based on strong notes of color, which in the case of the landscapes, and particularly of the still-life, are often pure and brilliant. Meanwhile, in his figure pictures, the color-scheme is usually low-tones; a figure, clad in black, gray, or dull blue, against a slaty-gray background, to which the flesh-tints offer the main contrast. Yet this scheme is not heavy or inert, as you might suppose from the description or even from a careless glance at the picture. It has at once an arresting quality and a vibrating animation, which, as you examine the canvas closely, you find to be the result of the blend of hues and tones. His grays, for example, reveal a blend of rose and blue, often threaded with yellow, and the flesh-tints present a correspondingly complex texture of hues and tones, as colorful and luscious as fruit.

But it is not alone by the intrinsic beauty of tone that these color-harmonies are distinguished. Their chief characteristic is the relation established between the hues and tones. How shall one describe it? In one word it is an organic relation. We know, for example, that an arch is supported upon its two columns or piers; it is their function to support the arch; and that the arch is composed of a series of stones or bricks, each of which is a necessary factor in the function of composing the arch's curve, and that the latter is completed by the keystone, until the arch is able to perform its function of supporting the superincumbent weight and of withstanding the various strains. It is an organic structure.

Now it is so that Cézanne constructs his color-harmonies. Their hues and tones are related as functionally as the bricks or stones of the arch and are built into a fabric of color, fully as compact and organic. But, more than this, the relations do not result in a fixed, organic structure; their interplay is elastic. They flow into one another, shall we say, as the movement flows through the muscles of a galloping race-horse. The color-harmony is a *living,* organic structure of sequences and rhythms. But, once more, and this is the final secret, the rhythms have an extraordinary *cohesion.*

How shall one suggest the force of this? Possibly, by

a comparison. One throws a stone into a pool, and sets in motion a series of rhythms, which flow outward in concentric circles that diminish in force until they finally disappear. On the other hand, in a running stream one has seen an eddy formed by a revolving twig or leaf. The movement of the rhythmic circles is now inward, their force increasing until a miniature whirlpool is formed, into which the leaf is sucked. In this case the movement is centripetal, pivoting about the center, whereas in the former it was escaping from the center—centrifugal. Now, in a way, this explains Cézanne's rhythms of hue and tone. Not only are they built into the structure of the composition, and are living, moving rhythms; but their movement is so concentrated, that they draw into their intense inward force the attention of the spectator. Hence the enthralling aloofness of his pictures, their self-contained completeness. "They have," as Mr. Roger Fry has said, "regained the epic aloofness and continuity of early art. . . . Their life is self-contained and self-sufficing; it is for us, not for them, to make advances."

To repeat, Cézanne was intent upon expressing the sensation that he received from the visual impression; but he analyzed the sensations and discovered by a severe logic the elements which, on the one hand, composed the sensation, and, on the other, would express the sensation. In a word, he intellectualized his sensations. And, in this way, he was, as he said, a primitive laying the foundation of a bridge which would lead back from modern naturalism and impressionism to the profound and noble painting of the great Italians and Flemish. We have space for only one more remark. Through Delacroix's example Cézanne was led to Rubens, and thus proved himself a true Frenchman by carrying on, in his own way, the great Rubens tradition.

While Cézanne intellectualized his color-sensations, the Neo-Impressionists may be said to have standardized theirs. That is to say, they have reduced color perception and color expression to a system, based upon scientific laws of light and color.

The basis of Neo-Impressionism is the use of the separate touch; that is to say, the placing of the colors pure upon the canvas, instead of previously mixing them upon the palette. Georges Seurat hit upon this method of applying the pigment after reading an experiment by the late Professor Rood, of Columbia University, New York. The latter, as we have said elsewhere, tested the luminosity and intensity of colors. He took two disks. The half of one of them he colored, for example, with yellow, the other half with blue. Then mixing an equal portion of the same yellow and blue on a palette, he covered the whole of the other disk with the resultant green. Next he placed both disks in a machine which revolved them simultaneously at equal velocity. The blue and the yellow on the one disk now blended into green, and he proceeded to compare the green of this disk with that of the other. The result showed that the green produced by the optical blend of the two hues was more intense and luminous than that which had been mixed upon the palette. Seurat saw the application of this to painting. He tried the effect of placing the pure colors side by side on the canvas in small touches, and trusted to the eye to blend them. The luminosity and intensity of his color-scheme were thereby enhanced. Accordingly he and others adopted as a principle of technique, "the suppression of all impure mixing and the exclusive use of the optical mingling of the pure colors." In a word, "division" of color.

Before going on to consider how the Neo-Impressionists applied this principle of technique, let us note, as Signac does in his book, that it was no new method. Delacroix had already observed the use of it by Constable, and had written: "The superiority of the green of Constable's meadows is due to the fact that it is composed of different greens. That which gives the lack of intensity and life to the verdure usually of the landscape painters, is the result of their habit of making it of a uniform hue." Elsewhere he wrote: "It is good that the touches should not be materially mixed; they blend naturally at the required distance by the sympathetic law which has associated them. The color obtains thus more energy and freshness." So Delacroix himself adopted the practice, and thus increased the intensity and luminosity of his own color-schemes.

Gradually the Impressionists adopted the method. Renoir was the first, and he seems to have derived it from the example of Delacroix. In 1871, however, Monet and Pissarro spent some time in London, where they discovered that Turner's wonderful color was produced by this division of color. When they returned home to proclaim their discovery, they found that the method had been worked out by the Dutch painter, Jongkind. Division of color thus became the general practice of the group of Impressionists.

In what respect, then, do the Neo-Impressionists represent an advance upon impressionism? They contend, in the first place, that the Impressionists are not absolutely consistent in relying solely upon the optical mingling of the pure colors; that occasionally they resort to impure mixing. Their second contention is that the Impressionists aim at fugitive or instantaneous effects and rely on instinct to guide them in their color-harmonies, whereas the Neo-Impressionists aim at permanent effects and reach their results by reflection, based on scientific principles. These laws of color, derived from the study of the gradations of hue and tone in natural light, as shown by the solar spectrum, can be learned, says Signac, in a few hours. "They are contained in two pages of Chevreul and Rood."

Nor need this reliance upon scientific laws enslave the artist, any more than a thorough knowledge of the laws affecting the structure of a sonnet need rob the poet of his liberty of imagination. On the contrary, in the security of his knowledge, the artist can compose his harmonies with greater freedom.

While Seurat started the Neo-Impressionist movement, the one who has contributed most to its advance, not only by his writings but also by his pictures, is Paul Signac. Signac has gone far, as Julius Meier Graefe says, to solve the problem of the modern painter—"'How to give us nature without hanging it bodily on the walls.' In his happiest moments he succeeds in giving the modern picture—that makeshift with which we beautify our dwellings—a brilliant and even ideal form, making it a beautiful spot on the wall, that lends itself readily to a frame, and represents, if not all, yet the most valuable thing we need in a rational home—beautiful color in a beautiful form."

CHAPTER XXX

HENRI MATISSE	PABLO PICASSO
1862–	*1881–*
French School	*French School,*
	although a Spaniard

THE motive-power of art as of life is instinct. We are born with the instinct to live, and each stage in our individual development is accompanied by a more fully developed instinct of what we need to realize our desire of life. If every individual life were *solely* intent upon its own self-realization, the result would be a continual conflict. Meanwhile man's instinct soon realized that man was not made to live alone. Early, therefore, there appeared the social instinct. Mankind banded together into families, communities, and nations; and gradually organized the social state. In doing so they had to adopt customs and laws which, in the interest of the social instinct, to some extent curbed the liberty of the individual instinct. Life became a compromise between the individual and the social instinct. An ideally perfect state or community would be one in which the organization were so perfectly adjusted that the utmost good to all would be secured with as little as possible infringement upon the self-realization of the individual.

But there never has been and probably never will be an ideally perfect community; the next best thing is a continual bettering of the conditions of life in the interests of each and all. Now in the striving for this gradual betterment, mankind has found from time to time that its growth is being checked by the very machinery designed to promote it. Laws lose their usefulness, customs harden into mere conventions; both have been standing still, while mankind continually goes forward. New laws have to be made, customs must be modified, so that both may be readapted to the progressive growth of the social and individual instincts.

Now the same forces and conditions have been operating in art, from its earliest dawn to the present day. The instinct in man led him to construct things that would contribute to his life; almost simultaneously the instinct prompted him to express his joy in life by decorating these things of utility. If one man showed superior imagination and skill, he at once became an artist whose example influenced others; so that in time what he and his followers did became accepted as a standard.

Certain principles gained the force of laws, and certain methods obtained the sanction of custom. Art, in fact, became organized. Then by degrees, as man's instinct of beauty grew in correspondence with his instinct of life, art would be found to be no longer a full expression of either instinct. Its own growth was being checked by inadequate laws and hard conventions.

We began our study with Giotto's revolt against the Byzantine conventions of painting. He began the work of restoring art to life; of wedding the instinct of art with that of life; of making art the expression of man's highest ideals of life. And the whole story since the thirteenth century has been a continual readjustment of art to the growth of life. In the twentieth century art entered a new phase which Cézanne helped materially to stimulate and of which Henri Matisse is a conspicuous representative.

The revolt was accomplished, as all revolts are apt to be, by excess. The revolutionists presented a disorganized band, united in nothing except a common hatred of convention. They were dubbed, and with no little justification, the "wild men." Meanwhile, out of this confusion Matisse stands conspicuous as one who has a reasoned faith which he has been following consistently.

Matisse has been impelled by a similar feeling for the primitive and elemental. His artistic creed, which he has practised in his own work and preached to numerous pupils, holds three articles—Simplification, Organization, Expression. If for the last we substitute a word of more universal application, Efficiency, we find it is the same creed that is coming to be held as the ground-principle of best achievement in every department of life. Let us examine Matisse's application of it.

The idea of Simplification is not new; we have met with it frequently in our story of painting. It was one principle of Giotto's treatment of form, and Puvis de Chavannes' decorations; it is an ingredient in the greatness of Frans Hals, of Velasquez and Millet. It is, indeed, involved in the Selection which we have seen is one of the two elements of all art.

The other, we recall, is Arrangement, which is only

a less specific word than Organization. The latter implies, as we have already noted, that the arrangement is organic; designed, that is to say, in order that each part may contribute its proper function to the structure and purpose of the whole. So Matisse's second tenet also is as old as humanity. In what then does the significance of his creed consist? In the principle which guides his Simplification and the motive with which he employs Organization; and the clue to both is to be found in the meaning which he attaches to Expression.

Matisse has no interest in the use of painting as a means of representing the external appearances of life and nature. He has no desire to compete with the camera. If he were to paint a man in an airplane, it would be with no purpose of showing how the machine is constructed or the man is operating the cranks, but to try to express the exaltation of spirit which the act of aviation involves. No doubt you will say that, so far, his motive is scarcely distinguishable from that of Millet. When the latter painted *The Sower,* he did indeed show, not how the act of sowing is usually performed, but how it would be if the highest possible efficiency were attainable; yet his chief motive was not representation, but the expression of the significance with which the idea of labor impressed him.

Matisse's expression is much less profound than Millet's, yet not less abstract or elementary. It deals with sensations, especially those derived immediately from instinct. For his aim has been to recover for himself, as far as possible, the promptings of instinct. He has been in his art as eager to escape the sophistications of modern civilization as was Gauguin, and, like the latter, sought suggestion, not indeed in the life of primitive people, but in their rude expression of it in art; for example, in the wood-carvings of African savages. His idea was to get in touch, if possible, with the attitude of mind and the method of a child-man, facing nature with untutored eyes and trying to give expression to what instinct told him about life.

So for a while Matisse, though an accomplished draughtsman in the manner of the schools, drew his forms rudely and uncouthly. Critics declared that any child could draw as well as he did. In this they encouraged Matisse. For he knew that if a child's instinct prompts it to draw, and it is left to itself, it will often display a surprising ability to render the essential facts of form and of form in movement; and this is precisely what Matisse has aimed to render.

The work which we illustrate is a large decorative panel for the embellishment of the staircase of a house in Russia. The theme embodied was *The Dance.* Now his intention was not to represent a number of nude female figures in the act of dancing, but to express that instinct for rhythmic movement which from earliest ages has inspired humanity. It has, from age to age, in folk-dances and in ballroom dances, found diverse forms of expression; but the elemental feeling that breathes through all is to-day what it was in the case of primitive man, the product of an instinct permanently fixed in human nature. Rather, then, than illustrate any one form of the dance, Matisse would suggest, as Millet did in *The Sower,* the elemental idea involved.

THE DANCE   HENRI MATISSE

MUSEUM OF MODERN WESTERN ART, MOSCOW

PIERROT   PABLO PICASSO

SOLOMON R. GUGGENHEIM FOUNDATION, NEW YORK

I can imagine him putting the problem to himself in this way: If I give my figures the finish of outline demanded by academic training, I shall run the risk of centering the attention of the spectator on the forms themselves. But it is the movement within the forms that I am solely interested in suggesting—in fact, the elemental principle of rhythmic movement; I will, therefore, give my figures something of a primitive suggestion—that is to say, I will simplify them until, as far as possible, they convey no impression but that of the elemental fact of bodies, organically related to one another, in a unity of rhythmic movement. Accordingly, no one figure shall single itself out for personal notice; in no one of them shall the movement be complete; it shall be in the way in which the movement of one flows into that of the others, throughout the circle formed by the linked hands, that I will suggest the elemental principle of rhythm involved in *The Dance*

The decoration, as I saw it hanging in his studio nearing completion, had, as it was intended, a certain savage force; for, after all, there is a strain of savagery in all the elemental instincts. But, for myself, there was no question of the enthusiasm it aroused. One was face to face, not with the local, the personal, and the temporary, but with the abstract suggestion of something permanent and universal in human instinct.

The abstraction of suggestion was reinforced by the color-scheme. The figures were circling on a knoll of green grass against the blue of the sky, and the hue of their bodies was vermilion. It is a union of colors much appreciated in Russia, and was chosen for its decorative possibilities. Possibly the choice of vermilion for the figures was assisted by Matisse's desire to make it absolutely clear that there was no thought of representation in his mind; that his sole purpose was, on the one hand, to create a handsome decoration, and, on the other, to make it expressive of an abstract idea.

At present, of course, we are so habituated to the naturalistic, representative kind of art, and so accustomed to judge a painting by its resemblance to the external facts of the visible world, that many people find it impossible to enter into Matisse's point of view.

But, on the one hand, the camera has done much to oust painting from its position as an art of representation; while, on the other, the world is beginning to react from excessive materialism; and the counterpart of the latter in painting has been too largely represented in the Naturalistic, Impressionistic, and so-called Classical-Ideal schools. In every direction men and women are beginning to demand some recognition of the needs of the spirit and intellect. Moreover, philosophy, as well as education, is taking more account of human instincts as the basis of sound and high living. The tendency also is to intellectualize the relations of life; and, further, to help everyone to extract out of life the utmost of social and individual betterment. The world is consciously moving toward a higher efficiency in the science and art of living; and the equivalent of Efficiency in art is, as we have said, Expression.

While Picasso had in the first decade of our century his period of expressionism not unlike that of Matisse, there was a distinct difference. Like Matisse, Picasso used arbitrary colors partly to emphasize the non-realistic purpose of his painting but his expression was more superficial. He expressed human emotions through forms which were calculated to play on human sympathies. In the *Sorrowful Mother* and in many of the famished Harlequins, Picasso's Expression is one of sentiment verging on sentimentality.

Picasso was in his early twenties when he turned to Expressionism; in his mature thirties he abandoned the very moving but still rather youthful tragic view of life for an exploration of the principles of order that lie under the surface. Almost as fundamental to human life as the driving instincts which Matisse expressed as forces, is the instinct to order and organization. As we have seen the second principle on which Matisse based his art was that of Organization, and it is this principle which, first enunciated by Cézanne when he said that "all nature is based on the cube, the cone, the cylinder and the sphere," a mathematical set of relationships, lies behind the system of painting known as Cubism.

It has been suggested that the rejection of concrete objective reality as the stuff of art is the natural result of the bankruptcy of 19th century materialism. A further development of this idea and a very thorough canvassing of the factors responsible for abstract art may be found in a little book published in 1934 by the Renaissance Society of Chicago University, written by Edward F. Rothschild, "The Meaning of Unintelligibility in Modern Art." The usefulness of Mr. Rothschild's study is in clearing our minds of the prejudice against non-objective art which is, I think, entirely natural and understandable. But the way to study the pictures of these modern painters is not to read about them but to look, and look again, with a mind alert to feel and to see that organization which is at once both intellectual and emotional. Never was there an art which could less well be represented by a colorless reproduction. One must see Picasso in the original or one is defeated at the outset.

Abstract expression in pictorial terms is in no sense new. Looking back at the period in which abstract painting preoccupied the ablest painters of our day on both sides of the Atlantic, one sees it now in relation to the main stream of art history. To-day we are already aware of a strong movement back to objective reality; pure abstraction seems, to this writer at least, to have passed its peak of importance and to be giving place to a new mode of artistic expression. At various times and in various places throughout the world man's need for the expression of intangible qualities and verities has given rise to a pictorial art bearing only a very slight relation to the objective environment in which the artist moves and has his being. If you will turn back to the first illustration in this book you will see that here is abstract or non-objective art. But, you demur, Cimabue painted a woman and a child, strange though they may be to our eyes, and in Picasso no recognizable creature or object is descernible. True. But is not space in which we see people, in which we move ourselves, quite as real as a three dimensional object? And is there any space as we know it, forward and back, in the picture of the *Madonna Enthroned?* No, Cimabue's concern with objective reality is only relatively greater than

[506]

Picasso's. Also the expressive or telling qualities of the Madonna picture have little to do with the painter's visual experience of the real world. The quality of cool remote dignity and queenliness, full as it is of tender awareness of mortal needs and hopes and fears, lies in those elements of arrangement, of relationships between the various parts of the composition, and in the wholly abstract expressive quality of the line itself.

All art is to a very great extent abstract, must be by the very nature of the conventions which man accepts when he undertakes to create a pictorial world of his own on a flat canvas or panel or wall. The habit of counterfeiting the objectively real world, of giving an illusion into which we can enter sympathetically is a local, European development of the past five hundred years, not a universal norm from which the 20th century has abruptly revolted.

The human activity which we recognize as that which produces art objects is essentially an ordering process. The artist takes from the chaos of human experience those elements which seem to him important and makes of them a pattern or form which is really a symbol of the meaning of life to him. On a very much lower level in the scale of quality the good housekeeper is an artist who makes out of the helter skelter of family living an orderly peaceful household with rooms that are not only good to look at but that express in some measure the people who live in them. The difference between orderliness, enriched with meaning, and disorder, is the difference between art and experience. The materials for the one lie in the other but must be organized into formal or abstract relationships in order to convey the meaning which the artist has felt in his experience and wishes to objectify, that is express. Therefore the distinguishing mark of art is its order, and order is an abstraction. It is the relation between two sets of three apples each that we express when we say that three plus three equals six. And when we arrange six chairs around four sides of a rectangular dining table we bring into a formless collection of chairs an abstract relationship of order, two balancing two and one opposite one.

When Picasso painted the picture illustrated, he used a seated figure of a man as his starting point in experience, in objective reality. But he saw no purpose in reproducing the visual appearance of the man exactly. If there were some need of reproducing that visual image the camera could be used to produce an entirely satisfactory result at great saving of time and materials. To the artist what was of interest was the whole complex of related colors and shapes, planes and solids that the eye could glimpse in seeing the seated man, and that the mind could elaborate in working over and over that initial image. The development of the relationships, the emphasis on the wholly formal aspects of the thing seen quickly transforms it into something else, into a work of "non-objective" art. He created it out of the materials of his own world of experience, but it expresses for him certain deeply felt and verbally inexpressible values. One cannot give words to the feeling or sense that such a work of abstract art gives one. It is not a thing that can be explained in verbal concepts because the artist is expressing certain felt relationships and meanings for which we have no language other than the artist's own. The advice which any critic or teacher who is not a hypocrite will sooner or later fall back upon is that which I suggested above. You must look for yourself. And looking involves really trying to see what is there, not merely to identify it but to see it. Mr. Rothschild in his book "The Meaning of Unintelligibility in Modern Art" describes our usual way of looking at art as that of the person who looks for a friend in a crowd. He notes each face in succession as unfamiliar and so passes on without having seen any one. Because we fail to find anything familiar in this Picasso painting we dismiss it as meaningless. We must look at it again and again to discover wherein lies the basis for an understanding and enjoyment of this stranger. Only in this way can one learn to see the order and feel the expressive quality that is there to be seen and felt and enjoyed.

CHAPTER XXXI

AMERICAN PAINTING TO-DAY

IN our discussion of Cézanne on page 476 we quoted the painter as having called himself " a primitive " laying the foundation of a bridge which would lead back from modern naturalism and impressionism to the profound and noble painting of the great Italians and Flemish. The bridge did indeed reach back, but, to change the figure, the pendulum of artistic style swung back farther than Cézanne had dreamed, back to the abstract formalism of the Byzantine, back to the primitive arts of Africa. Once the tradition of naturalism, of fidelity to objective appearance was overthrown, and it was Cézanne among the moderns who first had the courage to distort appearance for the sake of expression, the vast body of modern knowledge, of archæology and of anthropology was open to the artist. True to the inquiring spirit of the age, he ranged freely among the exotic art forms, exotic to us because lying outside our own immediate tradition, and as we have seen, he explored for the better part of a generation the realm of purely abstract art.

But the pendulum has already begun to swing back. To-day there is a strong reaction against unintelligible painting among artists themselves. This may be largely due to the changing economic position of the artist. Since 1929 he has had increasingly to rely on public support: he can no longer look forward with much degree of hope to finding enough private patronage to support him. And to appeal to this new and wider public he has realized the necessity of saying something in language which is understood, something which matters more widely than do his personal emotions and reactions to his environment. Social and economic conditions throughout the world have forced the artist, who is first and last a sensitive human being, to concern himself with issues and with vital social currents which are not readily expressed in abstract terms. The artist's feeling, his sense and awareness of the injustices in his world may well be expressible in terms of sheer, abstract pictorial form, as in music, but they will be richer, *more* meaningful because more directly communicable, through representational forms. And so a great many painters to-day have turned back to a new kind of realism: not to impressionism, which captured an elusive beauty in the momentary appearances of things, but to the realism of the old Italians to whom Cézanne looked back, a realism which is of the mind, not alone of the eye. The mental image with all the enrichment of emotion "recollected in tranquility," of repeated experience, of knowledge embracing the internal structure, the unvarying essence of the thing represented—this is the new material of art.

In this sense, if Cézanne was the primitive of the new style, our painters to-day are perhaps the classics, although facile labeling of styles is dangerous and misleading. In so far, however, as the classic style of European painting has been defined, its characteristics are, first and foremost, clarity of form, perfect readability; second, a reliance on line both for definition of form and for expression; and third, a marked tendency to measure off the picture space in a series of planes, the figures and objects occupying positions in bands parallel to the picture plane.   Such an arrangement of space can be seen in the illustrations of Fra Angelico and Jan van Eyck on pages 42 and 43, or in the Raphael Madonna on page 90.   This corresponds to the way we think of space, not the way it appears.   We think and speak of a foreground, a middle, and a background.   To arrange one's picture in this way is to increase the clarity, the readability of the composition.   This is clear if you contrast the David *Oath of the Horatii* on page 336 with the Delacroix *Dante and Virgil* opposite.   David arranges his figures across the stage of his picture so that they are parallel both to the arcade behind them and to the picture plane which is an imaginary forward limit where the footlights would be if the picture were a stage. Delacroix turns the boat of Dante back into the picture and suggests the murkiness of the infernal regions by the darkness into which the bow shoves its way.   The figures of Dante and Virgil give the composition some stability by their firm frontal position, but all the others cling and snatch at the boat's gunwales in agonizing confusion. Delacroix's purpose is to emphasize the murky unclearness and confusion; David's, to tell the story of the taking of an oath in as clear and as definitive pictorial form as he can manage.

This composing in planes parallel to that of the picture, with the clarity and often the lineal definiteness that go with it, is coupled in classical painting with the representation of types in preference to individuals. This we saw in Degas, and this is again becoming apparent in the painting of the present day. Thus we find the American painter, Joe Jones, in a painting at the Metropolitan Museum called *Threshing,* generalizing, to a certain extent, idealizing the worker in the wheat fields.

But an important factor in style that cannot be overlooked is that only by an act of artificial rejection can an artist forget and ignore what has stylistically preceded him. Therefore, while one may find in American painting to-day tendencies which reach back to the art of the Renaissance and earlier, our painting bears in its style the mark of the late nineteenth century impressionism. In rare instances one comes across a picture which is in effect a colored drawing, but in most of the best painting of the new realistic mode the artist treats the color as a living shifting element, subject, as it was in the work of Rubens and Renoir alike, to the local conditions of light and of environment.

It is a perilous task to attempt a classification by schools or by types of such a many faceted art as that of contemporary America. The new realism, which as we have indicated has much in common with the classical style of the Italian Renaissance, is a recognizable trend. It is to be found both among the Paris-trained painters of the eastern states and among the representatives of that "sectional painting" which has sprung up all over the country in answer, very largely, to the stimulation of government patronage. But there are deeper-seated causes at work even than the vivifying factor of government support. It is a strongly felt American nationalism, a new self-confidence which has been manifested since 1930 and is to be found in every aspect of our contemporary culture. At last we are throwing off the few remaining vestiges of provincialism: we are finally aware of a culture of our own that can be matched with that of Europe not alone on a materialistic level (of course, it is years since we considered ourselves their equal and superior in matters of plumbing and efficiency of telephone service) but also in the realm of spiritual and artistic values.

The art which is an expression of this new cultural nationalism is characterized by clarity and definiteness. Among the more pedestrian painters it descends to a kind of literalness which is very little relieved by imaginative insight and perception. In other words, to some it is enough to paint as faithfully and clearly as possible the American scene without bothering to interpret it. But among the more sensitive and more mature—not necessarily older—painters the faithful rendering of reality takes on a meaning which varies in richness with the personality of the painter.

In the picture called *View from Williamsburg Bridge,* Edward Hopper does not paint the flash past the car window of tenement houses vague and indefinite as the view from a moving train is apt to be; but those same houses as he has seen them time after time, as we have all seen them, ugly and raw, yes, but with a kind of dignity of their own; solid, four-square, and unequivocal.

VIEW FROM WILLIAMSBURG BRIDGE

EDWARD HOPPER

METROPOLITAN MUSEUM, NEW YORK

HOMELESS

METROPOLITAN MUSEUM, NEW YORK

WILLIAM GROPPER

As one studies the picture these two tenements come to stand for their whole genus: they are not individuals but types. We are not proud of the aspect of our civic life and history which has produced this type of architecture, and yet the painter accepts it as the embodiment of a kind of truth which we might better recognize and then proceed to alter. And as one studies the painting in the original the colors seem less harsh, almost lovingly applied to the canvas, and subtle harmonies become apparent which were not at first glance visible. The abstract relationships between the planes of the buildings across the picture and back into the picture space, the relation of the imagined movement of the bridge up and to the left, to the static solidity of the building itself— these give one a feeling of order and firmness that is comparable to the effect of Picasso's abstraction.

The painting of the American scene is not new in our history. In the first half of the nineteenth century there was a strongly developed taste for American landscape and American genre. William S. Mount and George Caleb Bingham are the spiritual forebears of many of our "sectional painters" to-day. In the best of these moderns you find the flavor of an intimately known place, a local tang, the sense of the personality of a Connecticut farm or of a California ranch which is a matter of the painter's very personal feeling transmitted through the paint.

In sharp contrast to this, which may be called the native trend, is the more sophisticated, more cosmopolitan, on the whole less vital though more accomplished art of the men and women who find in the technical problems of studio arrangements of still-life or of figure studies, the sustained interest and fascination that keeps them working. Here one would find such men as Kroll or Karfiol. The subject matter tends to range outside of the studio into the artificial lights of the theatre and dance halls; or into very personally rendered landscape as in the work of Weber and Levi. On the whole, this type of American art tends toward decorative subtleties and frequently has retained more than a little of the abstract, non-realistic character of the twenties.

Among the mural painters the influence of the Mexican Rivera—of his use of the fresco medium and of his "social consciousness"—is very apparent. It results in a clear-cut, lineal style, wherein types of men and types of social forces, like the machine, are confronted in a not altogether realistic setting. Here one finds the liberating effect on American painting of the period of abstraction through which the school if not the individual has passed. The direct, expressive qualities of form and color are constantly made use of in connection with otherwise naturalistic material.

A fourth type may be thought of as a cross between the realistic painting of the American scene and the abstract and decorative studio painting of the ardent individualists. It is represented by the work of such men as Thomas Benton and William Gropper. Particularly in Gropper's painting one finds the use of non-realistic, abstract forms in the service of an idea. Where a painter like Morris Kantor or Vincent Van Gogh will stylize the shape of trees until they express the very essence of a tree's growth, Gropper in the picture called *Homeless* stylizes mountains to symbolize the loneliness of refugees, distorts the normal image of a running child in order to express the terror which drives him along. Color is put on in patches. Lines and shapes all combine to express an idea which to Gropper is something which matters deeply.

The knowledge that emotions can be conveyed directly through the abstract elements of painting is not new. Like the eloquent scribbles on a telephone pad which record clearly the indolence of an unhurried conversation and the staccato nervousness of the mother getting a doctor, the painter's line conveys to the sensitive observer a direct perception of the emotions he wishes to convey. But when painting is engrossed with the problems of scientific rendering of natural appearances, the painter finds it difficult to free his line and color from their representational duties and allow them to perform their equally important task of direct communication. This is one of our most important inheritances from the period of abstraction through which twentieth-century painting has come. Cubism and all the fantastic vagaries of the first quarter of our century served to give us back the freedom of the painter, a freedom to paint in whatever way seems to him best fitted to interpret the relationship between him and his world.

A READING LIST

General Books on Art History and Appreciation

ABBOT, E. R.—*The Great Painters* (New York, 1927).
MATHER, F. J., JR.—*Western European Painting of the Renaissance* (New York, 1939).
ROBB, D. M., and GARRISON, J. J.—*Art of the Western World* (New York and London, 1935).

.   .   .

HOLMES, SIR CHARLES—*A Grammar of the Arts* (London, 1931).
READ, H.—*The Anatomy of Art* (New York, 1932).
ROTHSCHILD, E. H.—*The Meaning of Unintelligibility in Modern Art* (Chicago, 1934).
WÖLFFLIN, H.—*Principles of Art History* (New York, 1932).

Italian Schools

BERENSON, BERNARD—*The Italian Painters of the Renaissance* (revised edition, Oxford, 1930).
BURKHARDT, JACOB—*The Civilization of the Renaissance in Italy* (New York, 1928).
MATHER, F. J., JR.—*A History of Italian Painting* (New York, 1923).
VAN MARLE, RAIMOND—*The Development of the Italian Schools of Painting* (The Hague, 1923-38).
VASARI, G.—*Lives of the Painters,* edited by E. H. and E. W. Blashfield and A. A. Hopkins (New York, 1926).
WÖLFFLIN, H.—*The Art of the Italian Renaissance* (New York, 1928).

Flemish School

CONWAY, SIR MARTIN—*The Van Eycks and Their Followers* (New York, 1921).
FROMENTIN, E.—*The Masters of Past Time* (London, 1913).
MATHER, F. J., JR.—*Western European Painting of the Renaissance* (New York, 1939).
ROOSES, M.—*Rubens,* 2 volumes (Philadelphia and London, 1904).

A READING LIST

German School

MATHER, F. J., JR.—*Western European Painting of the Renaissance* (New York, 1939).

MOORE, T. S.—*Albert Dürer* (New York and London, 1905).

Dutch School

BODE, W.—*The Great Masters of Dutch and Flemish Painting* (New York and London, 1909).

FROMENTIN, E.—*The Masters of Past Time* (London, 1913).

HOFSTEDE DE GROOT, C.—*Catalogue Raisonné of the Works of Eminent Dutch Painters of the Seventeenth Century* (London, 1908-1927).

MATHER, F. J., JR.—*Western European Painting of the Renaissance* (New York, 1939).

VAN MANDER, CAREL—*Dutch and Flemish Painters,* translated by Constant van de Wall (New York, 1936).

WILENSKI, R. H.—*An Introduction to Dutch Art* (New York, 1929).

Spanish School

Burlington Magazine—Spanish Art Monograph (New York, 1927).

COSSIO, M. D.—*El Greco* (Madrid, 1908).

DE BERUETE, A.—*Velasquez* (Paris, 1898).

HARRIS, E.—*Spanish Painting* (Paris, 1937).

MATHER, F. J. JR.—*Western European Painting of the Renaissance* (New York, 1939).

STEVENSON, R. A. M.—*Velasquez* (New York and London, 1899).

French School

FRY, R.—*Characteristics of French Painting* (New York and London, 1933).

MEIER-GRAEFE, J.—*Cézanne* (New York and London, 1927).

———— *Modern Art* (London, 1908).

MOORE, G.—*Modern Painting* (New York, 1893).

Museum of Modern Art—*Picasso: Forty Years of His Art* (New York, 1939).

WILENSKI, R. H.—*French Painting* (Boston, 1931).

[524]

A READING LIST

English School

COLLINS-BAKER, C. H., and JAMES, M. R.—*British Painting* (Boston, 1933).

MEIER-GRAEFE, J.—*Modern Art* (London, 1908).

WILENSKI, R. H.—*Masters of English Painting* (Boston and New York, no date).

American School

BURROUGHS, A.—*Limners and Likenesses* (Cambridge, 1936).

CHENEY, M.—*Modern Art in America* (New York, 1939).

ISHAM, S., and CORTISSOZ, R.—*The History of American Painting* (New York, 1927).

Museum of Modern Art—*New Horizons in American Art* (New York, 1936).

Eastern Painting

FENOLLOSA, E. F.—*Epochs of Chinese and Japanese Art* (New York and London, 1921).

HEARN, LAFCADIO—*Kokoro* (Boston, 1896).

OKAKURA-KAKUZO—*Ideals of the East* (New York, 1904).

INDEX

INDEX

ā, fāte; ă, făt; ä, fäther; â, fâre; à, sodà; ē, wē; ĕ, mĕt; ē, hēr; ī, fīle; ĭ, fĭll; ō, nōte; ŏ, nŏt; ô, ôr; ŏ, whŏlly; ōō, fōōl; ŏŏ, lŏŏk; ū, ūse; ŭ, ŭs; ü, Fr. sür, Ger. über.

INDEX

---

ch, choose; ċh, Ger.aċh; g, get; n, Fr.bon; sh, show; y, you; zh, azure;
= indicates two syllables run together, as Daumier, dō-mē = ā';
' indicates principal accent; " indicates secondary accent.

INDEX

ā, fāte; ă, făt; ä, fäther; â, fâre; ȧ, sodȧ; ē, wē; ĕ, mĕt; ē, hēr; ĭ, fīle; ĭ, fĭll; ō, nōte; ŏ, nŏt; ô, ôr; ŏ, whŏlly; ōō, fōōl; ŏŏ, lŏŏk; ū, ūse; ŭ, ŭs; ü, Fr. sür, Ger. über.

INDEX

---

ch, choose; ċh, Ger. aċh; g, get; ṅ, Fr. boṅ; sh, show; y, you; zh, azure; = indicates two syllables run together, as Daumier, dō-mē = ā; ' indicates principal accent; " indicates secondary accent.

INDEX

ā, fāte; ă, făt; ä, fäther; â, fâre; å, sodà; ē, wē; ĕ, mĕt; ẽ, hẽr; ĭ, fīle; ĭ, fĭll; ō, nōte; ŏ, nŏt; ô, ôr; ŏ, whŏlly; ōō, fōōl; ŏŏ, lŏŏk; ū, ūse; ŭ, ŭs; ü, Fr. sür, Ger. über.

INDEX

ch, choose; ċh, Ger.aċh; g, get; ṅ, Fr.boṅ; sh, show; y, you; zh, azure;
= indicates two syllables run together, as Daumier, dō-mē = ā';
' indicates principal accent; " indicates secondary accent.

INDEX

ā, fāte; ă, făt; ä, fäther; â, fâre; ȧ, sodȧ; ē, wē; ĕ, mĕt; ẽ, hẽr;
ī, fīle; ĭ, fĭll; ō, nōte; ŏ, nŏt; ô, ôr; ŏ, whŏlly; ōō, fōōl; ŏŏ, lŏŏk;
ū, ūse; ŭ, ŭs; ü, Fr. sür, Ger. über.

INDEX

ch, choose; ċh, Ger.aċh; g, get; ṅ, Fr.boṅ; sh, show; y, you; zh, azure; = indicates two syllables run together, as Daumier, dō-mē = ā; ′ indicates principal accent; ″ indicates secondary accent.

ā, fāte; ă, făt; ä, fäther; â, fâre; á, sodá; ē, wē; ĕ, mĕt; ē, hēr; ĭ, fīle; ĭ, fĭll; ō, nōte; ŏ, nŏt; ô, ôr; ŏ, whŏlly; ŏŏ, fŏŏl; ŏŏ, lŏŏk; ū, ūse; ŭ, ŭs; ü, Fr. sür, Ger. über.

INDEX

ch, choose; ċh, Ger.aċh; g, get; ṅ, Fr.boṅ; sh, show; y, you; zh, azure;
= indicates two syllables run together, as Daumier, dō-mē = ā';
' indicates principal accent; " indicates secondary accent.

INDEX

rēl'-yō, 1617–1682, 179, 228–246

Music Master, by Steen, 268

Muther, Richard, 339 *n.*, 350, 396

Mystic Marriage of St. Catherine, by Correggio, 142–158; ill., 150

Naples, 179, 353

Napoleon, 204, 393, 340, 349, 384

National Gallery, 77, 121 *n.*, 268, 296, 325

Naturalism, 178, 381, 478, 504, 510

Neo-Impressionists, 476, 490, 492

New York, 204

Nieto, Don José, 198

Night Watch, The. See *Sortie of the Banning Cock Company.*

Normandy, 250

Northcote, James, 307

Norway, 95, 248

Nôtre Dame, Antwerp, 214

Nôtre Dame, Paris, 340

Novgorod, 140

Nuremberg (nōŏr'-ĕm-bĕrg), 93, 94, 96, 104, 110, 111, 118

Oath of the Horatii, by David, 329–346, 512; ill., 336

Odalisque, by Ingres, 374

Odyssey, 316

Œdipus and the Sphinx, by Ingres, 374

Oil painting, 45, 69, 147

Old Church at Vernon, by Monet, 455–475; ill., 464

Old Woman Spinning, by Maes, 265

Olympus, 106

Orcagna, 53

Orient, 9, 87, 160, 455

Orless, 243

Ornans (ôr-nôṅ'), 382

Ostrogoths, 86

Otho the Great, 86

Ovetari, 30

Oxford, 404

Padua, 18, 20, 30, 31, 32, 36, 71, 162

Palladio, 164

Pantheon, 34

Papacy, 86

Paradise, by Giotto, 18

Paradise, by Tintoretto, 175

Paris, 214, 251, 260, 302, 326, 345, 382, 394, 420, 423, 433, 441, 442, 454, 456, 479, 513

Parma, 157, 302

Parma, Duke of, 215

Parnassus, 106

Parthenon, 72

Pater, Walter, 318

Patrouille de Nuit. See *Sortie of the Banning Cock Company.*

Pepin, 160

Pericles, 112

Perugia, 31, 70, 84, 97

Perugino (Pietro Vannucci), pā-rōō-jē'-nō, 1446–1523, 68–84, 96, 97, 98, 104, 105, 106

Peruzzi Chapel, S. Croce, 18

Pescara, Marquis of, 155

Petrarch, 54, 106

Pheidias (fī̆d'-ĭ-ȧs), 72, 77, 384

ā, fāte; ă, făt; ä, fäther; â, fâre; ȧ, sodȧ; ē, wē; ĕ, mĕt; ē̆, hēr; ī, fīle; ĭ, fĭll; ō, nōte; ŏ, nŏt; ô, ôr; ŏ̄, whŏ̄lly; ōō, fōōl; ŏŏ, lŏŏk; ū, ūse; ŭ, ŭs; ü, Fr. sür, Ger. über.

INDEX

Philadelphia, 440

Philip, Duke of Orleans, 283, 343

Philip II of Spain, 181, 214, 215

Philip IV of Spain, 195

Picasso, Pablo (pä'-blō pē-cä'-sō), 1881– , 494–509, 519

Pierrot (pē = ĕr-rō'), by Picasso, 494–509; ill., 501

Pietà (pē-ā-tä'), by Michelangelo, 155

Pieve, 132

Pilatus, Leontius, 54

Pisa, 53

Pisano, Andrea, 24

Pissaro (pē-sä-rō'), 456, 457, 458, 491

Pizarro, 87

Pizzolo, Niccolo, 30

Plato, 55, 78, 106, 142, 469

Pleydenwurff, Hans, 96

Plymouth, 302

Plympton, 302

Pointillism, 458, 462

Pollajuolo (pōl-lä-yōō = ō'-lō), 55

Polyphemus, 317, 318

Pope, 296

Port of Marseilles (mär-sā'-yŭ), by Signac, 476–493; ill., 484

Portuguese, 162

Poussin, Nicolas (nē-kō-lä' pōō-säṅ'), 1594–1665, 247–260, 282, 294, 326, 329, 333, 340, 352, 394

Prado, 213, 419

"Praise of Folly, The," 138

Praxiteles, 77

Predis, Ambrogio da, 121 *n.*

Pre-Raphaelite, 398, 399, 401, 402, 403, 417

Prophets, by Sargent, 447, 448

Provence, 478

Provincial Museum, Seville, 192

Psyche, 106

Purgatorio, 11

Pythagoras, 106

Raeburn, Henry, 313, 440, 447

Raphael, archangel, 69

Raphael Sanzio (rä'-fā-ĕl sänd'-zē-ō), 1483–1520, 20, 67, 81, 85–108, 112, 142, 159, 164, 178, 251, 257, 258, 302, 307, 365, 378, 384, 399, 400, 440, 449, 512

Realism, 128, 129, 211, 297, 381, 384, 419, 505, 513

Redemption of Man, by Sargent, 447

Reformation, 112, 139, 404

Regent. *See* Philip, duke of Orleans.

Rehearsal on the Stage, by Degas, 418–438; ill., 431

Rembrandt Van Rijn (rĕm'-brănt făn rīn), 1606–1669, 117, 188, 225, 228–246, 249, 252, 264, 265, 266, 267, 276, 314, 344, 412, 419, 461

Renaissance, 10, 19, 31, 38, 65, 78, 81, 83, 85, 86, 105, 106, 109, 111, 112, 118, 139, 141, 142, 143, 144, 159, 169, 176, 194, 365, 399, 402, 412, 417, 513

Reni, Guido, 251

Renoir, Auguste (ō-gōōst' rĕn-wä'), 1841–1919, 364–379, 434, 476, 491, 513

Restoration, 295

ch, choose; ċh, Ger.aċh; g, get; ṅ, Fr.boṅ; sh, show; y, you; zh, azure; = indicates two syllables run together, as Daumier, dō-mē = ā; ' indicates principal accent; '' indicates secondary accent.

INDEX

ā, fāte; ă, făt; ä, fäther; â, fâre; à, sodà; ē, wē; ĕ, mĕt; ē, hēr; ĭ, fīle; ĭ, fĭll; ō, nōte; ŏ, nŏt; ô, ôr; ŏ, whŏlly; ōō, fōōl; ŏŏ, lŏŏk; ū, ūse; ŭ, ŭs; ü, Fr. sür, Ger. über.

INDEX

ch, choose; ċh, Ger.aċh; g, get; ṅ, Fr.boṅ; sh, show; y, you; zh, azure;
= indicates two syllables run together, as Daumier, dō-mē = ā';
' indicates principal accent; " indicates secondary accent.

INDEX

ā, fāte; ă, făt; ä, fäther; â, fâre; à, sodà; ē, wē; ĕ, mĕt; ē̆, hēr; ĭ, fīle; ĭ, fĭll; ō, nōte; ŏ, nŏt; ô, ôr; ŏ, whŏlly; ōō, fōōl; ŏŏ, lŏŏk; ū, ūse; ŭ, ŭs; ü, Fr. sür, Ger. über.

INDEX

INDEX

Wesley, John, 296
West Front of Rouen Cathedral, by Manet, 460
West Indies, 214
Westphalia, 216
Weyden, Roger van der (vī'-dĕn), 66
Whistler, James Abbott Mc-Neill, 1834–1903, 241, 473, 439–454
Wilberforce, 187
Wilkie, David, 275
William the Conqueror, 250, 287
William the Silent, 215
Willy Lott's House. See Valley Farm.
Wilson, 326
Winckelmann (vĭngk'-ĕl-män), 344, 366, 374

Wolgemuth, Michael (vōl'-gä-mōōt), 1434–1519, 85–108–110
Woman, Portrait of a, by Hals, 214–227; ill., 220
Woolner, Thomas, 398
Wordsworth, 343
Wren, Christopher, 312
Wyant, Alexander, 363

Young Mother, by Dou, 265, 268
Young Woman With a Water Jug, by Vermeer, 279

Zola, 479
Zurbarán, Francisco de (frän-thēs'-kō dŭ thōōr-bä-rän'), 1598–1662, 177–196
Zurich, 394

(16)

ā, fāte; ă, făt; ä, fäther; â, fâre; à, sodà; ē, wē; ĕ, mĕt; ē̆, hēr; ĭ, fīle; ĭ, fĭll; ō, nōte; ŏ, nŏt; ô, ôr; ŏ, whŏlly; ōō, fōōl; ŏŏ, lŏŏk; ū, ūse; ŭ, ŭs; ü, Fr. sür, Ger. über.

[544]